# The New Urban Atlantic

Series Editor
Elizabeth Fay
University of Massachusetts Boston
Cambridge
MA, USA

The early modern period was witness to an incipient process of transculturation through exploration, mercantilism, colonization, and migration that set into motion a process of globalization that continues today. The purpose of this series is to bring together a cultural studies approach—which freely and unapologetically crosses disciplinary, theoretical, and political boundaries—with early modern texts and artefacts that bear the traces of transculturalization and globalization in order to deepen our understanding of sites of exchange between and within early modern culture(s). This process can be studied on a large as well as on a small scale, and this new series is dedicated to both. Possible topics of interest include, but are not limited to: texts dealing with mercantilism, travel, exploration, immigration, foreigners, enabling technologies (such as shipbuilding and navigational instrumentation), mathematics, science, rhetoric, art, architecture, intellectual history, religion, race, sexuality, and gender.

More information about this series at
http://www.springer.com/series/14425

*Creole Testimonies: Slave Narratives from the British West Indies, 1709–1838*
Nicole N. Aljoe
*Stumbling Towards the Constitution: The Economic Consequences of Freedom in the Atlantic World*
Jonathan M. Chu
*Urban Identity and the Atlantic World*
Edited by Elizabeth A. Fay and Leonard von Morzé
*The Transatlantic Eco-Romanticism of Gary Snyder*
Paige Tovey
*Hospitality and the Transatlantic Imagination, 1815–1835*
Cynthia Schoolar Williams
*Trans-Atlantic Passages: Philip Hale on the Boston Symphony Orchestra, 1889–1933*
Jon Ceander Mitchell
*Atlantic Afterlives in Contemporary Fiction: The Oceanic Imaginary in Literature since the Information Age*
Sofia Ahlberg
*Cities and the Circulation of Culture in the Atlantic World*
Edited by Leonard von Morzé
*The Rise of New Media 1750–1850*
Julia Straub

Chiara Cillerai

# Voices of Cosmopolitanism in Early American Writing and Culture

palgrave
macmillan

Chiara Cillerai
St. John's University
Staten Island, NY, USA

The New Urban Atlantic
ISBN 978-3-319-62297-2     ISBN 978-3-319-62298-9 (eBook)
DOI 10.1007/978-3-319-62298-9

Library of Congress Control Number: 2017948260

© The Editor(s) (if applicable) and The Author(s) 2017
This work is subject to copyright. All rights are solely and exclusively licensed by the Publisher, whether the whole or part of the material is concerned, specifically the rights of translation, reprinting, reuse of illustrations, recitation, broadcasting, reproduction on microfilms or in any other physical way, and transmission or information storage and retrieval, electronic adaptation, computer software, or by similar or dissimilar methodology now known or hereafter developed.
The use of general descriptive names, registered names, trademarks, service marks, etc. in this publication does not imply, even in the absence of a specific statement, that such names are exempt from the relevant protective laws and regulations and therefore free for general use.
The publisher, the authors and the editors are safe to assume that the advice and information in this book are believed to be true and accurate at the date of publication. Neither the publisher nor the authors or the editors give a warranty, express or implied, with respect to the material contained herein or for any errors or omissions that may have been made. The publisher remains neutral with regard to jurisdictional claims in published maps and institutional affiliations.

Cover illustration: Chronicle/Alamy Stock Photo

Printed on acid-free paper

This Palgrave Macmillan imprint is published by Springer Nature
The registered company is Springer International Publishing AG
The registered company address is: Gewerbestrasse 11, 6330 Cham, Switzerland

# Acknowledgements

I have been fortunate to have had the help of numerous individuals and institutions who have guided me and provided support for the completion of this book. My oldest debt goes to Myra Jehlen and Michael Warner, my advisers at Rutgers University, New Brunswick, who convinced me that I could write about cosmopolitanism and believed in this project before I did. During my time at Rutgers, a Mellon Foundation grant allowed me to attend Michael McKeon's seminar on Problems in Historical Interpretation, which initiated my thinking about what was to become the chapter on Thomas Jefferson and Enlightenment thought in this book. Another Mellon Foundation Grant at the Library Company of Philadelphia allowed me to read and transcribe the papers of Elizabeth Graeme Fergusson. Jim Greene and the library's staff, then and throughout the years that I have been doing archival research at the library, have been and continue to be an amazing resource. I also want to thank the Library Company for having given permission to print an image of Elizabeth Graeme Fergusson's commonplace book.

Thanks to a Mellon Postdoctoral Fellowship in the Humanities at the University of Pennsylvania, I was able to spend a year in Philadelphia doing essential research for completion of the first draft of the book. The conversations with the fellows throughout the year were among the most productive I have had, and I am particularly thankful for the discussions about cosmopolitanism with Peter Conn, who directed the Penn Humanities Forum at the time. Christopher Nichols' feedback on my work on Franklin helped me to think more deeply about the connection between Franklin's role as a founder and his version of cosmopolitanism. Participation in Encountering Revolution: Print Culture, Politics, and the British American Loyalists, a summer seminar at the American Antiquarian Society in 2011, helped me to gain perspective on my work on Elizabeth Graeme Fergusson and her loyalist connections. I am lucky to have encountered a true academic family in the members of the Society of Early Americanists who, at various conferences, have helped me to sharpen my arguments and provided welcome opportunities to reflect on thoughtful criticisms. Among this group I have found real friends and mentors. I met Zabelle Stodola at the beginning of my career, and her advice and model of scholarship and collegiality have provided me with an example to follow that has made me a better scholar. Carla Mulford has proven to be a most generous and caring friend and mentor, beginning with dragging me out of thinking that the book was never going to be finished, to sending feedback any time I asked for it, and to encouraging me throughout the past few years. Her work on Benjamin Franklin and early American literature and culture has provided an important intellectual context for my work and helped me to grow as a scholar. Thank you from the bottom of my heart, Carla. At those conferences, I also met Lisa Logan and Kacy Tillman who have proved to be great colleagues and friends. Our common interest in Elizabeth Fergusson has produced quite amazing conversations and scholarship. I am looking forward to more collaborative work in the future. I owe an extra debt of thanks to Ed Larkin, Palgrave's outside reader, for having given the most productive and wise feedback in later stages of revising the book before publication. I thank my friend Cathy Denning, indexer and editor *exceptionnelle*, for having helped me see the light at the end of the tunnel. She took on numerous tasks for me at the end of the project and quickly completed a job that I had thought undoable. My friends and colleagues, Catherine Lynes and Anthony Lioi, cheered for me when I was trying to formulate the initial thesis for this project. They still do, and I thank them for that.

An earlier version of Chap. 3 was published in 2006 in *Early American Literature* 41(1): 59–78. Sections of Chap. 5 appeared in *Correspondences: Essays on the History, Theory, and Practice of U.S. Letters, 1770–1860*, pp. 17–34 (Farnham: Ashgate, 2009), a collection of essays edited by Sharon M. Harris and Theresa Strouth Gaul. I am grateful to acknowledge the editor of the journal and press for permission to reprint the essays in a modified form. I also want to thank St. John's University for the institutional support they provided me over the years.

My parents, Anna Cini and Vasco Cillerai, were always there to support and help us and, when the work got too hard, they were ready to get on a transatlantic flight to make our life easier. My father passed away before the completion of this book. No day goes by without wishing that he could be here to see it. My in-laws, Anne and Jack Harrington and Richard and Carol Lockey were as supportive. They helped, cheered, and were always there to help. I dedicate this book to my husband and children. To Brian Lockey, life-partner, friend, and colleague, I owe a debt that nothing will ever repay. He is my most demanding and most rewarding reader, and I would not have been able to do any of this without him. My three children, Olivia, Benjamin, and William, are the greatest gift I have ever received and the light at the end of all my working days.

# Contents

1 Introduction     1

2 Caught in the Webs of Empire: Benjamin Franklin's Cosmopolitan Ideas for an American Self     17

3 Jefferson's Cosmopolitan Nature in *Notes on the State of Virginia*     59

4 Elizabeth Graeme Fergusson's Cosmopolis of Letters     99

5 'A Continual and Almost Exclusive Correspondence': Philip Mazzei's Cosmopolitan Citizenship     129

6 The Cosmopolitan Frame of Olaudah Equiano's *Interesting Narrative*     159

Index     201

CHAPTER 1

# Introduction

*"To be a cosmopolite is not, I think, an ideal; the ideal should be to be a concentrated patriot. Being a cosmopolite is an accident, but one must make the best of it."*
Henry James, "Occasional Paris," 1877

Although we most commonly associate cosmopolitan ideology with the tolerance for foreign lands, cultures and people, the word's historical origins point to an association with territorial colonial expansions. It is this second association that generates the conditions for cosmopolitanism to emerge and that provides a way to respond to the cultural exchanges and conflicts that inevitably follow colonial projects.[1] If the Ancient Greeks' coining of the term by combining the words κόσμος (cosmos) and πόλις (polis) was to describe interest and tolerance for different peoples and cultures outside the boundaries of one's own community, the reality of these encounters by

---

[1] Amanda Anderson gives a succinct description of this aspect of the history of cosmopolitanism when she writes: "Cosmopolitanism has repeatedly emerged at times when the world has suddenly seemed to expand in unassimilable ways; it is at these moments that universalism needs the rhetoric of worldliness that cosmopolitanism provides" (A. Anderson 1998, 272; see also A. Anderson 2001, 3–33).

© The Author(s) 2017
C. Cillerai, *Voices of Cosmopolitanism in Early American Writing and Culture*, The New Urban Atlantic, DOI 10.1007/978-3-319-62298-9_1

the time the Western world reached early modernity was accompanied by, or the result of, conflict over territorial and cultural dominance.[2] It was no coincidence then that early modern English writer John Dee, the first to use the expression "Brytish Impire," was also the first author in English to call himself a "cosmopolitan" (Netzloff 2003, 9). In a tract entitled, *General and Rare Memorials pertayning to the Perfect Arte of Navigation*, Dee promotes a naval force capable of defending Great Britain during a time of increasing geographical expansion. Dee describes himself as the observer of what Great Britain can accomplish, explaining he is a *"Cosmopolite*, a citizen and member of the whole and only one mysticall citie vniuersall, and so consequently [able] to meditate of the Cosmopoliticall gouernment thereof, under the King almightie" (Dee 1968, 3).[3] In presenting himself as a cosmopolite while discussing the establishment of a military force overseeing imperial expansion, Dee makes the idea of cosmopolitan world citizenship and travel dependent on the way in which the British Empire is beginning to form. His words not only reflect the ancient meaning of cosmopolitanism, but also anticipate the description of cosmopolitanism Immanuel Kant would offer at the end of the eighteenth century. The interdependence of cosmopolitan ideology and colonial expansion places a contradiction at the center of cosmopolitanism. The aspiration to universal

---

[2] Cosmopolitanism has a lengthy history beginning with Greek and Roman thinkers in the Cynic and Stoic traditions. Ancient philosophers such as Zeno, Marcus Cicero, and Seneca believed that humans were by nature inhabiting two communities, one local and determined by individual birth places, and one universal represented by the entirety of humankind. Tied to this idea of dual belonging was that of a set of universal laws for humanity to comply with. The tradition initiated in the last three centuries BC also affected the Judeo-Christian thought of early philosophers, such as St. Augustine and Thomas Aquinas, and continued through the early modern period when it reappeared in the thoughts of the Neo-Thomist Spanish thinkers Bartolomé de las Casas, Francisco Suárez, and Francisco de Vitoria. These philosophers responded to and criticized the contemporary civilizing missions in the Americas and the slaughter of native people using the idea of universal natural rights as applicable to all human beings, including the natives of the land their country was colonizing. The notion of the cosmopolitan that emerged during the Enlightenment belongs to this tradition and shows connections to the ancient ideas of universal citizenship, universal human rights, and communication. Enlightenment concepts of universal human reason, equal human worth, and the demands for universal justice directly derive from the Western thinkers of the previous centuries had developed and are also affected by the political, economic, and social structures of these periods (Heater 1996, 1–26; Brown and Held 2010, 1–14).

[3] This passage is also used in the *Oxford English Dictionary* as example of the first appearance of the word cosmopolitan in the English language.

understanding of differences at the core of cosmopolitanism is a response to the meeting of different cultures, ways of life, and ideologies that crossing borders causes. At the same time, this aspiration is a difficult goal to achieve when the parties involved are standing on unequal ground in a colonial landscape.

Cosmopolitanism in early American culture is part of this trend to reach for the ideal while struggling with colonial inequalities and violence. Cosmopolitanism presents itself as a cultural feature in early America. In his seminal study of the cosmopolitan ideal during the transatlantic Enlightenment, Thomas Schlereth wrote that contradiction was part of the ideal's "more symbolic and theoretical than actual and practical" nature. He explained:

> Often [cosmopolitanism] was only a highly subjective state of mind that sought to grasp the unity of mankind without, however, attempting to solve the relations of the part to the whole. ... As such the ideal usually allied with humanism, pacifism, and a developing (although ambivalent) conception of universal human equality. This abstract faith in the fundamental unity of mankind at times provided the rationale behind the philosophe's involvement in the numerous humanitarian reform movements of the eighteenth century. (Schlereth 1977, XII)

As Schlereth showed, eighteenth-century cosmopolitans were caught in this contradiction when negotiating between cosmopolitanism's aspiration and the colonial realities of their own world. Whereas Schlereth discussed the cosmopolitan ideal as pertaining to *philosophes* and their ideal republic of letters with a main focus on the European intellectual elites, this book explores the contradictions of cosmopolitanism in the context of early American writings. I show that the *philosophes* were not the only Enlightenment figures who used the language of cosmopolitanism. The late colonial North American environment and its transatlantic reach provide useful settings to understand the complexities of the connection between cosmopolitanism and colonialism. The writings of Thomas Jefferson, Benjamin Franklin, Elizabeth Graeme Fergusson, Philip Mazzei, and Olaudah Equiano show how cosmopolitanism emerged as an idea, as a set of inter-cultural standards and a way of life, as well as a literary trope that served the purpose of replacing what was missing within the emerging discourse of nationhood. To borrow the expression from Henry James' 1878 words placed as an epigraph to this introductory chapter, their early American cosmopolitanism is not necessarily a chosen ideological path, but an accident they "make the best of" (James 2004, 129).

The works of writers from the second half of the eighteenth century are exemplary of what eighteenth-century cosmopolitanism looks like in the North American colonial and transatlantic context, of the connection between cosmopolitanism and colonialism, and also of what happens to cosmopolitanism after the American Revolution establishes a state apparatus to replace colonial socio-political infrastructures. If there was a sense of nationhood before the nation was defined through the Declaration of Independence, the Constitution, and the other documents that accompanied them, this sense was inextricable from the sense of belonging established by the cultural and political entity they identified with. This entity was, of course, the British Empire. In this book I examine the language of cosmopolitanism visible in the context of empire. Colonial subjectivities overcame some of the marginality that living in the provinces generated through the ideals cosmopolitanism nurtured, such as the lack of boundaries and supranational impulses, among others. Although each of the writers discussed in this book experienced colonial marginality in different ways, cosmopolitanism generated a sense of communal identity.

The simultaneous marginalization and communal identity is also what makes cosmopolitanism particularly relevant as the rhetoric of nation-building rises during the final decades of the eighteenth century. Looking at texts composed during the period of transition from one political stage to another highlights what elements constitute cosmopolitanism and what determined its presence in the rhetoric of many early American texts. The relationship between cosmopolitanism and nationalism developed in the nineteenth century can be more fully understood by focusing on this period in America (Brennan 1997; Jacob 2006). In the context of the North American colonies the notion of nation (both as *patria* and state) was quite removed from the everyday life of a subject of the British Empire, if not alien to it altogether. Yet, as my analyses show, in an apparent contradiction, colonial Americans used the language of cosmopolitanism, albeit not all the time, as a stepping stone for imagining a national identity. What we find in the late colonial American contexts are different versions of cosmopolitanism determined by different contingencies all intertwined with the social, political, and cultural frameworks established by the British Empire.

The works of Franklin, Jefferson, Fergusson, Mazzei, and Equiano are representative of these widely varied social, cultural, and economic backgrounds in colonial America. These different backgrounds produced the contingencies that informed the way cosmopolitanism took shape in their writings, which serve to demonstrate the pervasiveness of the language of cosmopolitanism among eighteenth-century intellectuals and show how cosmopolitanism emerged in different forms as well as in different genres of writing. They also show that, although the language of the cosmopolitan ideal seems to be what allows the writer to overcome a cultural, political, or social constraint, the constraints vary dramatically for each of them. Thus the emerging forms of cosmopolitanism are quite different from each other and serve different purposes. In the writings of Thomas Jefferson and Benjamin Franklin, we find examples of the engagement with the cosmopolitanism of the republic of letters and the *philosophes*. Their works reveal the many ambivalences that stem from imagining nationhood as based on the principles of cosmopolitanism while actively involved in the political process of nation-building. Elizabeth Graeme Fergusson's manuscript poetry and her commonplace book writings show how the language of cosmopolitanism could defend, from a traditionalist perspective, the world destroyed by the War of Independence. Finally, the writings of Philip Mazzei and Olaudah Equiano present more complex versions of cosmopolitanism that serve the purpose of opening political, social, and cultural venues that dominant forces of power would otherwise impede.

In exploring the ways in which cosmopolitanism permeated the rhetoric of late eighteenth-century writings, I am participating in a conversation with other scholars of colonial American literature who have begun to understand that early representations of America are more than nationalistic. Scholars often mention the cosmopolitan as one of the factors that emerge in these early nationalistic representations (Shields 1997; Aravamudan 1999; Nwankwo 2005; Iannini 2012). Yet, none of these studies considers the role cosmopolitanism played in the culture of the period beyond a component of nationalism. My analysis of the particular manifestations of cosmopolitanism situates the phenomenon historically and theoretically within the frame of late eighteenth-century writings. Understanding the influence cosmopolitan rhetoric had on eighteenth-century writers within the transatlantic context contributes to the development of a better sense of what cosmopolitanism meant and provides a stronger foundation for the study of what the phenomenon developed into later (Wood 2013, 23–40).[4] The works I examine in this book show that early American writers identified their community through a dynamic relationship between the local contexts and the larger contexts of the British and European metropolises. Writers like Benjamin Franklin and Thomas Jefferson whom we have come to identify with the nationalistic process of "founding" America defined their community as both within and outside this larger context and made it what Benedict Anderson has said a nation cannot be: namely an entity "coterminous with mankind" (Anderson 1998, 6). In this respect, understanding what role cosmopolitanism played in late eighteenth-century American writings also contributes to understanding the often noted, but seldom studied, paradoxes that emerge when we consider how ambiguously many early American writers treated the idea of separation from the British Empire. Some of the difficulties that Americans experienced when imagining a non-British America can be better understood when we think of the cosmopolitan aspects of early colonialism. Ultimately, in engaging in this conversation, I aim at problematizing both the process of nation formation, as well as the meaning of cosmopolitanism and the role cosmopolitanism played in the late decades of the colonial period.

Recently, historian Philip Ziesche has argued that a cosmopolitan faith in universal principles of natural rights was one of the founding concepts of the American revolutionary movement. It was a faith that turned quickly into distrust and produced a new faith of exclusionary nationalism in the aftermath of the French Revolution. In his analysis, Ziesche explores how the coexistence and compatibility between forms of cosmopolitanism and patriotism decreased as the century ended (Ziesche 2010, 3–13). My readings here both extend and complicate Ziesche's point. In texts by writers such as Benjamin Franklin and Thomas Jefferson, not only had the principles of universal belief in human rights helped develop a form of national identity—they also contained the premises of a national subjectivity based on cosmopolitanism and the seeds for its demise by way of an exclusivist form of national identity because they

---

[4]While historians have also turned their attention to cosmopolitanism in early America, they have done so without paying enough attention to the rhetorical and literary aspects of the phenomenon. Using a literary study approach for my analyses, I expand and deepen what historian Gordon Wood has described as the exploration of how cosmopolitanism affected the way Americans "invented" their nation during the last decades of the eighteenth century.

originated in and depended on the transatlantic geopolitical and social infrastructures the British Empire had established. In addition, my readings of Philip Mazzei and Olaudah Equiano show how other writers enacted the terms of universal communication and understanding to find a place in a society keeping them at its margins. Although coming from two different backgrounds, one a member of the European intellectual elites and the other an ex-slave who spent most of his life working as a sailor and then as a member of the abolitionist movement, Mazzei and Equiano used the principles of cosmopolitanism to dismantle some of the universalizing notions that elitist forms of cosmopolitanism were fostering. Tropes related to the notion of world citizenship provided Mazzei and Equiano with new and critical terms to describe what being American and what being a citizen of the world meant. Fergusson's employment of a cosmopolitan language and imagery complicates the picture even further, as in her work cosmopolitanism functions as a catalyst for managing the loss of the ties her participation in the British Empire had guaranteed her previously and silently articulates a form of resistance to the nationalism of the revolutionary movement. In focusing on the forms literary cosmopolitanism took in eighteenth-century America—writings from a variety of social, cultural, and economic spheres—I extend the arguments made about the many faces of cosmopolitanism to the early American context.[5]

Cosmopolitanism offered a language to those who lived in the transatlantic world through which and with which to understand their position in the world, and it was a progressive force and a conservative force. Late eighteenth-century colonial writers used the rhetorical frame of cosmopolitanism that was at times multicultural and inclusive, and at times exclusive. At times, it was in dialogue with imperial discourses of hegemony, and at other times, in open resistance to the language of imperial domination. Eighteenth-century cosmopolitanism—because of this imbrication in the colonial project—worked as a force that went against imperialism and worked as a force that replicated it. Kant's words in one of the most cited representations of eighteenth-century cosmopolitanism provide an example of how it can be presented as a force that levels the disparities colonial expansion creates:

---

[5] Hollinger (2000), Cohen and Nussbaum (1996), Cheah and Robbins (1998), Dharwadker (2001), Breckenridge et al. (2002), Vertovec and Cohen (2002), Appiah (2006), Harvey (2009), Cohen (1992), Ackerman (1994), Nussbaum (2010).

> If we compare with this ultimate end the *inhospitable* conduct of the civilized states of our continent, especially the commercial states, the injustice which they display in *visiting* foreign countries and people (which in their case is the same as *conquering* them) seems appallingly great. America, the Negro countries, the Spice Islands, the Cape, etc. were looked upon at the time of their discovery as ownerless territories; for the native inhabitants were counted as nothing. In East India (Hindustan), foreign troops were brought in under the pretext of merely setting up trading posts. This led to oppression of the natives, incitement of the various Indian states to widespread wars, famine, insurrection, treachery, and the whole litany of evils which can afflict the human race … The people of the earth have thus entered in varying degrees into a universal community, and it has developed to the point where a violation of rights in one part of the world is felt everywhere. The idea of a cosmopolitan right is therefore not fantastic and overstrained; it is a necessary complement to the unwritten code of political and international right, transforming it into a universal right of humanity. Only under this condition can we flatter ourselves that we are continually advancing towards a perpetual peace. (Kant 1970, 106–107)

Kant's proposal that a cosmopolitan international law would counteract the oppression of colonial peoples is one example of the way in which cosmopolitanism is presented as a force to oppose colonial oppression and nationalistic enterprises. But Kant's representation is not the summation of all Enlightenment cosmopolitanism and its manifestations. In Chap. 2, as my analysis of Benjamin Franklin's essay "Observations Concerning the increase of Mankind", Peopling of Countries, etc shows, the language of the cosmopolitan ideal serves the purpose of imagining a form of nationalism based on a concept of ethnic superiority that embodies what Kant's discussion of cosmopolitanism rejects. In his 1750s essay, for example, Franklin uses the rhetoric of cosmopolitanism to show how erecting boundaries, divisions, and hierarchies is necessary to protect the interest of mankind. Franklin's essay turns the cosmopolitan idea of universal camaraderie among human beings on its head. This contradictory character of cosmopolitanism is, as I suggested earlier, part of its core structure. It is the result of cosmopolitanism's intrinsic connection to coloniality, as well its connection to the process of a national formation that took place during the late part of the eighteenth century in America (Mignolo 2002, 157–188). To overcome the otherness of the colonial world, Franklin reimagines the local as unbounded and cosmopolitan.

My analysis of Benjamin Franklin's writings also shows the depth of the interconnection between rootedness and cosmopolitan realities, between the nationally oriented and the international that characterized the trajectory cosmopolitanism followed throughout the eighteenth century in American culture. The texts I examine were written in various periods of Franklin's long writing career: the proposal for the establishment of an American branch of the Royal Philosophical Society written in the 1740s, the queries for the members of the well-known Junto club drafted in the 1730s, and two sections of the *Autobiography* in the second and third parts that Franklin composed a few years before his death and that also include writings from the early 1730s. Franklin's memoir is particularly useful to understand the complexities of late eighteenth-century manifestations of cosmopolitanism as readers find references to the earlier writings. The rhetoric of cosmopolitanism permeated the way in which Franklin imagined himself as part of the American cultural community in different stages of his writing career. This is not only because the autobiography is the work that recounts Franklin's life as a cosmopolitan, but also because he wrote it at the juncture between the pre- and post-revolutionary moments. The act of remembering and writing about his life in the colonial setting, while engaging in the process of establishing an identity that fits the new republican stage in American history, produced a series of breaks with similar representations in earlier writings. These narrative features show the role cosmopolitanism played in the formation of a sense of America, as well as how this role was always ambivalent. Franklin's writings from the early part of the century and those he composed after the split from England show how his cosmopolitanism produced representations of a proto-national entity based simultaneously on a universal and inclusive idea of caring about humanity and, as I suggested earlier, on an imperialistic idea of the same based on exclusion. The *Autobiography* and its dialogues with the textual materials that informed Franklin's writing present the complexities and duplicities of cosmopolitanism, its simultaneous resistance and interconnectedness with imperial politics and ideas (Ziesche 2010, 5–13).

In Chap. 3, I examine how, in the representation of his home in *Notes on the State of Virginia*, Thomas Jefferson merged the languages of cosmopolitanism, of the "New Rhetoric" movement, and of contemporary scientific debates to ensure America's representative position in the republic of letters. In this work, a localized, contained space with its natural components and its archeological findings serves the purpose of representing a supranational America. Jefferson places Virginia at the center of a cosmopolis with no centers and no margins. From this new position, the American landscape can be both continuous with Europe and exceptional. Because of these features, the form of cosmopolitanism that emerges produces a model of cosmopolitan nationhood that criticizes the conceptual boundaries of nationhood as it portrays an idea of America (embodied in his home state of Virginia) potentially unbounded. Although Jefferson's representation of a cosmopolitan American identity is not one that ever fully materializes in a theory of nation formation, it does contain foundational terms that characterize later versions of American exceptionalism. The scientific community and its cosmopolitan framework make it possible for Jefferson to create an idealized portrait of an American landscape in *Notes on the State of Virginia*.

Similar in importance to cosmopolitanism's relationship to colonial expansion is its relationship to both the locality of one's origin and the universality of humanity that characterize the history of Western thought. This duality gives this concept its dialectical structure. Its etymological roots in "cosmos" and "polis" reflect the universe and the urban space required to understand its meaning. The local is essential to an understanding of how and why colonial American writers were cosmopolitan as the location of the colonies in relation to the center of imperial power is one that lends itself to the imagining of a world with fluid borders. While this duality is a relevant feature in all the texts I examine in the book, the local is particularly significant when seen in the writings of Elizabeth Fergusson not only because it highlights the connections between cosmopolitanism and the imperial networks of the colonial world (as is the case with Franklin and Jefferson), but also because cosmopolitanism was both a progressive force and an embodiment of conservative tendencies that ultimately blurred the line that separates patriotism from loyalism during the early republican years (as is the case of Fergusson's work). Fergusson's cosmopolitanism originates in the sociocultural environment of colonial Philadelphia and informs her as a poet and as an intellectual. Fergusson's cosmopolitanism is interdependent with the social interactions and the intellectual exchanges her environment provides. Her cosmopolitanism becomes a form of intellectual, if not political, loyalism. And in the 1780s and 1790s, her cosmopolitanism opens up a space in which the world and language the Revolution had taken away from her could survive. In a side note, in a commonplace book that Fergusson composed for her long-time friend Annis Boudinot Stockton in 1787, the writer refers to the war of the previous decade as a civil war that had torn families and friends apart.[6] Although Fergusson never openly shares her husband's loyalism, when she recovers her lost familial and friendship ties in the books that she composes, her mourning for the past and her cosmopolitan attitude translate into a type of loyalty which, if not political, is certainly cultural. The books and her poetry become the space where the cosmopolitan world of imperial Philadelphia continues to live.

Cosmopolitanism is what allows Fergusson to reimagine friendships, intellectual exchanges, and the borderless environment of her youth. It also identifies her longing for a system that was in place because of the imperial government over Pennsylvania. The cosmopolitanism in Fergusson's writing, which I call "creative cosmopolitanism," echoes the principles in Kant's representation of a "cosmopolitan law," but could also be described as "loyalist" as it clearly reminds us of her reliance on the colonial world to perform it. For Fergusson, the cosmopolitan social laws that organized the world in which she grew up were determined by an imperial system of cultural and material exchange. And here lies cosmopolitanism's most significant contradiction. What we see as "cosmopolitan laws" in Fergusson's writings can also be seen as the cause of the problems that a few years later Kant's "cosmopolitan laws" were devised to solve. While the conservatism of Fergusson's cosmopolitanism might seem unusual, it is part of what I have already identified as its intrinsic contradictory nature. In a recent study of the connection between cosmopolitanism and Catholicism during the British Renaissance, Brian Lockey has shown that for many early modern English writers, cosmopolitanism functioned in a similar way as we see in early American writers like Fergusson. Lockey showed that the early modern period secular cosmopolitanism emerged out of a medieval religious transnational realm headed by the Pope (Lockey 2015, 1–23). In Fergusson's work, cosmopolitanism bridges the gap the Revolution and its politics have brought into her life and allows her to revive her lost social and intellectual colonial environment.

---

[6]The manuscript book containing the reference is located at the Dickinson College Library and it accompanies a letter that Fergusson's nephew (a loyalist) wrote from England after the revolution.

Examining what cosmopolitanism looked like in the variety of texts produced in late colonial America also places this book in dialogue with postcolonial studies, a field that recently and frequently has engaged with the study of cosmopolitanism. Postcolonial theorists have utilized and redefined the concept in order to examine the geopolitical and cultural transformations that followed the dismantling of the various European empires. The "new" cosmopolitanism that has emerged from post-colonial analyses has been described as "actually existing," "rooted," "vernacular," and "managerial and critical."[7] Scholars have used these more complex definitions to assess how cosmopolitanism works and manifests itself in different colonial and post-colonial historical and cultural contexts. (Lockey 2015; Ramachandran 2015) Using postcolonial work on cosmopolitanism as a theoretical framework, the eighteenth-century meaning of the American expression "citizen of the world" needs to be interpreted differently because it is similarly historically contingent. The early American political and cultural context was also rooted in a modern transatlantic and cosmopolitan humanism. As I have already argued, by participating in the transatlantic republic of letters, American writers such as Mazzei and Equiano were concerned about place and nation in ways that differed from people located at the center of imperial metropolises. Mazzei's and Equiano's versions of cosmopolitanism are the last two examples I examine in this book.

In the fourth chapter, my analysis of Philip Mazzei's writings shows how the correspondences and his commercial exchanges that established his status of European intellectual formed a cosmopolitan foundation for this early Italian immigrant's representation of American identity. In his letters and letter-form writings, Mazzei represented a cosmopolitan ideal subjectivity based on dialogue and comparative analysis. He developed this view while he travelled and experienced life as a citizen of the British colonial world. During his experience in the revolutionary period, he represented an ideal American citizen based on this model. Mazzei's American is a citizen of the world who claims his identity based on the eighteenth-century cosmopolitan ideal of tolerance and understanding of others. Ultimately, his faith in being a citizen of the world, while also being an American, proved impossible. The views that had allowed him to become a cosmopolitan American were the ones that stopped him

---

[7] See footnote 5.

from having the American political career to which he aspired. Mazzei's American could be an American only while he is moving from one place to reach another one. Nation-building hindered that mobility.

The methodologies used in postcolonial studies shape my analyses of how cosmopolitanism manifested itself in the early American context. The supranational and universalist appeal of the cosmopolitan accompanies empire building and defines narrative aligned with the cosmopolitan perspective of global understanding and cooperation with Western political ideology. Writers located on a variety of cultural, social, and political margins found a voice with which to identify themselves and their American and transatlantic worlds with the language of cosmopolitanism. Cosmopolitanism formed a foundation of a rhetoric to resist imperial expansion for those on the edges of empire. The ex-slave Olaudah Equiano's autobiographical narrative I examine in the last chapter of this book is a case in point. Equiano's social and cultural background do not fit the cosmopolitanism model of the period and force us to find other ways cosmopolitanism played out during the eighteenth century, thus enriching our understanding of its cultural significance.[8] Equiano's worldliness and his commitment to the world's community are not solely a matter of choice or a reflection of his interest in mankind's welfare, which is traditionally considered at the center of cosmopolitanism. If these factors enter the narrative of Equiano's life, they do so because of Equiano's marginalized place in colonial society. As the language of cosmopolitanism emerges in the narrative, it generates a rhetorical frame in which readers are directed to imagine an eighteenth-century that is multicultural and inclusive, and thus, understanding the limitations abiding solely by one's contemporary cultural standards establishes. The language of cosmopolitanism Equiano uses not only helps him to condemn

---

[8] In describing Equiano as cosmopolitan, I am taking a position that differs from that of some postcolonial scholars such as Srivinas Aravamudan. Aravamudan describes figures like Equiano as "tropicopolitans" and opposes them to Enlightenment cosmopolitans because of their geographical position and, especially, because they challenge the privilege of contemporary cosmopolitans. I do so because I see Equiano's developing narrative identity as being generated using terms that belong to the rhetoric of Enlightenment cosmopolitanism and rather than seeing the narrative subject as working to debunk the concept, the narrative reshapes the concepts itself within its own rhetorical frame (Avaramudan 1999, 1–25 and 2001, 615–619).

slavery from the standpoint of the abolitionist movement in which he participates and whose rhetoric he is employing, the language of cosmopolitanism also allows Equiano to resist the limits abolitionist rhetoric places on him as a black writer and an ex-slave. This language of cosmopolitanism allows Equiano to avoid the creation of a narrative subject based on racial hierarchies the abolitionist movement supports which would inevitably place such a subject at the bottom. That model leaves the narrative subject in a state of perpetual captivity. Equiano creates a cosmopolitan subject in his autobiography (both as the autobiographer and as the autobiographical subject) reflective of a model of subjectivity that promotes cultural and ideological equality and that engages in dialogues and exchange of ideas. In the end, this subjectivity and its world remain virtual, but the challenges they perform constitute the core of the *Interesting Narrative*. The critical subjectivity Equiano develops demonstrates the power a cosmopolitan perspective offered individuals whose social and cultural position was one of submission and dependence by default.

The texts I examine in this book suggest that the forms of cosmopolitanism that emerged in the North American colonial environment were at times the result of impulses aimed at generating exclusive forms of identity. At other times, cosmopolitanism was the result of desire to overcome cultural and socio-economic boundaries, and still at others, it was a way to mourn the loss of social interactions being part of an empire made possible. Cosmopolitanism was at times a way to look forward to better and more inclusive forms of social and cultural interaction, and at times it was a means to bring back an uncontested imperial past that encompasses the entirety of North America.

## REFERENCES

Ackerman, Bruce. 1994. Rooted Cosmopolitanism. *Ethics* 104: 516–535.
Anderson, Amanda. 1998. The Divided Legacies of Modernity. In *Cosmopolitics: Thinking and Feeling beyond the Nation*, ed. Pheng Cheah, and Bruce Robbins, 265–289. Minneapolis, MN: University of Minnesota Press.
———. 2001. *The Powers of Distance: Cosmopolitanism and the Cultivation of Detachment*. Princeton, NJ: Princeton University Press.
Anderson, Benedict. 1998. *Imagined Communities: Reflections on the Origins and Spread of Nationalism*. New York: Verso.
Appiah, Kwame Anthony. 2006. *Cosmopolitanism: Ethics in a World of Strangers*. New York: W.W. Norton and Co.

Aravamudan, Srivinas. 1999. *Tropicopolitans: Colonialism and Agency, 1688–1804*. Durham, NC: Duke University Press.
———. 2001. Equiano Lite. *Eighteenth-Century Studies* 34: 615–619.
Breckenridge, Carol A., Sheldon Pollock, Homi K. Bhaba, and Dipesh Chakrabarty. 2002. *Cosmopolitanism*. Durham, NC: Duke University Press.
Brennan, Timothy. 1997. *At Home in the World: Cosmopolitanism No*. Cambridge, MA: Harvard University Press.
Brown, Garrett Wallace, and David Held. 2010. *The Cosmopolitanism Reader*. Cambridge: Cambridge University Press.
Cheah, Pheng, and Bruce Robbins (eds.). 1998. *Cosmopolitics: Thinking and Feeling beyond the Nation*. Minneapolis, MN: University of Minnesota Press.
Cohen, Joshua, and Martha Nussbaum. 1996. *For Love of Country: Debating the Limits of Patriotism*. Boston, MA: Beacon Press.
Cohen, Mitchell. 1992. Rooted Cosmopolitanism. *Dissent* 39 (fall): 458–483.
Dee, John. 1968. *General and Rare Memorials pertayning to the Perfect Arte of Navigation*. New York: DaCapo Press.
Dharwadker, Vinay. 2001. *Cosmopolitan Geographies: New Location in Literature and Culture*. New York: Routledge.
Harvey, David. 2009. *Cosmopolitanism and the Geographies of Freedom*. New York: Columbia University Press.
Heater, Derek. 1996. *World Citizenship and Government: Cosmopolitan Ideas in the History of Western Political Thought*. New York: Continuum.
Hollinger, David A. 2000. *Postethnic America*, 10th anniversary edition. New York: Basic Books.
Iannini, Christopher P. 2012. *Fatal Revolutions: Natural History, West Indian Slavery, and the Routes of American Literature*. Williamsburg VA: University of North Carolina Press.
Jacob, Margaret C. 2006. *Strangers Nowhere in the World: The Rise of Cosmopolitanism in Early Modern Europe*. Philadelphia, PA: University of Pennsylvania Press.
James, Henry. 2004. Occasional Paris. In *Americans in Paris: A Literary Anthology*. New York: The Library of America.
Kant, Immanuel. 1970. *Kant's Political Writings*. trans. H.B. Nisbet, and ed. Hans Reiss. Cambridge: Cambridge University Press.
Lockey, Brian. 2015. *Early Modern Catholics, Royalists, and Cosmopolitans: English Transnationalism and the Christian Commonwealth*. New York: Ashgate/Routledge.
Mignolo, Walter. 2002. The Many Faces of Cosmopolis: Border Thinking and Critical Cosmopolitanism. In *Cosmopolitanism*, ed. Carol Breckenridge, et al., 157–188. Durham, NC: Duke University Press.

Netzloff, Mark. 2003. *England's Internal Colonies: Class, Capital, and the Literature of Early Modern English Colonialism*. New York: Palgrave Macmillan.

Nussbaum, Martha. 2010. Kant and Cosmopolitanism. In *The Cosmopolitan Reader*, ed. Garrett Wallace Brown and David Held, 27–44. Cambridge: Cambridge University Press.

Nwankwo, Ifeoma. 2005. *Cosmopolitanism: Racial Consciousness and Transnational Identity in the Nineteenth-Century Americas*. Philadelphia, PA: University of Pennsylvania Press.

Ramachandran, Ayesha. 2015. *The Worldmakers: Global Imagining in Early Modern Europe*. Chicago: University of Chicago Press.

Schlereth, Thomas J. 1977. *The Cosmopolitan Ideal in Enlightenment Thought: Its Form and Function in the Ideas of Franklin, Hume, and Voltaire, 1694–1790*. Notre Dame, IN: University of Notre Dame Press.

Shields, David S. 1990. *Oracles of Empire: Poetry, Politics, and Commerce in British America, 1690–1750*. Chicago: University of Chicago Press.

Shields, David S. 1997. *Civil Tongues and Polite Letters in British America*. Williamsburg, VA: University of North Carolina Press.

Vertovec, Steven, and Robin Cohen. 2002. *Conceiving Cosmopolitanism: Theory, Context, and Practice*. Oxford: Oxford University Press.

Wood, Gordon. 2013. The Invention of the United States. In *Cosmopolitanism and Nationhood in the Age of Jefferson*, ed. Peter Nicolaisen, and Hannah Spahn, 23–40. Heildelberg: Universitätsverlag Winter GmbH Heidelberg.

Ziesche, Philipp. 2010. *Cosmopolitan Patriots: Americans in Paris in the Age of Revolution*. Charlottesville, VA: University of Virginia Press.

CHAPTER 2

# Caught in the Webs of Empire: Benjamin Franklin's Cosmopolitan Ideas for an American Self

In the following two chapters I illustrate how cosmopolitanism allows two of the often-called founding fathers of the United States to negotiate the global as well as the local in the colonial context. For both Benjamin Franklin and Thomas Jefferson, the language of cosmopolitanism works as a tool to carve out a central space in a world in which they inhabit geographical and cultural margins. Both writers were prominent figures in the intellectual, political, and scientific communities that composed the transatlantic environment of the republic of letters and both of them played a central role in the transition of the American colonies into nationhood. They lived abroad for long periods of time, were highly engaged in crossing borders, and, eventually, in imagining new borders for the nation they helped found. These shared features of their lives constitute what is cosmopolitan about Franklin and Jefferson and it is what enables them to re-center their own worlds. Their writings allow us to understand the interdependence of eighteenth-century cosmopolitanism with imperial structures and national formation. These two figures are the authors of texts that contain seminal representations of a newly formed American national identity, Franklin's *Autobiography* and Jefferson's *Notes on the State of Virginia*. In these two texts, cosmopolitanism functions as a building block for the articulation of an early notion of American national identity. And since cosmopolitanism is by definition a notion that aims at overpassing boundaries of culture, place, and politics, the fact it can offer elements with which to imagine what it is not supposed to produce may appear quite a contradiction. These two works, however, show this contradiction is as intrinsic to the notion of eighteenth-century cosmopolitanism as it is the aspiration to cherish all mankind and its differences.

In these chapters I show how eighteenth-century cosmopolitanism in the North American transatlantic context cannot simply be seen as a force that overcomes national identification because it is produced by and responds to the socio-economic and cultural conditions that the British Empire imposes on its subjects. Rather, cosmopolitanism works as a force that allows national identities to form. Franklin and Jefferson's sense of identity is grounded in the British commonwealth. As British subjects in colonial America, their sense of identity exists in the fluid space they inhabit and in the sense of Britishness that imperial culture projects onto its members. Within this world their position is two-sided. On the one hand, their Britishness places them in the privileged position of the colonial elites. On the other hand, they live and work on the margins of a geographically extended world where they have limited access to the resources and engagement with other members of the elites with whom they identify. This dichotomy is evident in all the works by the two authors I examine in this chapter and Chap. 3, and it is the reason for many of the ambiguities we find in Franklin's and Jefferson's writings. The ambiguity is visible in Franklin's employment of cosmopolitanism as both a vehicle to represent a supranational form of local government and as a way to assert the role that Britishness (as a distinctive pseudo-ethnic and cultural characteristic) should have in the expansion of a future American nation. The tension is equally visible in Jefferson's writings. Jefferson's cosmopolitanism straddles two positions in his representation of a unique American voice that speaks to the European elites while employing a voice that replicates and appropriates the Native peoples of North America.

Franklin's cosmopolitanism permeates all aspects of his life and writings. From his childhood reading experiences that spanned historical and geographical lengths to the continuous traveling that brought him back and forth from colonial Pennsylvania to England and to continental Europe, Franklin's life and work reflect the transnationality that characterizes the Enlightenment ideal of the cosmopolitan. The transnationality of Franklin's life is also reflected in the amount of correspondences he maintained throughout his life. The many letters, essays, and other writings he composed and circulated provide testimony of this cosmopolitan character. While the cosmopolitan traits of Franklin's work and life are manifest, his memoir, the work that represents the life and the man who lived it, portrays an individual who identifies with the local; one who is rooted in place rather than spread across many places as the man Franklin actually was. The story of "the circumstances of [Benjamin Franklin's] Life," in his own words, as he describes it, reflects this cosmopolitan attitude based on a sense of transnational belonging that is, at the same time, rooted in place. The genesis of the book's publication is also a reflection (albeit posthumous) of this reality of Benjamin Franklin's life and work.[1] The work we now know as *The Autobiography of Benjamin Franklin* was published for the first time in France as a French translation of the original manuscript in 1791, the year that followed his death. Translations of this edition in English followed those in German and Swedish (Green and Stallybrass 2006, 152–153).[2] Like the life of the cosmopolitan who is, at least in theory, a polyglot of sorts and a man at home in the world, it is through a series of linguistic translations and continuous geographical movements that the story of Franklin's manuscript memoir began.[3]

---

[1] James N. Green and Peter Stallybrass have pointed out Franklin's cosmopolitanism in one of the essays collected in the book that accompanied the catalogue of an exhibit held at the Library Company of Philadelphia in 2006, celebrating the tercentenary of Franklin's birth. In the chapter entitled "Making and Remaking Benjamin Franklin: *The Autobiography*," the writers discuss how the re-naming of Franklin's last work and the genesis of its posthumous publication have affected the ways in which the work has been historically read and interpreted. Although the scholars highlight Franklin's cosmopolitanism, they do not seem to see it reflected in the trajectory the text followed from its original manuscript form to the published work that we know today (Green and Stallybrass 2006, 145–171).

[2] Of the various translations and editions that followed the first ones, the authors say: "Franklin's book was a British book before it was an American one and, more importantly, it was a foreign language book before it was an English one. Finally, the first French translation [based of one of Franklin's manuscripts] was closer to what Franklin wrote than any of the English versions, which were drawn straight from the printed French *Memoires* and had no relation to any of the manuscripts. Here again, the history of the memoir's reception partially replicates the history of its writing, Europe preceding America as the place of its printing as it had been of its composition" (Green and Stallybrass 2006, 156).

[3] Throughout this chapter I will refer to the work as either the *Autobiography* or memoir/s. Although "autobiography" is not the word that Franklin would have used to address his work, the title that Bigelow gave it in 1862 is the one with which most readers are familiar and that, to a twenty-first-century readership, defines this work's generic realm.

## 1 AN AMERICAN REPUBLIC OF LETTERS

Franklin wrote the blueprint for the American Philosophical Society, entitled "A Proposal for Promoting Useful Knowledge among the British Plantations in America," in 1743, five years before he retired from operating his printing business. In the autobiography, he describes this period as one in which his attention turned to Pennsylvania's lack of "Provisions for Defense" and "a complete Education of Youth. No Militia nor any College" (Franklin 1987, 1410). Although the time frame for creating both the "academy" and the American branch of the philosophical society had to be extended, both institutions eventually came to life. In his autobiographical reminiscence, Franklin misses the date of publication of the broadside that contains the proposal by one year and says it was printed in 1744 (Hindle 1974, 127–145).[4] The proposal begins with a description of the colonial geography that emphasizes the physical extension and the natural wealth of the North American territories. The description of the large British dominions of North America, their powerful economic capacity in producing wealth that can be exported to England, and an acknowledgement of the hardship entailed in establishing successful colonial plantations open the first paragraph:

> The English possess'd of a long Tract of Continent, from Nova Scotia to Georgia, extending North and South thro' different Climates, having different Soils, producing different Plants, Mines and Minerals, and capable of different Improvements, Manufactures, &c. (Franklin 2: 380)

It is evident here that from the beginning Franklin identifies the development of an intellectual colonial elite with the economic mechanism that makes the empire flourish: the exploitation of American natural resources. The colonies' economic power and their geographical extension are the first features employed to attest to their viability and recognition among other knowledge-producing communities. Such an opening evokes the language of the colonial tracts generally aimed at obtaining financial or political support for the provinces as well as those

---

[4] Friends and correspondents in both the colonies and in England warmly supported Franklin's plan and the circulation of materials among those involved began right away, but they were not able to translate it into a material organization until 1769.

designed to invite new settlers. The description of the geographic extension of the North American territories and their productive power, especially Franklin's reference to "manufactures," also introduces a sense of completion and the implicit readiness to embark in new enterprises. Using the word "manufactures," Franklin evokes the process that transforms raw materials into finished products and the consequent potential economic independence such a process can provide. The entire productive cycle from the prime materials to their finished state is or should be in the colonies and the conditions for their economic independence are outlined in the list Franklin provides. Following the publication of the broadside of the proposal, the establishment of manufactures in the colonial territories became a major conflict between Great Britain and its North American colonies. The central government thought it an economic disadvantage and a cause of excessive emigration to establish manufactures in America and in 1750 passed the Iron Act, one of the Trade and Navigation acts that forbade American iron manufactures to expand beyond the production of basic materials (Mulford 2015, 75–182).[5]

In his proposal, Franklin does not present his comments about prime materials and manufactures as propaganda for any form of political independence from Great Britain. As this is a proposal for the establishment of an American equivalent of the Royal Philosophical Society, American material resources become what produces the knowledge for society to independently exist. The independence to which Franklin refers from the beginning of the proposal is what can allow America to be included within the international community of letters and science in which he claims an independent place. The aim of his prospective society is to claim the intellectual independence that comes from economic prosperity. Such prosperity produces a class of individuals who can access European elite communities that societies similar in structure and purpose have already established. The position for the American

---

[5] In these years, England was becoming more and more resistant to the idea of an industrial development of the colonies which was seen as a means of increasing emigration and creating the risk of losing its own sources of wealth. The 1750 Iron Act prohibited the exportation of any form of industry that could attract English workers. Franklin responded to such a decision with his ambivalent essay "Observation Concerning the Increase of Mankind, Peopling of Countries, & …" See the end of this chapter. Mulford's study traces the development of the position that culminated in the writing of the 1750s essay.

Philosophical Society Franklin will articulate in the proposal depends on giving the society itself a cosmopolitan shape.

Similar to the eighteenth-century ideal of the cosmopolite who needs to disengage from a home country in order to become a free citizen of the world, Franklin posits that the American intellectual community needs to achieve independence from the colonial system (at the economic and at the intellectual level) that controls its entrance to the international community and gives its work its appropriate value. There is no revolutionary spirit in Franklin's aspiration to create an independent American Philosophical Society. This imagined American community does not reject its attachment to the imperial elements that have generated the conditions for its prosperity. In the second, longer, paragraph of the proposal, in fact, Franklin explains how the economic prosperity of the colonies is the necessary condition for America to be considered as a member of the literary and scientific international community. The outline that Franklin generates also describes the connection between economic prosperity, and scientific and literary advancement:

> The first Drudgery of Settling new Colonies, which confines the Attention of People to mere Necessaries is now pretty well over; and there are many in every Province in Circumstances that set them at Ease, and afford Leisure to cultivate the finer Arts, and improve the common Stock of Knowledge. To such of these who are Men of Speculation, many Hints must from time to time arise, many Observations occur, which if well-examined, pursued and improved, might produce Discoveries to the Advantage of some or all the *British* Plantations, or to the Benefit of Mankind in general. But as from the Extent of the Country such Persons are widely separated, and seldom can see and converse or be acquainted with each other, so that many useful Particulars remain uncommunicated, die with the Discoverers, and are lost to Mankind; it is, to remedy this Inconvenience for the future, proposed. [...] (Franklin 2: 380)

Economic development and stability are essential to the development of knowledge. Economic development, the passage explains, generates the conditions (wealth and leisure time) for people to exercise their studies and "cultivate the finer arts." Now that these conditions have been achieved, the American Philosophical Society should be established and recognized. Such a trajectory replicates Franklin's own life experience, of course. His "retirement" from active participation in the printing business follows the essay by only a few years. His career as public official had begun and he had already become involved with his scientific inquiries, which were to be soon published and circulated internationally (Lemay 2005–2008, 452ff).

In Franklin's representation, an American cosmopolitan project depends on the success of colonial ventures and the establishment of a prosperous class of colonials. The combination of pursuing and improving knowledge and economic gain is central to Franklin's cosmopolitanism. What emerges in the proposal for the establishment of the American Philosophical Society is a significant example of the way in which, for Franklin, the burgeoning notion of a philosophically independent American community, which is at the basis of what he represents in the broadside, develops out of a dialogue between the terms of the Enlightenment representation of cosmopolitanism and those of commerce and empire (Mignolo 2002, 157–159).[6] The terms that relate to these different categories speak to each other throughout Franklin's proposal and form the basis of a vision of America as an entity that exists within the British Empire and its functional infrastructures (Shields 1990, 13–35). Franklin represents an American philosophical society that places itself simultaneously within and above the structures of the British Empire for the universal purpose of serving humankind using the universalizing terms of the cosmopolitan ideal and engaging with the ideas that the Enlightenment version of the republic of letters promoted. Franklin's view of the American branch of the society makes its independent identity more valuable at both the intellectual and economic levels.

Franklin takes colonial intellectuals away from their place and into the ephemeral and universal world of the republic of letters with this model. As historian Dena Goodman has shown, the Enlightenment republic of letters could claim independence from any state-based structures because of the way in which it imagined itself as a universal entity that could not be represented by any constituted body, be it academic or political, although it was based on a representation that replicated the modern political state, and therefore could be implicated in the actions of its power structures. This sense of independence was based on the concept

---

[6]Walter Mignolo retraces the history of this interdependence throughout modernity and finds the roots of modern cosmopolitan thinking within those of Western early modern colonial projects. Mignolo describes this kind of cosmopolitanism as "emancipatory," that is, it aims at generating independence from the economic and ideological forces that make it possible.

of a republic founded on an ideal of knowledge as collaborative enterprise, correspondences, association, and exchange of ideas (Goodman 1994, 15–22). Cosmopolitan notions of universal friendship, cooperation, understanding, and exchange of ideas served the republic and its members as means to identify themselves as well as their scope. They also become the means by which the culture of imperial expansion and commerce become tangled in Franklin's representation of an association of men of letters. The community Franklin represents in his proposal is part of such a republic of letters and thus depends on the exchange of letters and the exchange of goods, and on an open commerce of both. Franklin argues from the opening of the proposal that the imperial economy is an essential component of the future American Philosophical Society. At the same time, this economy generates the conditions for the society to nurture a community that, by principle, is not functioning for the improvement of a single nation, such as Great Britian , its colonies, or an independent America, but the community of humans it represents (Schlereth 1977, 1–24; Goodman 1994, 23–52).

Franklin makes clear from the opening paragraph of the proposal that the cosmopolitan role of the society is subordinate to the role it would have within the limits of the "*British* Plantations," to which the most important discoveries of the society would be directed. The cosmopolitan alternative to the first possibility is introduced by the conjunction "or" in the concluding sentence of the passage cited earlier: "or to the Benefit of Mankind in general." It is with supranational terms Franklin defines what the American society should represent as his description proceeds. In the following part of the proposal, the conjunction "or" that marks the difference between the imperial territories and human kind is removed, and the colonial space becomes a reflection of the world. Colonials, British subjects, and mankind come together in the actual proposed format of the society:

> That One Society be formed of Virtuosi or ingenious Men residing in the several Colonies, to be called The American Philosophical Society. Who are to maintain a constant Correspondence.
>
> That Philadelphia being the City nearest the Centre of the Continent-Colonies, communicating with all of them northward and southward by Post, and with all the Islands by Sea, and having the Advantage of a good growing Library, be the Centre of the Society.

That at Philadelphia there be always at least seven Members, viz. a Physician, a Botanist, a Mathematician, a Chemist, a Mechanician, a Geographer, and a general Natural Philosopher, besides a President, Treasurer and Secretary.

That these Members meet once a Month, or oftener, at their own Expence, to communicate to each other their Observations, Experiments, &c. to receive, read and consider such Letters, Communications, or Queries as shall be sent from distant Members; to direct the Dispersing of Copies of such Communications as are valuable, to other distant Members, in order to procure their Sentiments thereupon, &c. (Franklin 2: 380)

Virtuosi devoted to the improvement of mankind form the society and their "constant Correspondence" keeps it together. The colonies' geographical extensiveness and their marginality in the metropolitan context are now reversed. Philadelphia is constructed as the center that will produce and circulate knowledge, and the philosophical society would institutionalize collaborative research, discoveries, and their powers. The American intellectual who lives and operates within this environment will be more American because he now possesses distinctive features that make him recognizable outside of his own world as an American intellectual. This intellectual, however, also becomes what Diderot called "a citizen of the great city of the world," because the community he forms and improves is a community of humans, not of nationals (Diderot 1955, 8: 16).[7] The colonial world and European metropolitan centers are now subordinate to the overarching republic of letters that exists within them but is located at a superior level. Franklin's description of the scope of the American Philosophical Society in the central part of the proposal outlines this process: the colonial world and its ideas have progressed within and exceeded their imperial surroundings. Now they are beneficial to "Mankind in general."

In the latter part of the document, Franklin describes the administrative positions the philosophical society will require and reserves the role of secretary to himself:

---

[7]With these words, Denis Diderot addressed David Hume in a letter written on February 22, 1768. Hume is another cosmopolitan figure whose life as well as performance within the international intellectual circle closely followed the trajectory of colonials like Franklin. Hume overcame the marginality of his being Scottish by presenting himself as a supranational figure.

The Business and Duty of the Secretary be, To receive all Letters intended for the Society, and lay them before the President and Members at their Meetings; to abstract, correct and methodize such Papers, &c. as require it, and as he shall be directed to do by the President, after they have been considered, debated and digested in the Society; to enter Copies thereof in the Society's Books, and make out Copies for distant Members; to answer their Letters by Direction of the President, and keep Records of all material Transactions of the Society, &c.

Benjamin Franklin, the Writer of this Proposal, offers himself to serve the Society as their Secretary, 'till they shall be provided with one more capable. (Franklin 2: 382–383)

As its secretary, Franklin performed fundamental editorial work while remaining at the margins of the publication process (Grabo 1993, 31–39; Thomas 2012, 103–118). The marginal position he acquires as secretary/editor of the society's papers, like the position of the American Philosophical Society on the margins of the British metropolitan space, turns into a central one when one thinks of the power such a position gives Franklin.[8] Franklin produces the essential features of the society's

---

[8] The ambivalence and multiplicity of terms that Franklin employs to portray the individual and the group identity that we have seen in this text so far has been read in a variety of ways. They have often been related to the protean character of the personas and literary devices that Franklin employed and to the duplicity that they generated. Most convincingly, Michael Warner has described this literary strategy as determined by Franklin's "instrumental relation to discourse." Such a relationship generates what Warner has called a "manipulating self," whose sense of identity develops in rhetoric, and which, in order to exist, needs the printed form, the texture of the work that produces it. Instead of thinking of a self as an abstracted matter that is external to the text that produces it, Warner argues that Franklin's sense of identity exists within the printed material, the text itself. Because of these generative circumstances, Warner continues, Franklin's subjectivity "assumes this absent agent in the same way that print, so conceived, postulates a generative agent not immanent in it" (Warner 1990, 76–79). Warner's view of Franklin's subjectivity is useful to understand the narrative form that Franklin uses in "A Proposal for Promoting Useful Knowledge." Warner shows that the printed discourse of the public sphere is the principal factor in producing this type of subjectivity. However, the public sphere that Warner recognizes as determining Franklin's particular strategy of self-representation is also interconnected with the other eighteenth-century discourses that I have discussed earlier such as those of cosmopolitanism, empire, and colonial economy, as well as the networks of manuscript materials that were constantly circulating among the representatives of the republic of letters. Franklin's connections to the environment that surrounds him are, I would

papers and of the society itself as the secretary when he edits and revises for publication. These features constitute the body of knowledge that the society supplies to the public. Franklin can achieve this goal because of his ability to control both the internal and the external workings of the organization as both secretary and, one would assume, the printer of its proceedings.[9] These movements replicate those of the society and of its materials and, ultimately, those of the colonial world and its inhabitants. Colonial networks of exchange are based on the principles that Franklin's description reflects. The "hints" that men of science and letters have accumulated over time to which Franklin refers in the opening of the proposal become the correspondence that ties the colonial space to the European centers.[10]

---

suggest, more grounded in the reality of life than hidden in the texture of the page. As I have shown, the particular context in which Franklin writes, and which is affected by his colonial intellectual position, determines the way he presents subjectivity as an entity fluid and in movement yet in conversation with the socio-historical circumstances that surround it. The rhetoric that reproduces this view on the page reflects these features as well.

[9] On this point, I find my argument progressing in the same direction as scholar Ed White when he argues that Franklin's scholarship has often had too much of a tendency to separate him from the actual historical and political circumstances that surrounded the production of his writings (White 1999, 1–33).

[10] Franklin's narrative strategy in this part of the proposal—the ideal critical distance that derives from his positioning himself within and without both the textual space and the local context of colonial Philadelphia—is a common strategy used in works that have a cosmopolitan figure at their center. In works such as Thomas More's *Utopia*, for example, the principal character is distinguished by his ability to be both an insider and an outsider of the societies that he observes and to which he addresses his criticism and judgments. These qualities determine Raphael Hythloday's cosmopolitanism, and give this central narrative figure of More's work the ability to provide the reader with the most objective view of the two countries he observes and compares (Hallsberg 2012, 578–606). Similarly, the narrator's principal task in the Baron de Montesquieu's *Persian Letters*, or Oliver Goldsmith's "Citizen of the World," to cite two examples from the "foreign letter" genre that employed the figure of the cosmopolitan and were closer in time to Franklin's work, is to organize the material they have collected and the letters that they have found for their audience (Watt 2005, 56–75). These are cosmopolitan characters because their experience with other people and cultures has given them knowledge and an ability to judge that they can use in many different directions, including toward their own people, with a detached and objective point of view. Their experiences have given them knowledge, which they then share with their audiences. From these figures' perspective forms and conventions can thus be assessed and, possibly, be transformed for the better through the narrative they construct.

The colonial infrastructure that created the possibility for the philosophical society to exist is, as Franklin's opening words in the proposal suggest, also blocked in its progress because of the lack of interest in importing and exporting knowledge from the colonies. The work of the structures Franklin represents stands at the basis of the cosmopolitan community that the American Philosophical Society establishes. A member of the society needs the fluid space, the openness of borders (both geographical and intellectual) that such a space offers in order to redefine the role it plays within the British Empire. We begin to see here how cosmopolitanism's aim of overpassing various boundaries easily germinates within the colonial environment. It can be useful to a writer like Franklin to free his imagined society of its dependence from its British counterpart while at the same time asserting membership within the established imperial frame. Imagining the creation of an intellectually cosmopolitan American Philosophical Society is in fact what makes it possible for Franklin to eventually employ cosmopolitanism at the local level to create a virtual form of citizenry for the colonial subject.

## 2 THE WORLD MOVES WITHIN: COSMOPOLITANISM AND PLACE

The proposal for the American Philosophical Society is not the first instance in Franklin's works where we find him describing an association and how it works using a cosmopolitan model. In the queries for the members of the Junto, the society for mutual improvement he founded in the late 1720s, Franklin represented the citizen of the world as the ideal creator of local communities. Unlike the later work that presents an American cosmopolitan intellectual projected outward and thus in search of a larger community to belong to, the earlier representation illustrates how an ideal American local community can be created only by bringing the cosmopolitan within the community itself. In the series of questions known as "Standing Queries for the Junto" drafted in 1732 for the purpose of introducing the weekly meeting of the mutual improvement society, the terms of the cosmopolitan ideal become the ones to define the way a local community operates. The combination of cosmopolitan notions of friendship and exchange, of commerce, and of virtue are evident in the questions the members of the Junto were required to use in order to prepare for their Friday meetings (Grimm 1956, 437–462).[11] The group's structure, as well as the questions that constitute the introductory ritual to each meeting, are based on the model of contemporary Masonry (Hans 1953, 513–524). Like a Masonic association, Franklin's mutual improvement club is an association in search of public recognition at the same time that is not open to the general public (Bullock 1996, 50–82). This society is inclusive and exclusive simultaneously; it works to create moral and intellectual opportunities for its members and it is clearly focused on individuals' economic growth.

The twenty-four questions address topics ranging from general knowledge, to manners, and sociability, from virtue and its lack, wealth, personal moral growth, financial gain or loss, and, as I mentioned earlier, the cosmopolitan. By meeting each week, asking the questions, and considering their answers, Junto members are required to employ their knowledge and expertise in an odd variety of areas in order to establish themselves in a world with no well-established intellectual and commercial centers. The questions are worth quoting in their entirety:

1. Have you met with any thing in the author you last read, remarkable, or suitable to be communicated to the Junto? particularly in history, morality, poetry, physics, travels, mechanic arts, or other parts of knowledge?
2. What new story have you lately heard agreeable for telling in conversation?
3. Has any citizen in your knowledge failed in his business lately, and what have you heard of the cause?
4. Have you lately heard of any citizen's thriving well, and by what means?

---

[11] The group began to meet in 1727 and was initially also called "Leather Apron Club," a name that highlights its members' societal standing. The better-known name "Junto" derives from the Spanish "junta" or fraternity, and its structure was visibly similar to that of the contemporary speculative freemasonry whose main focus was to experiment and disseminate knowledge. The queries themselves and the rules they establish derive from a proposal for neighborhood societies in Cotton Mather's 1724 Religious Societies and from John Locke's 1720 essay "Rule of a Society which met once a Week for the Improvement of Useful Knowledge, and the Promoting of Truth and Charity" (Lemay and Zall 1986a, 47).

5. Have you lately heard how any present rich man, here or elsewhere, got his estate?
6. Do you know of any fellow citizen, who has lately done a worthy action, deserving praise and imitation? or who has committed an error proper for us to be warned against and avoid?
7. What unhappy effects of intemperance have you lately observed or heard? of imprudence? of passion? or of any other vice or folly?
8. What happy effects of temperance? of prudence? of moderation? or of any other virtue?
9. Have you or any of your acquaintance been lately sick or wounded? If so, what remedies were used, and what were their effects?
10. Who do you know that are shortly going [on] voyages or journeys, if one should have occasion to send by them?
11. Do you think of any thing at present, in which the Junto may be serviceable to mankind? to their country, to their friends, or to themselves?
12. Hath any deserving stranger arrived in town since last meeting, that you heard of? and what have you heard or observed of his character or merits? and whether think you, it lies in the power of the Junto to oblige him, or encourage him as he deserves?
13. Do you know of any deserving young beginner lately set up, whom it lies in the power of the Junto any way to encourage?
14. Have you lately observed any defect in the laws, of which it would be proper to move the legislature an amendment? Or do you know of any beneficial law that is wanting?
15. Have you lately observed any encroachment on the just liberties of the people?
16. Hath any body attacked your reputation lately? and what can the Junto do towards securing it?
17. Is there any man whose friendship you want, and which the Junto, or any of them, can procure for you?
18. Have you lately heard any member's character attacked, and how have you defended it?
19. Hath any man injured you, from whom it is in the power of the Junto to procure redress?
20. In what manner can the Junto, or any of them, assist you in any of your honourable designs?

21. Have you any weighty affair in hand, in which you think the advice of the Junto may be of service?
22. What benefits have you lately received from any man not present?
23. Is there any difficulty in matters of opinion, of justice, and injustice, which you would gladly have discussed at this time?
24. Do you see any thing amiss in the present customs or proceedings of the Junto, which might be amended?[12] (Franklin 1: 255)

The first two questions give the reader a sense that knowledge in all its aspects is essential to the group. Members should communicate to each other any newly acquired knowledge of history, morality, poetry, physics, mechanics, and travels. The intellectual growth of each group member is first and foremost in the list. And by the third question readers are reminded of the role financial prosperity plays in the exercise of the intellect as it will be the case in the writings about the philosophical society Franklin wrote twenty years later. What follows is a series of questions that ask to share information about manners and sociability, about business failures and successes, virtue and its lack, health, and justice.

The eleventh question on the list is the one in which the reader encounters cosmopolitanism and the role it plays in the enrichment of the society's members and in the formation of communities: "Do you think of any thing at present, in which the Junto may be serviceable to mankind? to their country, to their friends, or to themselves?" In the manuscript draft of the same query held at the Historical Society of Pennsylvania, the language of the cosmopolitan ideal is even more striking: "Do you think of anything at present, in which the Junto may be serviceable to Mankind? to their Country consistent with their Duty to Mankind; to their Friends consistent to their Duty to Mankind and their Country; to themselves consistent with their Duty to Mankind, their Country and their Friends?" In this version, the questions the query includes almost literally replicate the terms used by Denis Diderot in the description of the notion of cosmopolitanism he will publish in

---

[12]This version of the queries reflects the order in the collection of Franklin's writings that Benjamin Vaughan published in London in 1779 with the title *Political, Miscellaneous, and Philosophical Pieces*. There is also a manuscript, earlier text of the queries that is held at the Historical Society of Pennsylvania. The order of the queries in the manuscript draft, compared to that in Vaughan's text and in the *Autobiography*, is the following: 1, 12, 3, 4, 5, 9, 10, 2, 13, 11, 6, 23, 14, 15, 16, 17, 18, 19, 20, 21, 7, 8, 22, 24.

the French *Encyclopédie* in 1751. Diderot's definition summarizes what the concept meant for the international community of men of letters of which Franklin was to become one of the most prominent members. The *Encyclopédie* described the cosmopolitan as "A man who does not have a permanent home, or rather a man who is not a stranger anywhere. It comes from ... κόσμος and πόλις ... When asked, an old philosopher since dead answered: I am cosmopolite, which means, citizen of the universe. I prefer said another, my family to myself, my country [patrie] to my family. And humankind to my country."[13] According to this definition, the individual does not have geographical fixity and yet, as the coordinate sentence that follows the first definition shows, he is not a foreigner anywhere ("n'est étranger nulle part" the original text in French says). Despite his itinerant lifestyle, Diderot's *cosmopolite* is not homeless; his home is the entire world. And as the rest of the definition explains, the cosmopolitan man is also the man who puts his family above himself, his country above his family, and mankind above his own country. Thus, his lack of a geographical rootedness is paired to a civic involvement that translates the notion of civic involvement itself outside the contained space of a single country to the comprehensive space of the cosmopolis. In fact, Diderot's parenthetical etymological reference brings together the two concepts that conflate in the eighteenth-century definition of cosmopolitanism: the idea of polis, the metropolitan centers of Western civilization centered in cities such as Paris and London, and that of cosmos, the entire world where such a civilization should be propagated and reproduced.

The duty of Franklin's Junto members is to overcome the insularity of local allegiances to work for the improvement of their society, which is, the queries show, both continuous with mankind and its own distinct entity. The following thirteen queries remind the Junto members of the need for mutual help by asking them for information about possible useful new friendships and if they need help to improve their standing in society or with "weighty affairs." Characteristic of the language of the queries, and the eleventh in particular, is also the gesture toward a

---

[13] "*Un homme qui n'a point de demeure fixe*, ou bien *un homme qui n'est étranger nulle part*. Il vient de ... κόσμος et πόλις ... Comme on demandoit à un ancient philosophe d'où il étoit, il réspondit: je suis Cosmopolite, c'est-à-dire, citoyen de l'univers. Je préfere, disoit un autre, ma famille à moi, ma patrie à ma famille, & le genre humain à ma patrie" (the English translation is mine).

disinterested form of good that addresses a large and a small community simultaneously. For these men, community does not differentiate itself from humankind. In fact, it can be imagined as both the particular locale of metropolitan Philadelphia as well as the entire world. The civic duty of these American representatives of the world community moves from the polis and its locality to embrace the universal community of mankind, the cosmopolis, yet they remain rooted in their community and the common purpose of the society they represent. Philadelphia is the center of this cosmos and each individual's task is not only to improve mankind, but also to do so by improving himself both intellectually and economically, thus enriching the communal good for which the society works. The thirteenth query addresses this in particular by saying: "Do you know of any deserving young beginner lately set up, whom it lies in the power of the Junto any way to encourage?" (Franklin 1: 255). The prospective member of this community moves from the outside in. He might bring necessary strength to the community and might profit from it himself. The cosmopolitan features of the project behind these queries consists of bringing outsiders, the men of the world, within the community in order to enrich both. And, as the opening question about intellectual improvement and wealth reveals, this enrichment is both intellectual and material (Bullock 1996, 58–59). The queries portray a cosmopolitan that transfers the transnational onto the grounds of a specific community so the citizen of the world is one who is able to positively affect the intellectual and economic welfare of those who live in a specific locale. This model of citizenry and civic engagement is still visible in the autobiographical account of this early period. However, the contingencies surrounding the later account play a role in the way Franklin presents the figure of the citizen of the world as model for a national subject. By the time the colonies have declared themselves an independent republic, the cosmopolitan citizen becomes anachronistic and a thing of a past to remember and cherish—but to also keep in the past.

## 3 Virtue Remembered: Cosmopolitanism and Franklin's *Autobiography*

The four parts of Franklin's autobiography, composed between 1771 and the months before he died in 1789–1790, were written in England, France, and the United States—the three geographical locations where he spent most of his life. As his correspondence about this text attests, Franklin drafted it with a specific purpose in mind: providing his posterity with a text that could instruct young men in the skills necessary to be good workers, good citizens, and good Americans.[14] The first young man he had in mind was his son William, to whom the first part of the manuscript is addressed. As we know, Franklin drafted the first part of this work in 1771 while residing in England. He was still a colonial American and still close to William, the Royal Governor of New Jersey. William and his descendants (the "dear son" and the "posterity" of the autobiography's opening paragraph in the first part) were the direct addressees of his writing. When Franklin composed the second part of the manuscript in 1784, he was living in France, the Treaty of Paris had been signed and American independence made official. His familial situation had changed as well; William had remained loyal to the British Crown throughout the revolutionary period and Franklin had severed all his ties with him. Although Franklin was at this point raising William's son, William Temple Franklin, he did not continue the memoir in a similar fashion as its first part by addressing it to his grandson, the representative of the younger generations of Franklins. Instead his addressee broadened into a much more generic new generation of young men. Franklin introduced the new part of the manuscript with two letters he had received in the previous months from two friends who, knowing he had drafted an initial section of a memoir, asked him for more.

As a transition to part two of the manuscript and as a directive for the reader, Franklin added a short note at the end of part one explaining the difference in addressee from the first to the second section. Here he also cites the two correspondents' suggestions contained in the attached letters as the reason for writing the new draft and for addressing it to a general public. Franklin now gives credit to the letter writers for the inspiration to continue writing his memoirs. A final and abrupt sentence with no mention of his son charges the revolution as the reason for the thirteen-year gap between part one and part two:

> Thus far written with the Intention express'd in the Beginning [of this manuscript] and therefore contains several little family Anecdotes of

---

[14] The complete correspondence is included in the Norton edition of the *Autobiography* edited by Leo J.A. Lemay.

no Importance to others. What follows was written many Years after in compliance with the Advice contain'd in these Letters, and accordingly intended for the Publick. The Affairs of the Revolution occasion'd the Interruption. (Franklin 1987, 1372)[15]

Franklin had begun the first part of the manuscript with a brief history of the family's British origins and a genealogy.[16] Franklin dismisses any autobiographical reasons for the change in the writing style and cites the revolutionary turmoil as the cause for the interruption in his writing process. With this transformative action, from letter to his son to a more generic response to a suggestion from two friends to recount the story of his life, Franklin bestows on the letters some of the agency he had earlier bestowed on his son; the letters' requests become the reason why he writes. This change in addressee signals a series of changes that, I demonstrate, relate to the shift in Franklin's attitude that an American subjectivity based on the notion of cosmopolitanism is possible to one that only thinks of this type of subjectivity in mnemonic terms. In the autobiography, cosmopolitanism collapses if imagined as a force for nation formation when the openness of the colonial world no longer forms the underlying socio-political frame.

Part two begins with the text of the two letters Franklin mentions in his concluding note to part one. The author of the first letter, Abel

---

[15] The brief and stark reference to the revolution speaks to the complex and conflicted story of Franklin's relationship to William. As is the case with the abruptness of this sentence, so too was the way in which their final separation took place. After Franklin left England and became fully involved in revolutionary politics, he never spoke publicly about his son and their relationship.

[16] The more personal audience of the first part of the text should not be confused with a more intimate or personal character of the narrative. As Stephen Carl Arch has recently explained, Franklin's autobiographical style is not the confessional one with which the tradition that began with Rousseau has made us familiar. Arch argues that, in the autobiography, "Franklin had continued the classical and early modern tradition in which the individual self is de-emphasized in order to praise God (as in St. Augustine's *Confessions*) or to typify human behavior (in Franklin's case)" (Arch 2008, 166). The scope of his writing then becomes an explanation of what one can observe in one's self from a more or less objective standpoint. This note is an exemplification of this feature of the subsequent sections of the autobiography, but the first part also needs to be read in these terms. What appears as the more personal undertone of addressing the letter to his son and his direct descendants is in fact a literary convention that belongs to the earlier type of personal narrative that Franklin employs here.

James, was the person who had recovered Franklin's original manuscript in Pennsylvania after the war had ended. Abel James suggests that Franklin continue to write and then publish his memoirs. Franklin shared the copy he received in France with another friend, Benjamin Vaughan, who wrote the second of the letters included as a preface to part two. Vaughan was living between Paris and London and had been Franklin's emissary during the peace talks before the 1783 Treaty of Paris. Vaughan wrote his letter after having read both the letter Franklin had received from James and the manuscript of the autobiography. Vaughan's letter is written with a purpose similar to James's, to invite Franklin to complete and to publish the autobiography and a book entitled *The Art of Virtue*. The two works, Vaughan says, will improve "the features of private character, and consequently of aiding all happiness both public and domestic" (Franklin 1987, 1374). Vaughan cites several reasons why the books, and especially Franklin's recollections, will be important, but the main ones are the increase of good feelings toward America, the attraction of "settlers of virtuous and manly minds," and the crucial role his work will play in the formation of future generations of Americans. The focus of the first part of Vaughan's letter is on the potential of Franklin's work to produce a stronger American nation and positively influence England's perception of the ex-colonies, which at the time was still affected by the antipathy the revolution had left between the two countries. As Vaughan's letter proceeds, however, the author's aim becomes less nationally oriented and exclusive. After having discussed the memoirs' potential to produce a strong American self, Vaughan continues:

> Let Englishmen be made not only to respect, but even to love you. When they think well of individuals in your native country, they will go nearer to think well of your country; and when your countrymen see themselves well thought of by Englishmen, they will go nearer to thinking well of England. Extend your views even further; do not stop at those who speak the English tongue, but after having settled so many points in nature and politics, think of bettering the whole race of men. (Franklin 1987, 1378)

Vaughan's suggestions in this passage shift the book's goal from nation-building, implied in his suggestion that the newly formed country will acquire legitimate status in the eyes of British subjects, to a universal goal, implied in the new suggestion that humanity in general will benefit from Franklin's work.

Franklin's editorial choices for parts two and three of his work reflect both Vaughan's quasi-nationalistic message in the first part of his letter to Franklin and the universalizing gesture in the last part of the passage quoted above. Vaughan's words and Franklin's interpretation of his suggestions in the formal organization of the last sections of the *Autobiography* introduced in the brief postscript to part one begin to reflect the fluid distinction Franklin made between the national and the cosmopolitan. Parts two and three of the manuscript show the important and multifaceted role the rhetoric of cosmopolitanism played in Franklin's representation of American subjectivity and it shows how cosmopolitanism's roots in the colonial environment both make it possible to imagine a cosmopolitan form of national subjectivity and make it an unsustainable one. Franklin also points out the irony of the ideal American subjectivity he represents in his memoir, namely a form of identity that immediately becomes unstable when placed within the boundaries of a socio-political structure narrower than an empire.

Vaughan's letter becomes the blueprint for part two. The addressee of this later section, and of the subsequently written parts three and four, as stated before, is a generic young American man whom Franklin addresses and instructs with the example of his own life (Breitweiser 1984, 202–230). In addition, just as Vaughan's words suggest that Franklin's work should have a nationalistic as well as a universally oriented aim, Franklin organizes his text according to principles that connect to the national as well as to the international and universal. Part two of Franklin's autobiographical account is an example of how the changing historical circumstances surrounding the composition of the autobiographical narrative also shifted in its relationships between cosmopolitanism and American nationhood. The book becomes the embodiment of the Enlightenment ideal of the man of letters as the *cosmopolite*. As Franklin in the 1780s embarks on a discussion of the period that surrounds and follows the 1720s and 1730s, the time when his role of man of letters was solidified, the narrative also demonstrates Franklin's reluctance to link the models of civic involvement he describes to an idea of the American subject as a citizen of the world—a reluctance that, we have seen, did not emerge in the writings of the period in question. This reluctance is especially evident in Franklin's references to the idea of virtue and to the societies for mutual moral and practical behavior he established, or planned to, during this time and which he discussed in the second and third parts of the manuscript.

When Vaughan refers to the drafting of a book in addition to the autobiography, the book, he says, is to be titled *The Art of Virtue*; and Vaughan attributes to it the same importance as the memoir itself. Franklin reminds readers he never wrote this book: "But it so happened that my Intention of writing and publishing this Comment was never fulfilled" (Franklin 1986, 74). This comment appears in the manuscript soon after the section in which Franklin describes his attempts at "arriving at moral perfection" with the daily practice of the now-famous thirteen virtues (Lemay and Zall 1986a, 59).[17] Practice is what, in the end, transforms his experiment of internalizing the virtues into a success because it makes him "a better and happier Man."[18] This is also what

---

[17] Lemay and Zall (1986) have made a case for this in the Norton edition of the *Autobiography* and in the genetic edition of the same text.

[18] What Franklin wrote in a letter to Lord Kames in the 1760s is perhaps the most indicative example of how Franklin imagined virtue as a practical art. The letter to Lord Kames is dated May 3, 1760 and a part of it is dedicated to the outline of his plan to write a book that would provide young individuals with rules to follow in order to become virtuous. Here is how Franklin describes his project:

[A] little Work for the Benefit of Youth, to be call'd The Art of Virtue. From the Title I think you will hardly conjecture what the Nature of the Book may be. Most People have naturally *some* Virtues, but none have naturally *all* the Virtues. I must therefore explain ... To *acquire* those [virtues] that are wanting, and *secure* what we acquire as well as those we have naturally, is the Subject of *an Art*. It is as properly an Art, as Painting, Navigation, or Architecture. If a Man would become a Painter, Navigator, or Architect, it is not enough that he is *advised* to be one, that he is *convinc'd* by the Arguments of his Adviser that it would be for his Advantage to be one, and that he resolves to be one, but he must also be taught the Principles of the Art, be shewn all the Methods of Working, and how to acquire the *Habits* of using properly all the Instruments; and thus regularly and gradually he arrives by Practice at some Perfection in the Art. If he does not proceed thus, he is apt to meet with Difficulties that discourage him, and make him drop the Pursuit. My Art of Virtue has also its Instruments, and teaches the Manner of Using them. (Franklin 9: 103)

The virtue that Franklin describes in this section of the letter is a practical art that can be internalized through habit and repetition and that conflates the moral value of virtue with the practical value of mechanical arts. It is easy to recognize how scholars have generally agreed that this passage summarizes the overt intent of Franklin's autobiographical accounts. Franklin's description of his practice with the thirteen virtues reflects what the passage from the letter describes. Franklin, however, is not unique in portraying the works of virtue and art as interconnected. His usage reflects how contemporary encyclopedic dictionaries record the meaning of the terms. In Ephraim Chambers's dictionary of 1728

makes it possible for the story to be told and the experience turned into a model for the audience. Before returning to a description of the virtues themselves at the end of part two of the manuscript autobiography, Franklin introduces a more specific reason for not writing a book on the art of virtue.[19] He explains that because of the time he has had to dedicate to business, he could not succeed in performing a larger project planned about the book—a project designed to bring the experiment from a personal to a general level:

> But it so happened that my Intention of writing & publishing this Comment was never fulfilled. I did indeed, from time to time put down short Hints of the Sentiments, Reasonings, &c. to be made use of in it; some of which I have still by me: But the necessary close Attention to private Business since, have occasioned my postponing it. For it being connected in my Mind with a *great and extensive Project* that required the whole Man to execute, and which an unforeseen Succession of Employs prevented me attending to, it has hitherto remain'd unfinish'd. (Franklin 1986, 74–75)

Franklin describes the practical virtue here that would be at the center of his experiment and the subject of his manual. The virtue is not only what is at the basis of his personal experiment with the thirteen virtues, but it

---

(second edition 1738), for example, both virtue and art are described as activities that rely on habit and repetition. An art, Chambers describes, can be "active" or "factive;" the performance of an "active" art does not leave material effects, while "factive" arts produce an affect, such as is the case with painting. In both cases what makes an individual capable of exercising an art is his ability to assimilate it through repetitive practice. A similar involvement with the repetition of an activity is Chambers's definition of virtue: "in a more proper and restrained sense, [virtue] signifies a habit, which improves and perfects the haver, or possessor, and his actions." (Chambers 1738, 1: 2) The habit-forming practices that Franklin tells his reader he undertook while still a fairly young man, his insistence on the need for discipline and repetitive behavior in order to achieve virtue, and the description of the book project reflect these ideas of art and virtue.

[19] Douglass Anderson provides an interesting reading of Franklin's position regarding virtue. The scholar suggests that we should interpret Franklin's discussion of his failure to publish the book and his other comments regarding virtue throughout the memoir as an exercise in avoiding moralizing and in asserting a view of virtue and moral behavior based on the aggregate of thinking about and performing virtue itself. An internal and external reciprocity between the idea about virtue and its practice are essential for its existence and when the two cannot be achieved virtue remains ideal. Such an acknowledgement, Anderson argues is at the basis of Franklin's fundamental disinterest in completing his book project as well as the autobiography (Anderson 2008, 24–36).

is also the foundational text for the "great and extensive Project" that never materialized.[20]

This project, grander and farther-reaching than his individual plan to become virtuous, involves a large group of men who are first instructed to become virtuous and then, by forming a society, work together to propagate this virtue throughout the world:

> In this Piece it was my Design to explain and enforce this Doctrine, that vicious Actions are not hurtful because they are forbidden, but forbidden because they are hurtful, the Nature of Man alone consider'd: That it was therefore every ones Interest to be virtuous, who wished to be happy even in this World. And I should from this Circumstance, there being always in the World a Number of rich Merchants, Nobility, States and Princes, who have need of honest Instruments for the Management of their Affairs, and such being so rare, have endeavoured to convince young Persons, that no Qualities were so likely to make a poor Man's Fortune as those of Probity & Integrity. (Franklin 1987, 1392)

This passage, as does the one cited earlier, highlights the moral and the practical/economic value of Franklin's "great and extensive Project." The corruptible nature of man calls for the exercise of virtue. Moral integrity will make a young man profitable. The representation of these virtuous men as simultaneously morally strong and bent on making profit is based on the same idea Franklin's queries for the Junto revealed. It is only the combination of the possibly mutually exclusive features of eighteenth-century virtue and economy of profit that can bring power to a society of young men. If young men can make themselves become this particular type of virtuous young person, then "Merchants, Nobility, States and Princes" may all be their possible employers. The passage draws a link among commonly shared ideas of the corruptibility of human beings, the need to generate an elite of individuals whose special training is in exercising virtue, and an imagined colonial world in which

---

[20] Colleen Terrell argues that Franklin's sense of self and of virtuous behavior depend on his perception of the imaginative arts as material arts and virtue, like any other art, is itself a mechanical skill. Throughout his writings, Terrell claims, Franklin treats virtue as a systematic body of knowledge and virtue is the means to keep his behavior in harmony with the orderliness of nature's laws. When discussing how Franklin represents the way virtue works, Terrell adds that he attempts to internalize virtuous actions so that they can be performed reflexively (Terrell 2003, 100–132).

merchants, statesmen, and even nobles and royalty join together. It is this combination that produces a representation of a society that depends on the elements identifiable as an integral part of the cosmopolitan ideal. Such an ideal is, as I have already argued, embedded in the language of imperial expansion and of colonial economies, of international exchange and communication, and virtue is the practical art its representatives employ. What makes the society Franklin represents unique, however, is that, while originating in the transatlantic environment, it is deeply rooted in and operates at the local level.[21] The local character of this society emerges when Franklin returns to the subject in the opening of the third part of the autobiography.

The necessity to attend to other business that had stopped him from working on his project earlier on had not decreased in the 1780s when Franklin was writing his memoirs. It took him another four years before he could return to his manuscript and write another segment. He did so by going back to his memories about the "great and extensive Project" he had brought up at the end of part two: "I am about to write at home, August 1788, but cannot have the help expected from my Papers, many of them being lost in the War. I have however found the following." What follows is a short essay Franklin had kept as material for the book he never wrote. He introduces the piece with a reminder about the concluding comments from the previous section: "Having mentioned a great and extensive Project which I had conceiv'd, it seems proper that some Account should be here given of that Project and its Object. Its first Rise in my Mind appears in the following little Paper, accidentally preserv'd, viz." The copy of the essay, an example of what he has just described as "Hints of the Sentiments, and Reasonings" related to his discussion of the art of virtue, is copied immediately after. The document is entitled "OBSERVATIONS on my Reading History in Library, May 9, 1731." This essay, Franklin had explained earlier on, is one of those "Pieces of Paper" on which he put down "such Thoughts as occur'd to

---

[21] Scholars generally use the notion of "rooted cosmopolitanism" as a way to describe a postmodern sensitivity towards the ethnic and cultural diversity of our world and then place it in opposition to the way early modern and eighteenth-century cosmopolitanism was represented and performed, which is described as "rootless." By using the term in the context of Franklin's representation of the cosmopolitan, I aim to show that rootedness and cosmopolitanism precede our contemporary understanding of the Western world social and cultural make up. See introduction for bibliographical references.

[him] respecting [the project]" (Franklin 1987, 1396). This society, or "Sect" as he describes it, is deist in principle and follows the model that closely reminds readers of the Junto and of the Freemasonry, both relevant to Franklin at the time he composed this short essay. This "Society of the *Free* and *Easy*," he explains soon after the cited essay, is to propagate knowledge and moral goodness and generate a community of individuals who are interested in the welfare of human beings rather than being driven by partisan and local interests (Franklin 1987, 1395).

The essay presents readers a model of a society of virtuous men that reflects some of the ideas Franklin has outlined in the earlier section. The opening sentence is a consideration of the great powers that parties (both political parties and associations of citizens in a more general sense) have in societies: "That the great Affairs of the World, the Wars, Revolutions, etc. are carried on and effected by Parties" (Franklin, 1: 192). This statement is followed by the claim that parties are, in general, led by private interests: "That the different Views of these different Parties, occasion all Confusion. That while a Party is carrying on a general Design, each Man has a particular Private Interest." Franklin deplores the contemporary connection between parties and private interests, which he defines both in terms of personal and limited group interests. On this topic he says as follows:

> That few in Public Affairs act from a meer View of the Good of their Country, whatever they may pretend; and tho' their Actings bring real Good to their Country, yet Men primarily consider'd that their own and their Country's Interest was united, and did not act from a Principle of Benevolence. That few still in Public Affairs act with a View of the Good of Mankind. (Franklin, 1: 192)

As it had been the case in the eleventh query to be answered by the Junto members, the terms and the rhetoric in this passage anticipate those Denis Diderot will use twenty years later in the *Encyclopédie* to describe cosmopolitanism. Franklin's words in the passage underscore how the men who form contemporary parties fail to apply the standards that would make them fit the ideal cosmopolitanism presented. They fail to be productive at the civic level. Diderot's definition of the cosmopolite later in the century concluded by placing the greatest emphasis on one's allegiance to mankind. Franklin calls the reader's attention to the universal aim the party should have. Only a small number of individuals "act with a View of the Good of Mankind." The rest of the party leaders act against the principles that would make them cosmopolitans. However, as Franklin moves on to describe his own version of an ideal party of virtuous men, a party that functions in a cosmopolitan way and that fosters cosmopolitan virtue among its members, he does so by reversing some crucial elements of the structure he just described. Franklin's proposed revision of the way parties should be organized, although based on a cosmopolitan and universalizing model, ultimately makes the local, its features, and its improvement, the focus of the party of virtue's actions.

In the subsequent and final section of the short essay, Franklin in fact acknowledges that, despite his dissatisfaction with parties' structure and their employment, parties (in a general sense of the word) represent the most common way human beings associate and protect their interests.[22] Thus, rather than promoting their elimination, he promotes the revision of their standards through the establishment of another structure of this kind, a "Party of Virtue," he calls it. Such a party, Franklin says, would unite "the Virtuous and good Men of all Nations into a regular Body, to be govern'd by suitable good and wise Rules, which good and wise Men may probably be more unanimous in their Obedience to, than common People are to common Laws." (Franklin, Papers 1: 193) Franklin proposes a reformation of the elements that constitute such associations rather than considering the abolition of this form of association among humans. He suggests a change in the politics of their leadership so that parties' divisive and destructive power can be turned into a productive force—a force that unites people and engenders a sense of identity that is not national but instead human and universal. The men who compose this group are not only good and virtuous; they are selected according

---

[22] In a reading of the same essay, Douglas Anderson describes Franklin's attitude towards parties as ambivalent. In Anderson's analysis, Franklin's proposal of a party of virtuous men is seen as a model of Franklin's career, a model that derives from the practice of Shaftesburean brotherhood and Masonic organizations to which he had been introduced during his first stay in London in 1725–1726. I agree with Anderson's reading. The scholar, however, does not discuss the connection between the language that Franklin uses and the non-partisan and cosmopolitan ultimate goal of the party of virtue to generate a better humanity that, in my view, constitutes the most striking feature of Franklin's discussion of parties' reformation (Anderson 1997, 13–15).

to a standard that raises them above local environments and their particularities. They are "Men of all Nations" and are called to constitute a body of subjects who obediently follow the law by which this universal community should abide and set the example for those who might follow them. Through the form of the virtuous men's party, the founding tenets of Enlightenment cosmopolitanism find their way in the body of the society of learned men. Simultaneously, these men reflect the model Franklin assigns to his narrative persona in the memoirs. As he says in the opening paragraph of part one, the book's aim is to provide his own experiences as examples "fit to be imitated," first by his own descendants and then the larger and transnational audience he projects onto the latter parts of the work (Norton, p. 1).

This new version of the Masonic and Junto models is called the "Society of the *Free* and *Easy*." This group was, Franklin explains:

> To be begun and spread at first among young and single Men only; that each Person to be initiated should not only declare his Assent to such Creed, but should have exercised himself with the Thirteen Weeks' Examination and Practice of the Virtues as in the before-mention'd Model; that the Existence of such a Society should be kept a Secret till it was become considerable. To prevent Solicitations for the Admission of improper Persons; ... That for Distinction we should be call'd the Society of the *Free and Easy*. (Franklin 1986, 78)

The men Franklin envisages as the leaders of this society, a revised and improved type of party, are taken from all the nations and brought into a body that works for the universal good of humanity. It is from this universal model that such men can then have an effect on the local and on the universal. And although Franklin has admitted that time and business eventually kept him from putting this project into practice, he also adds: "And I was not discouraged by the seeming Magnitude of the Undertaking, as I have always thought that one Man of tolerable Abilities may work great Changes among Mankind" (Franklin 1987, 1307, 1397).

In an entry in his commonplace book, written in 1732 a year after the composition of the "Observations" and that the editors of Franklin papers included as a contemporary text related to the essay on reading history, readers find another set of ideas about the propagation of knowledge and virtue and a description of the society's representative men.

This memorandum is, as the editors note, obviously linked to the essay on reading history, and introduces the notion of correspondence as an essential component to the success of Franklin's project. The memorandum says the following:

> He may travel, every where endeavouring to promote Knowledge and Virtue; by erecting J[unto]s, promoting private Libr[arie]s, establishing a Society of Virtuous Men in all Parts, who shall have an universal Correspondence and unite to support and encourage Virtue and Liberty and Knowledge; [and then he adds in short hand] by all Methods. make m slf wrth 2 b mpld n s grt nd gd a Dsyn [make myself worthy to be employed in so great and good a Design]. (Franklin 1: 193)

The subject of this short passage provides another representation of the virtuous man, who has the same features as the one Franklin had described in the "Observations" written the previous year. Among the virtuous man's principal tasks are the promotion of virtue and knowledge through travel and the establishment of a universal correspondence, which will serve both as a promotion of and as a unifying structure for the society of learned men. Franklin enables the virtuous man to perform various functions by using the image of "universal Correspondence," intended as both the practical device of epistolary communication and an intellectual understanding among the members of the party.[23] Like the man described in the "Observations," this virtuous man will establish correspondences that generate a connective texture on a scale larger than country or city. Franklin stresses the transnational and trans-local role of the virtuous man in both the passage from the commonplace book and in the short essay included in the *Autobiography*. Yet, despite the universal foundations of the practice of broad generative correspondence, Franklin promotes the reproduction of the virtuous man's ideals at the local level. His final aim is similar the goal he held for the Philadelphians who joined the Junto years before.

---

[23] Jerome Christensen gives a lucid description of the fundamental role that the concept of correspondence played during the Enlightenment. Christensen refers to the definitions for the term that the *Oxford English Dictionary* reports as being in usage during the eighteenth century and notices how the concept describes the epistemology of the period in a variety of its aspects (Christensen 1987, 11–15).

The universal features of this society are validated only by its local application. Franklin notes that if a plan focusing on the local were applied societies of virtuous men would be established "in all Parts." The establishment of local Juntos and libraries propagates virtuous ideas and generates the correspondences necessary for such societies to flourish. Because the central task is to take care of the specific needs of each local entity, only in local embodiment can they be validated. The cosmopolitan ideals of universal dialogue and comprehension nurtured these communities and identified them, but this passage in Franklin's commonplace book grounded the most distinctive feature of the cosmopolitan community in the establishment and prosperity of a local community. This form of cosmopolitanism describes the colonial subject as able to engage above the colonial government imposed constraints, and, simultaneously, to be civically productive at a localized level.

In the memorandum from Franklin's commonplace book, the qualities of the local Junto club's members combine with those of the cosmopolitan men of letters sketched in his essay on reading history (Shields 2008, 50–62). The association of Franklin's imagined society with one of its material manifestations brings his local and universal aims together in a manner similar to that noted in "Observations" where he had stated that "Men from all Nations" were to operate "in all Parts" of the world. Associations like the Junto become connective links in the establishment of the "Society of Virtuous Men" Franklin imagines in these essays. These clubs' principal task is still the mutual improvement of their members. The creation of new Juntos, similarly to that of new libraries, the note in the commonplace book suggests, would encourage the promotion of ideals such as "Virtue, Liberty and Knowledge." These Enlightenment staples warrant the continuation of the process of further expansion of the virtuous society, this time from the local to the universal from where its roots have now been established.

The figure who represents this virtuous society and operates within local communities becomes what Diderot called "a citizen of the great city of the world" because the community he helps to form and improve is a community of humans, not of nationals (Roth 1955, 8:16). Yet, when embodied in entities like the Junto, Franklin's proposed society will raise the cultural level of America, it will enlarge its members' general knowledge, it will also legitimize the province, and finally it will make the center of imperial culture participate in the mobility of colonial America by seeing its forms reproduced. It is this multiplicity of functions and the fluidity they assign to the group identity in Franklin's representation of community and to the America it embodies that makes his sense of national identity a combination of the elements associated with the discourses of cosmopolitanism. It is cosmopolitan because it is based on an ideal that benefits humanity, and because it exists within colonial North America and within Philadelphia's city limits. This similarity allows for a reproduction as well as a challenge of the forms that generate it, because it relies on an idea of community that exceeds the cultural and political borders that would define the empire. Yet it is dependent on the imperial economic and political structure to exist because there would not be the possibility of real exchange unless the borders were made fluid by its geopolitical existence. This community of virtuous men (dubbed in the Junto) produces a dialogic bridge between center and periphery without necessarily originating constraints for either space and can thus exist without apparently interfering with or contradicting each other. It can be virtuous at the same time it works at producing wealth. Franklin's description of the society of virtuous men outlines this process: the colonial world and its ideas have progressed within their imperial surroundings and can be beneficial to "Mankind in general." Yet, they could not be so, unless they were produced by the culture that generates and sustains them locally.

In this view, Franklin's imagined community does not simply contribute to the formation of the idea of nation, since Benedict Anderson's employment of the expression has been identified with these terms. The image of community these texts present is not "both inherently limited and sovereign" (Anderson 1998, 6). The ideas of geographical and cultural closure Franklin employs in the early work cited in his memoir serve the purpose of imagining a community that, in reproducing the space of the metropolitan center, opens itself to the larger space of the "world" rather than simply thinking of itself as an exclusive and closed community. In the passage describing his idea of "imagined community," Anderson states: "the nation is imagined as *limited* because even the largest of them, encompassing perhaps a billion living human beings, has finite, if elastic, boundaries, beyond which lie other nations. No nation imagines itself coterminous with mankind" (Anderson 1998, 7). Franklin's description of a society of virtuous political leaders, his Junto members, and the idea of intellectual community behind them define an American identity based on what Anderson argues nations are not. Franklin was indeed, as Anderson claims elsewhere, one of those printer/

journalist and postmaster figures whose work put into motion the fundamental elements that generated a sense of national identity among people during the late colonial period in North America (Anderson 1998, 60–65). What is particularly interesting about the short "Observations on Reading History" and the related commonplace book entry is that they show that, for figures like Franklin, imagined communities in the early decades of the eighteenth century could be imagined both as independent, limited, and coterminous with the idea of mankind.

As I mentioned at the beginning of this chapter, there is an intrinsic irony in finding the outline of a cosmopolitan form of nationhood in a text that has come to be seen as one of the first representations of this kind of American national identity. Franklin himself seems to doubt the sustainability of an American national identity when he distances himself from his plan of forming the society of the "*Free* and *Easy*" and reminds his readers how it never materialized as: "an unforeseen Succession of Employs prevented [him] attending to [it]" (Franklin 1986, 75). While Franklin's words are simply a reflection of how personal and historical events interfered with his well-thought-out plan, it is also important to consider the role the changes in his life and the contingencies generated by them play in forming these views. The first change I want us to consider is the shift in the political frame surrounding the account. Franklin, as we know, is writing the latter parts of the memoirs after the end of the War of Independence. The various examples of cosmopolitan subjectivity within the memoir show that a large part of the constructed identity depended on a lack of well-defined national borders. The irony here, of course, is that, although the environment Franklin inhabits while a colonial subject lends itself to this type of representation, the cosmopolitan national identity is imaginable only when Pennsylvania is part of the British Empire and makes the cosmopolis nothing more than an amplified notion of nation embodied in an abstract representation of British Empire.[24]

---

[24] The representation of a virtuous American man, who was cosmopolitan, virtuous, and intent on making money, while viable in the 1720s, becomes so only when described as part of a never finished plan by the time Franklin drafts his memoirs at the end of the century. By the time Franklin wrote the account of his life there was a much more defined sense of the disconnection between the world of labor and economic profitability and that of intellectual enlightenment and the representation of a cosmopolitan citizen he had used earlier becomes anachronistic (Brewer 1989; Langford 1989).

## 4  OF WEEDS AND POLYPS: A NATIONALISTIC COSMOPOLITAN?

Franklin's well-known 1751 essay entitled "Observations Concerning the Increase of Mankind, Peopling of Countries, & ..." conflates the idea of cosmopolitanism with the British nation and provides a telling example of how cosmopolitanism can be the force to define and strenghten national borders. The cosmopolitanism that emerges in the essay becomes the vehicle for developing a nationalistic and ethnocentric portrayal of a proto-American sense of nationhood. Empire-building becomes a form of border crossing and transnational growth. The essay centers on the ideas of community, population growth, and national unity. It has been known as one of the most influential of Franklin's writings with figures such as Jefferson, Adams, and Washington in the list of individuals who knew the text and publicly appreciated it (Lemay 2005–2008, 3:260–64). In 1751, Franklin was a fully recognized member of the republic of letters and his professional career had begun to move in a new direction. In 1748 he had officially retired from actively participating in the printing business and his attention was focused on the civic and political issues of his home colony and in actively cultivating his interest in science. In his biography of Benjamin Franklin, Leo Lemay has described the year 1751 as Franklin's "annus mirabilis," not only because he was elected to the Pennsylvania House of Representatives and acquired the right to vote in it—two things he had been denied while he was the assembly's clerk—but also because Franklin wrote some of the most highly circulated and most influential essays of his career during this year (Lemay 2005–2008, XIV). In response to Great Britain's decision to transport felons to the North American colonies, Franklin first published the editorial "Jakes on our Tables" that compared the new practice of sending convicts to the colonies to dumping toilets on North American colonists' dinner tables, and then the satire "Rattlesnakes and Felons," which continued the protests against the transportation of convicts. As Franklin's writings became more engaged with current political controversies, his personal activism increased.[25] "Observations

---

[25] Franklin was in London from 1757 until 1762, and again from 1764 until 1775 when the political divergences with the British government became intractable and he left for Paris.

Concerning the Increase of Mankind" reveals this political engagement and it also provides a significant example of the ambivalent nature of Enlightenment cosmopolitanism and a sign of its interdependence on the cultural and political forces of the times. The essay shows us how the language of cosmopolitanism is inextricable from that of empire and thus blends with and sustains the rhetoric of nationalistic exclusivity and proto-ethnic superiority. In "Observations Concerning the Increase of Mankind," the rhetoric of cosmopolitanism helps Franklin suggest that, within an empire, the forces that produce necessary imperial structures can also weaken and eventually destroy them.

"Observations Concerning the Increase of Mankind" circulated in manuscript form until its 1755 publication in Philadelphia. Once it was published, Franklin reissued and included the essay in a number of different publications while he was in England actively working as agent for Pennsylvania.[26] The essay presents the North American colonies as part of a larger imperial body and Franklin describes this entity as a distinct ethno-political community that wants to establish well-defined ideological and geographical limits to the space it occupies. In order for this community to maintain its unique character, Franklin suggests, it should not be ethnically or culturally corrupted. In "Observations Concerning the Increase of Mankind" the interest of mankind is to make boundaries, divisions, and hierarchies visible. Franklin begins with a detailed analysis of population growth and a comparison between the overpopulated European regions and the underpopulated colonial spaces, and it ends with a racialized argument against non-British immigration.[27] According to Franklin's theorizing and calculations, the colonial population grew twice as fast as the European ones and such a growth could be easily maintained in the ever-enlarging imperial territories, if Great Britain

---

[26] The essay was first published in the November 1755 issue of the *Gentlemen's Magazine* in London and in the *Scots Magazine* in April 1756. It was often reprinted and Franklin added it as an appendix to the essay "The Interest of Great Britain Considered" that he published in 1760. He also included it in the fourth edition of his "Experiments and Observation on Electricity" in 1769 (Franklin 4: 225–234).

[27] In this part of the essay, Franklin wrote down the basis of a theory of social reproduction that later sociologists, such as Thomas Malthus, will embrace and develop. According to Franklin's calculations, the population grows twice as fast as in the colonies as in Europe because of the prosperity that allows for early marriages and a higher number of offspring (Lemay 2008, 3: XIV).

could establish what he calls "generative laws." These laws would help the generation of wealth and a larger number of children by preventing the importation of "Foreign Luxuries and needless Manufactures," and by avoiding the development of a lazy class of people who would be more interested in pleasure than in promoting the production of "manufactures."[28] The ethnocentricity of the argument becomes evident when, after maintaining that natural growth should be promoted, Franklin insists that immigration should also be strictly controlled so that a nation and its people could maintain their distinctive ethnic and cultural character.[29]

After having introduced the issue of natural population growth, in fact, Franklin says the introduction of foreigners to the colonies would not be encouraging the needed improvement. Foreigners, Franklin says, "will gradually eat the Natives out" (Franklin 4: 232). This eating metaphor that introduces Franklin's argument about keeping a "race of people" uncontaminated becomes a central theme in the representation of nation formation that follows.[30] Mixing people cannot form a nation, Franklin suggests, because the ethnocultural traits of the strongest group would prevail on the other. Under these circumstances, the risk of introducing a new group would be too high and could jeopardize the Britishness of the colonial territories and that of the mother country as well. To exemplify his words, Franklin uses the first of two images derived from the natural world:

---

[28] Here Franklin is also interested in promoting the production of manufactures in the colonies, which England is blocking (Franklin 4: 225).

[29] Carla Mulford offers an extensive discussion of Franklin's ideas as they developed out of his conversations with environmental, labor, societal, and economic theories. Mulford shows that Franklin's discussion was designed to prove to a British audience of specialists in those fields that they were ultimately mismanaging the colonies and risking losing profit and possibly the colonies as well. The racist language that Franklin uses, Mulford argues, reflects contemporary anxieties "born of population density, land and labor problems, health concerns, and language fears" that immigrant groups' (especially German) lack of interest in cultural and social integration in the English-speaking North American environment was causing among Franklin's contemporaries (Mulford 2015, 152–164).

[30] Leo Lemay and Douglass Anderson have argued that Franklin's comments are ironic and skeptical and thus reveal his quite ambivalent position regarding the position he seems to take in the essay. Here I am interested in analyzing the way in which the language of cosmopolitanism can easily merge with the nationalistic discourse Franklin develops (Anderson 1997, 158–168; Lemay 2005–2008, 3: 256–257).

There is in short, no Bound to the prolific Nature of Plants or Animals, but what is made by their crowding and interfering with each others Means of Subsistence. Was the Face of the Earth vacant of other Plants, it might be gradually sowed and overspread with one Kind only; as for Instance, with Fennel; and were it empty of other Inhabitants, it might in a few Ages be replenish'd from one Nation only; as for Instance, with Englishmen. (Franklin 4: 233)

In this passage the natural world becomes both the model on which imperial expansion should function and an example of how necessary it is to keep natural processes under control when it comes to developing a nation. The suggestion that the world could assume an entirely British character is introduced through a metaphor that shows how nature's course cannot be stopped and how human growth and reproduction also reflect the works of the natural world. Franklin assigns to the expansion of the British Empire an inevitability like the expansion of weeds in the natural world. However, his choice of the fennel as a means of comparison, a plant that reproduces itself as a weed and drives other plants out even though it is also used for cooking, introduces the sense that any form of expansion needs to be brought under a form of control that exceeds nature's powers. Here the cosmopolitan idea of the nation of humans Franklin seemed to envision in other places comes with an addition: humankind should have British features.

Franklin pairs the idea that the British Empire needs to be cautious when choosing the best way to increase the number of its subjects and its geographical extension with the celebrative idea that its greatness can be reproduced without interruption. Franklin stresses in the rest of the paragraph the need to continue the territorial expansion necessary to grant people enough room to reproduce themselves and in the paragraph that follows he employs a new natural world metaphor to further stress the problematic process that such an expansion could entail.[31] Franklin compares the well-functioning of nations to the hydra-like animal called "polypus." A well-regulated nation, Franklin says, is:

Like a Polypus; take away a Limb, its Place is soon supply'd; cut it in two, and each deficient Part shall speedily grow out of the Part remaining. Thus

---

[31] Here Franklin's description reflects the usage John Dee had done of the term in the sixteenth century. See Introduction.

if you have room and Subsistence enough, as you may by dividing, make ten Polypes out of one, you may of one make ten Nations, equally populous and powerful; or rather, increase a Nation ten fold in Numbers and Strength. (Franklin 4: 234)

Franklin's comparison between polypuses and nations offers two options: the production of other nations, potentially rival, or the extension of the original nation into a larger and stronger entity. In each case the community that would originate from Franklin's metaphorical description aims at reproducing itself politically as well as ethnically. It can become another self-sufficient nation or one that represents, like the North American colonies, the original one of which it is an extension. Ironically, the unlimited power to regenerate itself without interruption that Franklin attributes to this proto-national entity in the end produces the same image in his 1720s essays, namely one nation of humans. The peculiarity of the model that Franklin's comparisons to the fennel and the polyp produce is that these humans overtly share the cultural and racial traits of those who run the empire. The party of virtuous men offered a "revised" version of what parties had come to represent in history, and the philosophical society generated itself out of its roots in British expansion and its predecessor, the Royal Society. Yet the image Franklin's words produce here is not one of a process of communal improvement, but one of improvement that comes at the expense of the replacement of the weakest by the strongest, with the implicit sense that the strong should work to make themselves stronger and push the weak out of the picture.

As I said at the beginning of this chapter, Franklin's writings repeatedly show how complex terms that describe nationhood are, and, ultimately, how the concept of national identity and the process that defined it during the late colonial American period cannot be retraced without taking into account the inherent contradictions of the language in such a process. The language and imagery that derive from the concept of the cosmopolitan play an essential role in this construction. What the British Empire and a prospective American nation were for Benjamin Franklin is perhaps best articulated in the words of the author of the essay that might have inspired Franklin to use the image of the polypus in "Observations." This essay, which was published in the "Poor Richard Revisited" almanac of 1751, contains a description of the animal Franklin uses to represent the way an eighteenth-century nation should function.

The writer in the almanac—whom the editors of the Franklin's papers have not identified as Franklin himself but who obviously stirred in him a strong journalistic and scientific interest—says the polypus was the "most unaccountable of all Creatures," it had a:

> Manner of Production, Feeding and Digestion ... different from all other Animals. The young ones come out of the Sides of the old, like Buds and Branches from Trees, and at length drop off perfect Polypes. They do not seem to be of different Sexes. They take in Worms, and other Sustenance, by means of a Sett of long Arms or *Antennae*, which surround their Mouths, and after keeping them some Time in their Stomachs, throw them out again the same Way. The Animal's Body consists of a single Cavity, like a Tube or Gut, and what is wonderful, and almost beyond Belief, is, that it will live and feed after it is turned inside out, and even when cut into a great many Pieces, each several Piece becomes a compleat Polype. They are infested with a Kind of Vermin, as are almost all Animals from the largest down to Bees and other Insects. These Vermins sometimes in a long Time will eat up the Head and Part of the Body of the Polype, after which, if it be cleared of them, it shall have the devoured Parts grow up again, and become as compleat as ever. (Franklin 4: 93)

The detailed description of this strange animal offers another metaphor that as readers of Franklin's works we could use to describe his late eighteenth-century colonial American perspective of what national communities could be like and what role cosmopolitanism played in his views. Like the polyp, national communities and their members are the "most unaccountable of all Creatures." They can be turned upside-down and still survive and function, be separated and regenerate themselves and see each other as part of a whole and yet distinct and separate from each other. They exist as they form themselves and their features are those of becoming.

Franklin's complex and quite contradictory projections of models for national communities reminds us of what Walter Mignolo writes about the interlocking of coloniality and cosmopolitanism and the problems that this connection produces. Citing Francisco de Vitoria as the exemplar promoter of this type of cosmopolitanism during the Atlantic colonization, the first large project of globalization that we can identify in modernity, and Immanuel Kant as the one doing the same for the late Enlightenment, Mignolo argues such projects "can be complementary or dissenting with regard to global designs" of world domination and cultural homogeneity within the same body of thought. In this view, cosmopolitan projects "arose from within modernity, however, and, as such, they have failed to escape the ideological frame imposed by global designs themselves" (Mignolo 2002, 159–160). Though critical of the reality surrounding it, this type of cosmopolitan attitude remains connected to the world that has produced it and depends on it to exist. The cosmopolitan attitude and the language Franklin used to represent communities with national traits is similar to the one Mignolo describes when talking about cosmopolitan projects. Although in many ways Franklin's employment of cosmopolitanism fits what Mignolo calls an "emancipatory narrative," as was the case for the essay "On Reading History in the Library," Franklin's employment of the terms of the cosmopolitan ideal reminds us of the interdependence of the imperial infrastructure. This interdependence fosters both the ideas of inclusion and of a humanity that is homogeneous in both culture and ethnicity. Franklin's final refusal in the autobiographical account to link the image of the cosmopolitan subject he had produced in the 1720s with the idea of the virtuous man he described in the memoir can be seen as a signal that the idea of cosmopolitan inclusiveness has been taken over by one about homogeneity, which, however, cosmopolitanism itself also promotes.[32]

REFERENCES

Anderson, Amanda. 1998. The Divided Legacies of Modernity. In *Cosmopolitics: Thinking and Feeling beyond the Nation*, ed. Pheng Cheah, and Bruce Robbins, 265–289. Minneapolis, MN: University of Minnesota Press.

Anderson, Douglass. 2008. The Art of Virtue. In *The Cambridge Companion to Benjamin Franklin*, ed. Carla Mulford, 24–36. New York: Cambridge University Press.

———. 1997. *The Radical Enlightenment of Benjamin Franklin*. Baltimore, MD: The Johns Hopkins University Press.

---

[32] Anthony Appiah first described the cosmopolitan patriot as the individual who nurtures one's own cultural roots while also respecting those of others. With this description, Appiah replicates the same terms that the enlightenment writers used to describe the cosmopolitan. The limitation of this view is that it does not take into account the hegemonic power that certain cultural and ethnic traits have in our world and thus reflects the idealistic traits that the Enlightenment representation of cosmopolitanism has (Appiah 1998, 91–116).

Appiah, Kwame Anthony. 1998. Cosmopolitan Patriots. In *Cosmopolitics: Thinking and Feeling beyond the Nation*, ed. Pheng Cheah, and Bruce Robbins, 91–114. Minneapolis, MN: University of Minnesota Press.
Arch, Stephen Carl. 2008. Benjamin Franklin's Autobiography, Then and Now. In *The Cambridge Companion to Benjamin Franklin*, ed. Carla Mulford, 159–171. New York: Cambridge University Press.
Breitweiser, Mitchell R. 1984. *Cotton Mather and Benjamin Franklin: the Price of Representative Personality*. New York: Cambridge University Press.
Brewer, John. 1989. *The Sinews of Power: War, Money and the English State, 1688–1783*. New York: Alfred Knopf.
Bullock, Steven C. 1996. *Revolutionary Brotherhood: Freemasonry and the Transformation of the American Social Order, 1730–1840*. Chapel Hill, NC: University of North Carolina Press.
Chambers, Ephraim. 1738. *Cyclopædia, or a Universal Dictionary of Arts and Sciences*, 2nd ed. London: James and John Knopton.
Christensen, Jerome. 1987. *Practicing Enlightenment: Hume and the Formation of a Career*. Madison, WI: University of Wisconsin.
Diderot, Denis. 1955. Correspondance. ed. Georges Roth. Paris: Les Editions de Minuit.
——— and Jean le Rond D'Alembert. 1751–1765. Encyclopédie, ou dictionnaire raisonné des sciences, des arts et des métiers. Paris: Le Breton.
Franklin, Benjamin. 1959. *The Papers of Benjamin Franklin*. Edited by Ellen R. Cohn et al. New Haven, CT: Yale University Press.
Goodman, Dena. 1994. *The Republic of Letters: A Cultural History of the French Enlightenment*. Ithaca, NY: Cornell University Press.
Grabo, Norman. 1993. The Journalist as Man of Letters. In *Reappraising Benjamin Franklin: A Bicentennial Perspective*, ed. J.A. Leo Lemay, 31–39. Newark, NJ: University of Delaware Press.
Green, James N., and Peter Stallybrass. 2006. *Benjamin Franklin Writer and Printer*. Philadelphia, PA: Oak Knoll Press.
Grimm, Dorothy F. 1956. Franklin's Scientific Institutions. *Pennsylvania History* XXIII (4): 437–462.
Hallberg, Peter. 2012. Thomas More's Cosmopolitan Civil Science: The New World and Utopia Reconsidered. *History of Political Thought* 33 (4): 578–606.
Hans, Nicholas. 1953. UNESCO of the Eighteenth Century, La Loge Des Neuf Sœurs and Its Venerable Master, Benjamin Franklins. In *Proceedings of the American Philosophical Society*, XCVII: 513–524.
Hindle, Brooke. 1974. *The Pursuit of Science in Revolutionary America, 1735–1789*. New York: W.W. Norton and Company.
Langford, Paul. 1989. *A Polite and Commercial People, 1727–1783*. New York: Oxford University Press.

Lemay, J.A.Leo. 1981. *The Autobiography of Benjamin Franklin: A Genetic Text.* Knoxville, TN: University of Tennessee Press.

———. 1987. *Benjamin Franklin Writings.* New York: The Library of America.

———. 1991. Franklin and France. In *Benjamin Franklin: Des Lumières à nos jours*, ed. Gérard Hugues and Daniel Royot. Lyon: Didier.

———. 2005–2008. *The Life of Benjamin Franklin*, Vols I–III. Philadelphia, PA: University of Pennsylvania Press.

——— and P.M. Zall. 1986a. *Benjamin Franklin's Autobiography: An Authoritative Text.* New York: W.W. Norton.

——— and P.M. Zall. 1986b. eds. *Benjamin Franklin's Autobiography: An Authoritative Text, Backgrounds, Criticism.* London: W. W. Norton.

Mignolo, Walter. 2002. The Many Faces of Cosmopolis: Border Thinking and Critical Cosmopolitanism. In *Cosmopolitanism*, ed. Carol Breckenridge, et al., 157–188. Durham, NC: Duke University Press.

Mulford, Carla J. 2015. *Benjamin Franklin and The Ends of Empire.* New York: Oxford University Press.

Shields, David S. 1990. *Oracles of Empire: Poetry, Politics, and Commerce in British America, 1690–1750.* Chicago: University of Chicago Press.

Shields, David S. 2008. Franklin in the Republic of Letters. In *The Cambridge Companion to Benjamin Franklin*, ed. Carla Mulford, 50–62. New York: Cambridge University Press.

Terrell, Colleen. 2003. Republican Machines, Franklin, Rush, and the Manufacture of Civic Virtue in the Early Republic. *Early American Studies: An Interdisciplinary Journal* 1: 100–132.

Thomas, Douglas B. 2012. Recasting Benjamin Franklin as Printer: A Note on Recent Historiography. In *Benjamin Franklin's Intellectual World*, ed. Paul E. Kerry, et al., 103–118. Madison, WI: Farleigh Dickinson University Press.

Van Doreen, Carl. 1938. *Benjamin Franklin.* New York: Viking.

Warner, Michael. 1990. *The Letters of the Republic: Publication and the Public Sphere in Eighteenth-Century America.* Cambridge, MA: Harvard University Press.

Watt, James. 2005. Goldsmith's Cosmopolitanism. *Eighteenth-century Life* 30: 56–75.

White, Edward. 1999. Urbane Bifocals: The Federalist Sociology of Franklin's Autobiography. *American Literary History* 11 (1): 1–33.

CHAPTER 3

# Jefferson's Cosmopolitan Nature in *Notes on the State of Virginia*

Thomas Jefferson, like Benjamin Franklin, belonged in the liminal space inhabited by elite colonials. As an intellectual he was at the center of European Enlightenment culture and as an American he remained at the margins of that culture because of the distance and the lack of a metropolitan center, such as London or Paris, close to him. This marginality and his engagement with the discourses of the European elites are the two elements that bring the cosmopolitan into his writings. In particular, they constitute what makes the cosmopolitan an integral part of Jefferson's representation of an American national identity. Similar to Franklin's imagined nation of cosmopolitan men that ended up represented in his autobiographical account as an impossible reality, Jefferson's post-independence cosmopolitan American landscape in his only published book *Notes on the State of Virginia* is a belletristic exercise. Jefferson's representation produces a powerful image of exceptionalism that contains traits of a narrative that will characterize future representations of America. This second aspect of Jefferson's employment of cosmopolitan imagery gives us another example of eighteenth-century cosmopolitanism's origins in British colonialism and imperial expansionism. For Jefferson, the American cosmopolis exists because it is a part of the eighteenth-century republic of letters, yet within this larger entity, America stands out for its exceptional characteristics. The cosmopolis Jefferson places at the foundation of his idea of America is a reflection of the imperial connections that made the world he lives in possible. The republic of letters he converses with and into which Jefferson claims membership exists because of the way the colonial world has expanded and made their conversation possible. The republic of letters has for Jefferson the same shape as the colonial world, and depends on it for its existence. Thus cosmopolitanism, like nationalism, becomes essential to maintain the exclusivity of this world, rather than creating the inclusiveness it promotes.

Jefferson began to organize the materials for the first draft of *Notes on the State of Virginia* in the fall of 1780. The composition of the book began as a response to a questionnaire sent to governors about newly formed states by the secretary of the French legation François Barbé-Marbois. This was an uncertain time in Jefferson's personal history, as well as in the history of the War for Independence. In 1781 when he started writing, Jefferson's actions as Governor of Virginia were challenged and his conduct investigated. The outcomes of the war were still unpredictable, the unity of the colonies all but defined, and the much-needed Queryforeign support to fight the British was not yet entirely assured. During this time, his youngest daughter died and the health of his wife began the deterioration that would eventually cause her death. Answering the set of questions written by French authorities was both a distraction from his many overwhelming problems and a necessity for Jefferson (Peden 1982, XI–XXV).[1] The list of questions makes clear that the French are interested in knowing if the newly formed country would be able to pay back the large sums they had borrowed from the French government.

The questions that open each chapter of *Notes* consist of a revision of those questions originally in the list Barbé-Marbois sent to American governors. For his manuscript, Jefferson revised the order and changed the form of many of the questions.[2] Scholars have often looked at this reordering

---

[1] Joseph Jones, a member of the Virginia delegation to the Continental Congress and James Monroe's uncle, gave Jefferson the list of twenty-two questions that Barbé-Marbois had passed around in hopes to find somebody to write about America.

[2] Following is the text of Barbé-Marbois' queries:
1. The Charters of your State.
2. The Present Constitution.
3. The exact description of its limits and boundaries.
4. The Memoirs published in its name, in the time of its being a Colony and the pamphlets relating to its interiors or exterior affairs present or ancient.
5. The History of the State.

as a reflection of Jefferson's attempt to order and organize the raw material of a yet undefined national history—a history that was natural, political, and social simultaneously.[3] When Jefferson's changes are given close attention, the relationship between the form of this work and the historical,

---

6. A notice of the Counties Cities Townships Villages Rivers Rivulets and how far they are navigable, Cascades Caverns Mountains Productions Trees Plants Fruits and other natural Riches.
7. The number of its Inhabitants.
8. The different Religions received in that State.
9. The Colleges and public establishments. The Roads Buildings & c.
10. The Administration of Justice and a description of the Laws.
11. The particular Customs and manners that may happen to be received in that State.
12. The present State of Manufactures Commerce interior and exterior Trade.
13. A notice of the best Sea Ports of the State and how big are the vessels they can receive.
14. A notice of the commercial production particular to that State and of those objects which the Inhabitants are obliged to get from Europe and from other parts of the World.
15. The weight measures and the currency of the hard money. Some details relating to the exchange with Europe.
16. The public income and expenses.
17. The measures taken with regard to the Estates and Possessions of the Rebels commonly called Tories.
18. The condition of the Regular Troops and the Militia and their pay.
19. The marine and Navigation.
20. A notice of the Mines and other subterranean riches.
21. Some Samples of these Mines and of the extraordinary Stones. In short a notice of all what can increase the progress of human Knowledge.
22. A description of the Indians established in the State before the European Settlements and all those who are still remaining. An indication of the Indian Monuments discovered in that State (Jefferson 1951, 166–167).

[3] Scholars introduced this argument in the 1980s and early 1990s. Robert Ferguson, for example, has described the ideological placement of the republic as Jefferson's main theme in *Notes*, achieved through an organization of its materials in a form derived from seventeenth- and eighteenth-century law treatises (Ferguson 1984, 38). Christopher Looby has argued that, with the categorization of Virginia's natural order, Jefferson was indeed organizing and categorizing the raw material of American social and political order (Looby 1987, 260–261). Similarly, Susan Manning has illustrated Jefferson's ordering of the questions and his obsession with classification as an attempt to control the socio-political chaos of the early republican years. She has argued that "Jefferson transformed what appeared to be the neutral task of documentation into an intellectual and patriotic discovery of the emergent nation and a means of personifying one of the voices of what his correspondent Hector St. John Crèvecoeur characterized as 'the American, this new man'" (Manning 1996, 348–349).

political, and social circumstances of the country become evident.[4] In fact, the situation for American writers like Jefferson who wanted to discuss America at the transatlantic level was even more complex than scholars generally describe. Jefferson was writing both for and against a specific group of European intellectuals, namely those members of the republic of letters who were involved in the exchange of ideas in the cosmopolitan world of knowledge. This constrained Jefferson to write within a specific frame of reference that the European component of his audience could accept and understand. With this frame Jefferson merged the language of cosmopolitanism—the idiom this intellectual community shared—with that of contemporary scientific debates in a book whose purpose became that of ensuring America's representative position in the republic of letters, which, like the European communities of most of its members, was thought of as a cultural, political, and environmental periphery.[5]

## 1 Changing Frames: From Barbé-Marbois' Questionnaire to *Notes*' Publication to Remembering It All

Jefferson's reordering of Barbé-Marbois' queries is part of an overarching project of formal and linguistic revision of a model for writing natural history that the culture of the republic of letters gave him.[6]

---

[4] And the book's central aim has been seen as one of national identity development. The changes that Jefferson made to the order of the original "queries" reflect the concerns and the fears that American intellectuals like Jefferson had regarding Europeans' material and ideological support. They reflect assumptions about how to address those who wanted to be reassured about the feasibility of the revolutionary enterprise in view of the fact that France was the ex-colonies' largest economic supporter. In addition, Jefferson's organizational strategy in the book that his answers formed reflects a response to the standards and expectations of the international political and scientific community that he addressed.

[5] Years after the composition of *Notes on Virginia*, Jefferson wrote to correspondent John Hollins comparing the community of scientists to the "republic of letters" itself (Bergh 1903, XII: 253).

[6] Although the two main authors whose theories Jefferson engages directly in Query VI are de Buffon and Voltaire, the group of natural philosopher who theorized about the natural state of the Americas was much larger and involved a numbers of intellectuals from a variety of European countries, including the Dutchman Cornelius de Pauw, the Scotsman David Hume, the Frenchmen Guillaume Raynal and the Baron de Montesquieu, to name some of them. All of these writers developed theories about the climate, natural environments, animal, and people of the Americas. They exchanged ideas and argued over the variety of transformations or the lack thereof that took place once similar species developed in one or another place (Gerbi 1973).

The formal and rhetorical changes that begin with the reordering of the questions and continue throughout the book serve Jefferson the purpose of developing a picture of the American natural environment that is transatlantic and cosmopolitan. In organizing his personal notes into the book, Jefferson regrouped questions according to the two major categories of the natural and the socio-political, so that the work could be organized in the specific form of contemporary natural histories (Thomson 2012, 62–73). The natural is the first topic of discussion and the political follows it. This reorganization of the order of the queries de-emphasizes the economic interests at the core of the French representative's inquiries. Jefferson combines a number of different questions (1, 4, 5, and 6 from Barbé-Marbois' list) concerning the economic development of the state and the exploitability of its resources into one so the stress on the economic is displaced. In Jefferson's version of the questions, consistently with the generic rules of natural histories, the natural features play a larger role and are more visible than they would have been if the original order had been left unaltered. To further enhance this effect, he splits Barbé-Marbois' sixth question, "A notice of the Counties, Cities, Townships, Villages, Rivers, Rivulets, and how far they are navigable. Cascades, Caverns, Mountains Production Trees Plants Fruits and other natural Riches," into five different ones, developing the long section on Virginia's natural resources that constitutes a third of the book. The form that the answers to the questionnaire assume is that of a natural history that conforms to contemporary generic standards and whose main goal is the objective representation of the physical and political features of the region.[7] Jefferson's rearrangement and reformulation of the questions gives him a better foundation for the new representation of American natural and political history that is to follow. From the terms that Barbé-Marbois has already supplied and those of the culture that he represents, Jefferson is ready to develop the new ones that can articulate what America is.

---

[7] Susan Manning has described the results of this strategy as "a characteristic Enlightenment interaction of topography, climate, and culture" (Manning 1996, 348). Robert Ferguson has explained Jefferson's changes in the order of the queries as part of a larger unifying project by which *Notes* is to be organized like a legal treatise. In Ferguson's view, Jefferson's rationale was the following: "just as the multiplicity of human law might give rise to a science of jurisprudence, so the bewildering physicality of America could be made to yield a unified republic" (Ferguson 1984, 46).

This rearrangement reveals Jefferson's intention to respond to the French diplomat's inquiries and the concerns about the profitability of the political alliance between the ex-colonies and France, and it places his answer within a framework that could establish a dialogue, despite his characterization of it as a dispute, with the cultural and scientific context that had elicited Barbé-Marbois' questions. Jefferson's redistribution of the original questionnaire's words demonstrates how any disruptive effort on his part, if present, would not exceed the boundaries established by the genre of his narrative and by the ideas his audience was promoting. They are still there to frame his natural history, yet they are placed in an order that allows Jefferson to tell the story from his own perspective. The writing process for Jefferson signifies revision rather than creation. The integration and separation of the original questions set the foundation for a discursive innovative act, which rearranges the terms supplied by the French diplomat, the original questions, in a reflexive process that mimics the dialogue the work embodies.

Jefferson completed *Notes on the State of Virginia* between 1780 and 1781 and published it for the first time in a limited private edition in 1785 (Peden 1953, XI–XIX). At the time of this first publication, Jefferson was minister plenipotentiary in Paris, having inherited Franklin's position when Franklin retired and returned to Philadelphia. The year after this publication, a member of the French Academy, the Abbé André Morellet, offered to translate the work into French. Jefferson retells the story in a contemporary letter to James Madison:

> An Abbé Morellet, a man of letters here to whom I had given a copy, got notice of [a publisher's intent to issue a pirate edition]. He had translated some passages for a particular purpose: and he compounded with the bookseller to translate & give him the whole, on his declining the first publication. I found it necessary to confirm this, and it will be published in French, still mutilated however in it's freest parts. I am now at a loss what to do as to England. Everything, good or bad, is thought worth publishing there; and I apprehend a translation back from the French, and a publication there. I rather believe it will be most eligible to let the original come out in that country; but am not yet decided. (Papers 9: 265)[8]

---

[8] Letter to James Madison, February 8, 1786.

Jefferson's account describes a connection between the French translation, the damage that a bad representation of America could cause if printed and circulated, and his intention to publish the original. Part of his worries turned out to be justified. He found the translation to be inaccurate and he began to think about ways to correct it, as he explained in another letter to his former law teacher George Whyte written in 1786: "[The] bad French translation which is getting out here, will probably oblige me to publish the original more freely, which it neither deserved nor was ever intended"[9] (Papers, 10: 243). When a year later a British printer contacted him about publishing an English edition, Jefferson accepted, and the book appeared in London in 1787. During this period, Jefferson found himself face to face with often-hostile European presses and a public opinion that challenged the image of America as a unified and politically stable nation (Faÿ 1927; Echevarria 1957). Critics argued that the new nation was on the edge of collapse because of incipient anarchy and a lack of cohesion among its leading forces. The scientific theories of environmental and human degeneration in America promoted in the writings of the naturalist George Leclerc de Buffon, among others, had by that time been popularized and went hand in hand with the political attacks and the lack of trust promoted in the European press (Chinard 1947, 27–57). Given these premises, the series of decisions to have the book in which Jefferson worked on debunking many such theories published first in a limited edition for his friends in 1785, then in French in 1786, and eventually in the English edition of 1787 possessed an understandable logic.

In his 1821 autobiographical retrospective, Jefferson returns to the history of the publication of his *Notes on Virginia*. There he recalls that in 1780, he had welcomed Barbé-Marbois' questionnaire about his home state as a way to organize the memoranda he had compiled during the years: "I thought this a good occasion to embody their [the memoranda's] substance, which I did in the order of Mr. Marbois' queries so as to answer his wish and to arrange them for my own use" (Jefferson 1984, 55). After describing this dual purpose of satisfying the French diplomat's request and repurposing such answers for his "own use," Jefferson goes on to discuss the history of the book publication. The account reproduces that which Jefferson had articulated in the

---

[9] To George Whyte, August 13, 1786.

letters contemporary to the first printings in France and England and explains his decision to print a limited edition in 1785 as a choice dictated by friends' requests and by the economic advantage printing had over hand copying. Then, he describes his attempts at improving the French translation, and, finally, how he had decided to give the book to the British press in 1787: "A London bookseller, on seeing the translation, requested me to permit him to print the English original. I thought it best to do so to let the world see that it was not really so bad as the French translation had made it appear. And this is the true story of that publication" (Jefferson 1984, 55). In these two moments of his recollection, Jefferson presents himself as an authorial agent in the service of a series of separate entities: Marbois, Jefferson's friends, and the world. This distancing from the act of writing and the sharp language of these passages reflect the conciseness and the direct tone of the short sketch that constitutes Jefferson's memoir. The hasty ending, with the sentence "and this is the true story of that publication," however, evinces an anxiety in Jefferson that does not appear in other parts of the short memoir. The appeal to truth in Jefferson's concluding remarks evokes the appeals to factuality common to contemporary fiction and belletristic writing, and reveals Jefferson's uneasiness with the narrative he wrote four decades earlier.[10] The account's linguistic form and the use of the expression "true history" suggest that the writer seems to have a troubled relationship with the process of writing and making his work public. The relationship between *Notes* and the realm of *belles lettres* appears to be one of Jefferson's main preoccupations when he looks back at his work.[11]

---

[10] Jennifer Kennedy has raised the same questions about the last sentence of this passage. In her interpretation, however, Kennedy considers Jefferson's account in relation to his attitude towards the events that took place in France after the French revolution. Kennedy argues that the many imprecisions in the account are part of a pattern of forgetting and misremembering that Jefferson develops in order to "protect his legacy from the charge of fanaticism" after the failure of the French Revolution in which he had seen a projection of his own ideas. Kennedy reads Jefferson's remarks on *Notes* as a metaphor for the French Revolution. The bad translation of his ideas in the French context had caused the revolution's failure, thus Jefferson's resentment in his account (Kennedy 2000, 553–573).

[11] The question of truth relates to *Notes* in another way as well. Jefferson was accused of having forged the speech of the Native American Logan he quotes later on in Query VI in order to provide an example of Native American natural oratorical powers. The attacks against him had begun in 1797 when a Federalist opponent and son-in-law to Colonel Cresap (the alleged murderer of Logan's family in Jefferson's version of the episode), Luther Martin, had charged Jefferson of forgery and challenged him in a series of

I suggest the connection between the realm of *belles lettres* and the realm of science is not merely a feature of Jefferson's reminiscence about his work. Instead, it is central to the most scientific chapter of the book in which Jefferson responds to Louis Leclerc de Buffon's claims that American natural world and its creatures are degenerating. It is also connected to Jefferson's use of cosmopolitanism to introduce Virginia's exceptional representativeness within the republic of letters. Jefferson's portrayal of a cosmopolitan America in the book is preceded by a revision of many of the features of belletristic writing. It is in *Notes on Virginia*'s sixth chapter that Jefferson openly resorts to the language and ideas of the cosmopolitan republic of letters in order to analyze and discuss American nature. He identifies America as an abstract supranational entity by applying a static view of nature to his portrayal. Using a universalizing language that makes America part of a unified community of science and letters, Jefferson brings together eloquence and the scientific discourse and establishes America's representative position in the republic of letters. And this position is such that it ultimately sets America apart as the most significant exemplar of what's most valuable in the republic itself.

One of the most extensive sections in Query VI is dedicated to the discussion of Buffon's theories of degeneration. Jefferson claims that in his work Buffon has replaced scientific inquiry with eloquent fiction and

---

newspaper articles. At the time Jefferson had refused to take part directly in the dispute, which he had deemed offensive and argued that "forbade the respect of an answer" because of its partisanship (Peden 1953, 298). Nonetheless, his preoccupation with Luther Martin's accusations continued and resulted in an almost obsessive research, which lasted over three years, to find enough evidence to support the veracity of the facts he had described in the book, the authenticity of Logan's words, and Jefferson's own good faith in reporting them. He then attached all the documents he had collected, mainly letters in response to his inquiries, and published them in the 1800 reprint of the book as an appendix. Jefferson's worries about the veracity of his account of *Notes*' genesis in the autobiographical account were also probably related to this longstanding polemic about the veracity of that account which had brought the work to the center of Jefferson's conflict with his federalist opponents. The anxiety that prompted the decision to collect and publish evidence in his favor and information about the story after the accusation—the fear of having fictionalized the story of the murder—may be another reason behind the usage of the blunt expression in the *Autobiography*. In both cases Jefferson's preoccupation about the veracity of what he is recounting reveals his preoccupation with imaginative writing, the role that eloquence plays in such writing, and the production of discursive misrepresentations—a series of elements that, as I show later in this chapter, permeate the central section of *Notes*.

supported science with a proto-evolutionary view of nature. In opposition, Jefferson uses contemporary popular scientific views of "static nature" to propose an empirically based description of American nature. The espousal of these views enables Jefferson to reorganize the rhetorical foundations of the republic of letters. Jefferson remaps the metropolitan context in the terms of a cosmopolis, which has no center and no margins and he thus takes the idea of America away from its marginal position in the geographical, cultural, and political outskirts of the Atlantic world. The effectiveness of this strategic employment of rhetoric and eloquence, however, works in an ambivalent way because it blurs the distinction between the discourse of *belles lettres* and that of science that Jefferson wants to establish through a scientific empiricist approach to his analysis. It also highlights the interdependence of cosmopolitanism, nationalism, and the discourse of empire. The author still feels anxiety when he discusses his work forty years after its composition, writing "And this is the true story of that publication," which, in my view, is a sign of this conflict.[12]

## 2   Rhetorical Revolutions and Involutions

In Query VI, entitled "Productions Mineral, Vegetable and Animal," and subtitled, "A notice of the mines and other subterraneous riches; its trees, plants, fruits, etc.," Jefferson attacks Buffon's theory that excessive humidity in America causes a decrease in the size, lifespan, and ability to reproduce of American living creatures. Jefferson's criticism is subtle and

---

[12] In addition to the short autobiographical account, the anxiety concerning the relationship between the writer and his material characterizes Jefferson's references to *Notes* in writings that precede it in composition. When Jefferson gave a copy of the book to James Madison, he distanced himself from authorship and wrote "Do not view me as an author, and attached to what he has written. I am neither." Jefferson's reference to his book—characterized by an insistence on its being a compilation of informative notes and a wariness to attribute it any literary value—are significant. Describing himself a writer would have meant to draw a connection between his work, eloquence, and the literary world that he seems to be trying hard to avoid. In the enlightenment context the lines between disciplines such as history, literature, and science, had blurry separating lines, but here Jefferson seems to want to draw clear ones (Schlereth 1977, 17–25). Robert A. Ferguson notes how Jefferson's apparent disregard for his work was voiced in a number of letters he wrote at the time of *Notes*' publication (Ferguson 1984, 34 and ff). Ferguson also notes that scholarship (until the early 1980s) was accepting of Jefferson's claims and did not consider the text as a literary work.

weaves through the section until he suggests that Buffon's theory is a literary construction in which rhetorical manipulation replaces the exposition of facts (Chinard 1947, 34–40). Jefferson does not accuse Buffon of having privileged eloquence over scientific integrity until the end of the section of the chapter when he quotes from Buffon's *Histoire Naturelle*, and even in that context, his harshest comments are relegated to a footnote.[13] This reticence to address Buffon's so-called "abuse" of rhetorical misconstructions of the North American environment is however accompanied by the overarching presence of eloquent oratory throughout this section. Ironically, in fact, the part of the chapter in which Jefferson most visibly outlines his empiricist position, analyzes Buffon's measurement charts, and attacks his ideas is the place where eloquence and oratory stand at the basis of Jefferson's argument. In the last part of "Query VI," eloquence and empiricism become entangled to the point where eloquence becomes both the target of Jefferson's criticism and his strongest weapon in the scientific rivalry witnessed in these pages. Jefferson accuses the French scientist of having resorted to eloquence. Yet, since rhetorical eloquence is also fundamental to Jefferson's argument, in order to avoid the evident conflict, he aligns it with the leading scientific views of his time and with the language of the audience to which he wants to appeal. For this purpose, Jefferson relies on contemporary views of eloquence and science. Beginning with a precise application of the newest scientific methods, he intertwines them with notions of eloquence which he draws from the contemporary "new" rhetoric movement.

The section entitled "Animals" begins with a reference to the two most authoritative voices of Western natural science, the father of European scientific taxonomy, Carl Linnæus, and the Comte de Buffon himself, who, Jefferson states, provides readers with information on one of America's quadrupeds, the so-called mammoth. Jefferson follows this reference with another where he directs his reader to the authority of another source, a Native American chief whom Jefferson introduces by means of a reference to his eloquent oratory and formal rituals. Using the voice of this Native American chief, Jefferson introduces the central

---

[13] Buffon's work, entitled *Histoire Naturelle, générale et particulière*, was composed during a twenty-year period (1749–1779) and consisted of various volumes that Buffon never quite organized as a unified work. The result is a composite collection of information, often contradictory, which can be described as a work in progress (Gerbi 1973, 3–34).

topic of the discussion: the question of whether or not the American mammoth is extinct. With this example, Jefferson brings forward a contemporary discussion on the findings of prehistoric large bones in various parts of North America. The example also introduces Jefferson's most important evidence for supporting his views of a perfected unchanging nature: the measurements of the animals Buffon had claimed were smaller in the American continent than in Europe. The passage begins with the reference to the two European scientists:

> Our quadrupeds have been mostly described by Linnæus and Mons. De Buffon. Of these the Mammoth, or big buffalo as called by the Indians, must certainly have been the largest. Their tradition is, that he was carnivorous, and still exists in the northern parts of America. A delegation of warriors from the Delaware tribe having visited the governor of Virginia, during the present revolution, on matters of business, after these had been discussed and settled in council, the governor asked them some questions relative to their country, and, among others, what they knew or had heard of the animal whose bones were found at the Saltlicks, on the Ohio. Their chief speaker immediately put himself into an attitude of oratory, and with a pomp suited to what he conceived the elevation of the subject, informed him that it was a tradition handed down from their fathers, "That in antient times a herd of these tremendous animals came to the Bigbone licks, and began an universal destruction [...] that the Great Man above, looking down and seeing this was so enraged that he seized his lightening, descended on the earth, seated himself on a neighbouring mountain, on a rock, of which his seat and the print of his feet are still to be seen, and hurled his bolts among them till the whole were slaughtered, except the big bull [that] bounded over the Ohio, over the Wabash, the Illinois, and finally over the great lakes, where he is living at this day." (Peden 1953, 43)

Jefferson's argumentative strategy in this passage is not unique to his text. Other early American writers used prehistoric findings to argue over the existence of this animal; its relationship to the elephant, or to other animals living in Europe and Africa; and its presence in North America to defend themselves and their colonies when accused of being second-tier subjects of the British Empire. Beginning in the early eighteenth century, in fact, many American writers had developed hypothetical constructions of American identity around arguments over the discovery of mammoth bones.

On one side were writers like Cotton Mather, who had claimed the bones pointed to the existence of a great and glorious biblical past

(Mulford 2001, 88–98). In a letter to the Royal Society written in 1712, Mather appealed to Christian history and called for a place among and above biblical figures for what he called the "American giant," a giant that, he said, made the "*post-diluvian Giants*" mentioned in the Bible "puisny Things" in comparison to the ones that had inhabited North America. Not only did the giant that Mather described raise America from its inferior position; it simultaneously elevated it above other nations. Mather's description established continuity between the biblical figures and the one whose remains had been found near New England, and it made America better than those European places where no such remains were ever found:

> Of all those *Curiosities*, I know none that exceeds what has lately been found in an *American* plantation, adjoining to *New England*. And its being found in *America* makes it yet the more curious and marvellous. For I beseech you, How did the *Giant* find the way hither?
>
> The *post-diluvian Giants* mentioned in the Sacred Scriptures, were puisny Things in comparison to one of One above Seventy Foot High; and yett we have here the undoubted Reliques of Such an One. (Levin 1988, 764ff)[14]

On the other side of the argument were people like Buffon who saw the existence of the mammoth as scientific evidence of degeneration or lack of development within the Americas (Chinard 1947, 33). Benjamin Franklin, who shared this position, argued that the remains showed that at some point in the past, the earth had "been in another position, and the climates differently placed from what they are at the present," and as a consequence these animals, probably giant elephants, had died and remained in the locations where the bones were found.[15]

---

[14] The first bones of mammoths were found near Albany, New York, in 1705.

[15] Benjamin Franklin's British correspondent Peter Collinson had described the bones as those of an antediluvian animal. The anatomist William Hunter called them the bones of "the American incognitum," to indicate a different species not yet identified. Jefferson was probably aware of Collinson's and Hunter's hypotheses or he just argued following the same lines. It was only between 1796 and 1806 that the French naturalist Georges L.C.F.D. Cuvier named the animal mastodontis (now mastodon) and distinguished the ones found in America from those found in Siberia, which he called Mammoth. Daubenton, Buffon's associate and contributor to the *Histoire Naturelle*, was the first scientist to study American fossils in 1762 (Franklin 14: 222; Bedini 1990, 97).

Although the remains of the mammoth were taken as examples either to prove the continuity between America and Europe or to be placed as a symbol of American exceptionalism, the naturalists who discussed the findings considered the remains relics of a faraway historical past. The position Jefferson supports by quoting Native American tradition and by maintaining its existence in the late eighteenth century exists somewhere between the two described above. Using the words of the Native American speaker as a form of evidence, Jefferson assumes the animal still exists because nature has a never-changing character and the Native American speaker's words contribute to support this idea. This particular character determines continuity between America and Europe, and, it elevates America as the country where the largest animal on earth still lives.

In the history of the various findings of mammoth bones Jefferson gives after the passage quoted on p. 43, he highlights the fundamental role that empirical study has in determining the validity of a scientist's argument. Jefferson cites a series of empirical data regarding the size of the bones, their geographical location, and physical qualities:

> The skeleton of the mammoth (for so the incognitum has been called) bespeaks an animal of six times the cubic volume of the elephant, as Mons. De Buffon has admitted. The grinders are five times as large, are square, and the grinding surface studded with four or five rows of blunt points: whereas those of the elephant are broad and thin, and their grinding surface flat. ... The obliquity of the ecliptic, when these elephants lived, was so great as to include within the tropics all those regions in which the bones were found; the tropics being, as is before observed, the natural limits of habitation for the elephant. (Peden 1982, 45)

In this passage, the data Jefferson supplies is specific. His claim that the mammoth cannot be an elephant is based on the measurements of a material sample of its bones and on the observation of the place where such a species can live. The series of empirical data he offers in the passage supports Jefferson's case and starkly contrasts with his criticism of the scientific argument in Buffon's work that, Jefferson will argue, is based on a fundamental lack of empirical analysis. Jefferson's reliance on the idiom of scientific empiricism should not, however, obscure the form in which he deploys his language. The discussion that includes the quotes above offers a picture in which America is not defined through its differences, especially in animal size, from the European continent, but rather through the unifying power of nature and the continuities it establishes.

Jefferson throughout his discussion employs a language of cosmopolitan inclusiveness that invokes ideals of universal communication and mutual understanding. The mammoth, therefore, is both a means of comparison and a unifying symbol. Jefferson's tool for achieving such a goal is the Native American tradition of eloquent oratory that the account of the speaker's words quoted earlier evokes. The native speaker's oratory offers Jefferson a universalizing image of immutable nature, which he then deploys as the American nature that is at the basis of his representation.[16] In this manner, he makes of America the entity that produces natural and linguistic forms recognizable by the entire scientific community. Indian oratory, with the help of the evidence "found at the Saltlicks, on the Ohio," enables Jefferson to make America and its creatures lose their local and exceptional character and become part of an overarching environmental unity the cosmopolitan intellectual seeks.[17]

Both the speaker's words and the context of their utterance, a council in the presence of the Governor of Virginia, generate a link between Jefferson and his readership that relies on commonly assumed notions of native eloquence as representative of a uniquely American spirit and its integrity. Jefferson does not begin his scientific argument against Buffon with the solid evidence of the comparative examples shown above and

---

[16] Charles A. Miller has described Jefferson's approach to nature "deistic science," and argued that it derives from Jefferson's elaboration of the Lucretian premises that matter and motion always have a primary cause in a natural law and that each biological species is fixed in such laws. To the Lucretian position, Jefferson adds a Christian belief that such a state is determined by the overarching power of God. Miller argues that Jefferson's representation of *Notes*' semi-perfect nature originating in the deity's harmonious design of the universe derives from such a view (Miller 1988, 23–55).

[17] Denis Diderot's definition in the *Encyclopédie* states that to be a cosmopolitan meant to be a "man at home in every country, a man who placed his family above himself, his country above his family, and humanity above his country" (Diderot 1751, 4: 297). See Chap. 2 for a discussion of Diderot's definition of cosmopolitanism and its connection to eighteenth-century culture. This attitude was the premise for the approach to the study of the natural world as well that naturalists like Jefferson adopted. Scientists, in the words of the members of the Royal Society who presented the Copley Medal to Benjamin Franklin, needed to "consider themselves and each other, as Constituent Parts and Fellow-Members of one and the same illustrious Republic," and thus abide by impartiality both towards the republic's members and the subject matter they studied (Schlereth 1977, 37).

the comparative tables demonstrating that most American animals are superior in size to their European counterparts. Rather, he begins the discussion with a claim based on a visibly mythological character. The use of a Native speaker plays a peculiar role in the context of Jefferson's argument and is a common literary trope employed by early American and European writers since the beginning of the colonizing process. Native American oratory was used to assert a new, distinctive trait of an emerging American identity. Its original function as a diplomatic tool between Natives and settlers had been displaced during the colonial period and were later used in a different form of diplomacy between Anglo-Americans and Europeans.[18]

The imagery Jefferson uses in "Query VI" belongs to the model of diplomatic exchanges described above. It functions as a diplomatic tool between the American writer and his European audience, and it provides a familiar portrayal of Early American integrity. The portrayal Jefferson offers, with the Native American speaker resuming the official attitude of the council when he has to recount the story of the mammoth, would have been familiar to his audience. Most significantly, the manner in which the speaker narrates the story also validates the claims he makes. Rather than reproducing the speech of the Native, as he will do later when quoting the renowned "Logan speech," Jefferson summarizes it. However, he provides a lengthy description of the man's act of utterance during the official meeting in which the information was translated. Jefferson first draws the reader's attention to the tradition of the Indian speaker with a sentence that associates Native American mythology with oratorical skills:

> Their tradition is, that it [the mammoth] was carnivorous, and still exists in the northern parts of America. ... Their chief speaker immediately put himself into an attitude of oratory, and with a pomp suited to what he conceived the elevation of the subject, informed him that it was tradition handed down from their fathers .... The formality of the Native

---

[18] Sandra Gustafson has documented how Anglo-American colonials were first fascinated by Native American oratorical performances used in their formal interactions with the colonists and then had appropriated these practices to define the traits of an American colonial spirit, later interpreted as the spirit of independent America. Jefferson's use of the Native voice as a marker of an American distinctive past implies a similar assumption and elevates America to a level of common understanding (Gustafson 2000, 111–139).

American's attitude conveys the notion of tradition and recalls the expressive manifestations of Native American eloquence during formal interactions with the colonists, both of which, in Jefferson's presentation, constitute a model for narrative integrity.[19]

Jefferson's presentation of the Native American speaker, however, does more than evoke the imagery of the official councils and their modes of communication. In his introduction, in fact, Jefferson makes the Native American speaker a member of the republic of letters and sciences. Jefferson's opening sentences, in fact, align "Indian tradition" with the most eminent scientific tradition of the Enlightenment represented by the taxonomist Linnæus and Buffon himself. The speech of the Native American immediately follows the sentence, "Our quadrupeds have been mostly described by Linnæus and Mons. De Buffon. Of these the Mammoth, or big buffalo as called by the Indians, must certainly have been the largest" (Peden 1953, 43). From this position, the Native American speaks the same idiom as the two scientists and the community they represent—an idiom that reaches above particular interests and to a scientific community that declares itself as the speaker for humankind and its development. Like them, the man who tells the story about the mammoth speaks a language—the language of the republic of letters—spoken across national, cultural, and linguistic borders and has the same cosmopolitan traits of the republic itself. As he invokes Native American oratory, Jefferson translates it into cultural terms his European audience of intellectuals understood because they had developed them. From such premises, the words the Native American speaks as well as the rhetorical strategies Jefferson employs to discuss them become foundational features of Jefferson's argument and allow him to prevent criticism his ideas might raise. In particular, they allow him to ally his argument with widely accepted notions associated with the "great chain of being" (Lovejoy 2001, 183–207).

The distinctive Americanness of the Native voice associates his rhetoric with the eloquence that the European intellectual community can use to understand what Jefferson says in the rest of the chapter. Such rhetoric

---

[19] Peter S. Onuf has argued that Jefferson saw Native American people and culture as the disappearing ancestors of the Europeans who currently inhabit North American territories. This imagining allowed Jefferson to reframe past and contemporary events and claim ownership of the stories he tells (Onuf 2000, 18–52).

becomes the foundation of Jefferson's counter-discourse.[20] Jefferson does not simply conclude that, because Native Americans can naturally master the art of public speaking, they have at least as much credibility as any other European speaker. He also relies on his contemporary readership's ability to associate Indian oratory with America and its recognition as an entity capable of producing a form of speech that is commonly recognizable in both environments. Then he assigns this idiom a cosmopolitan feature, and he gives it back to the republic of letters.

In this respect, Jefferson's strategy is also reminiscent of the technique used by many of his contemporaries who employed the voice of "exotic" speakers to generate a commentary addressed to a supranational audience. Examples are Montesquieu's Persian letter writers, and Philip Freneau's Native Americans like Tomo Cheeki.[21] These figures' linguistic and cultural otherness allows for the establishment of the cosmopolitan point of view of the author, who, by embodying exotic literary personas and simulating a different cultural background, can thus speak about local topics using a detachment he could not have shown otherwise. With the figure of the Native American and his eloquence, Jefferson can use the cosmopolitan level of his discussion to make, albeit indirectly, the political argument that republican America possesses the same productive power as Europe. Jefferson's confidence in the unquestionability of the speaker's words is related to the significance that the rhetorical form of his argument and the formality of its performance had for his eighteenth-century audience. His description of the speaker's attitude during the act of utterance validates Jefferson's account for such an audience.

This particular use of rhetoric as expressive of the Native American's sincerity, and thus a warrant of his information's reliability, also links Jefferson's usage of the notion of eloquence to contemporary debates over oratory and elocution. As scholars have shown in regard to

---

[20] Myra Jehlen has also noted the connection between oratory and the legitimacy of native American eloquence and argued that: "Eloquence, the *locus classicus* for the expression of intellectual power, is granted to an Indian [Jehlen refers to Logan's speech at the end of the chapter] in the same measure as the greatest ever possessed by white men in the highest moments of the golden age of their culture" (Jehlen 1989, 48).

[21] Philip Morin Freneau's stories of *Tomo Cheeki, the Creek Indian in Philadelphia* were published in the *New Jersey Chronicle* (1795) and in *The Time Piece, and Literary Companion* (1797). *The Persian Letters* by Charles de Secondat, Baron de Montesquieu, were published in French in 1721.

Jefferson's first draft of the Declaration of Independence, he was deeply influenced by the ideas of Scottish Enlightenment philosophers, such as Henry Home, Lord Kames (Wills 1978, 111–216). Jefferson's interest in this movement is reflected in the role it played in the rhetorical structure of his draft of the founding document. Kames' work, *The Elements of Criticism* (1762), proposed a view of rhetoric as centered in human nature rather than in the authoritarian rules of literary composition. This work and that of other important figures of the Scottish Enlightenment, such as Adam Smith and the rhetoricians James Burgh and John Rice, among others, brought together *belles lettres*, rhetoric, and eloquence in the study and in the teaching of language. The ideas of these intellectuals reflect what contemporaries called the "elocutionary revolution" and a new understanding of rhetoric as a manifestation of the speaker's inner senses.[22]

In general terms, the elocutionary revolution (begun in the first and matured during the second half of the eighteenth century) proposed a revision of the role oral performance played in the traditional views of rhetoric, and thus a revision of the meaning of rhetoric itself. Elocution, which in the Ciceronian tradition plays a secondary role within rhetoric, becomes central in the understanding of what rhetoric should do during this period. Language and its operations, the basic elements of rhetoric, rather than being interpreted as forms of linguistic expression, become forms of self-expression (Fliegelman 1993, 28). As a consequence, what takes place in verbal expression becomes a symptom of the speaker's internal status, of his emotions as well as of his thoughts. The Aristotelian and Ciceronian traditions of rhetoric as the expressive and highly stylized means for political, forensic, and ceremonial discourse were thus altered by adding to the picture elements that can lead back to the influential practices of Baconian empiricism (Fliegelman 1993, 29). Such practices produced a view of rhetoric based on the idea that an argument should be developed according to a scientific process and does not involve a highly stylized set of terms but, rather, terms are to

---

[22] My understanding of the historical development of the notion of eloquence, as well as of the process that brought together eloquence, *belles lettres*, and pedagogy derives from the work of the following writers who have analyzed the history of rhetoric and its development in the North American colonies during the eighteenth century (Guthrie 1951, 17–30; Howell 1971; Fliegelm 1993; Warnick 1993).

be drawn from the individual experience in question. Because Jefferson shared such a view of rhetoric and elocution that privileges oral delivery and because the *Declaration* was a document imagined as oral communication, scholars have often argued, its readers should pay attention to the performative signs of the speech Jefferson marked on his draft as much as to the written words themselves (Fliegelman 1993, 30).

The arguments scholars have made regarding Jefferson's relationship to the elocutionary movement are strictly related to the *Declaration*. Despite the generic difference between such a document and *Notes on Virginia*, the role that contemporary debates over rhetoric played in this later work should not be discounted. The oral performances mentioned in Jefferson's account make his interest in the debates over rhetoric relevant to our understanding of the role the oral performances play in the text. Jefferson includes the Native American's ability to eloquently communicate within a set of evidential elements in support of his argument. This move reflects his reliance on the model of affective rhetoric the elocutionary movement described. The Native American and Jefferson's sincerity of expression are just as important as the scientific reliability of the data he collects and describes in the chapter. According to what the members of the elocutionary movement termed a "mechanistic" position, Jefferson's trust of the Native speaker's words reveals a sense that both the words he speaks and the manner in which he speaks them reflect the natural laws underscoring the world (Guthrie 1954, 56–59). In the rest of this section of *Notes*, Jefferson places Buffon on the opposite sides of the debate and attributes to him the negative qualities that the representation of rhetoric as self-expression also implies—deception and scientific imprecision. He accuses Buffon of having broken the Baconian empiricist principle that should have sustained his eloquent exposition and he argues that instead of using material facts to develop his argument, Buffon has employed the stylized prose (and therefore empty of effectual meaning) that the new rhetorician should discard.

## 3 Invalidating Buffon's Theory

If Jefferson's view of eloquence reflects the contemporary changes in the field, the view of nature that underscores his scientific analysis presents change as an enemy. As I suggested earlier, when Jefferson brings in the statement of the Native American regarding the existence of the "great buffalo" and uses it as a supportive claim to his idea that the mammoth could still exist in North America, he begins to align his views of American natural history with the European scientific tradition that he wants to support. The claim that the animal still exists, in fact, serves Jefferson the twofold purpose of supporting America's greatness in a way similar to what Mather had done when discussing the "American giant," but also to present American nature according to the standards of the scientific views of many of his European colleagues who saw nature in a static form unaffected by change.[23] The immemorial character of the Native American tradition, which attests to the existence of the mammoth in the speaker's eloquent exposition, contributes to such a model of nature. Later in the chapter Jefferson describes this view as the "economy of nature," where a species cannot simply be extinct or evolve into something else.[24] Through this section of the query, Jefferson puts the native speaker's eloquence at the service of a static view of nature in line with the conservative scientific position he embraces.

The philosophical method Jefferson presents as the most appropriate and with which he wants to captivate his European audience comprises the eloquence of the native speaker. With this, Jefferson introduces the empirical data in support of America's physical natural strength and unchanging character. In his analysis of the data that Buffon had provided him, Jefferson speaks of scientists who have proven Buffon's measurements wrong, discusses the difference in the habitat and size between the elephant and the mammoth, which Buffon has failed to discuss, and argues against the French naturalist's claim that the remains of the animal can be found only below a certain latitude. Then he finally returns to the opening point about the mammoth and places it against Buffon's theories of degeneration. As he proceeds in his long digression on the largest American quadruped, Jefferson summarizes what he sees as the reality of Buffon's argument, namely that Buffon's conclusions rely on

---

[23] Buffon's proto-evolutionary views of nature had been harshly criticized by the established French scientific community and his position of director of the royal gardens had been in jeopardy because of it. Jefferson was probably well aware of this episode (Chinard 1947, 28; Gerbi 1973, 30–31).

[24] The relationship between Jefferson's appropriation of the Native idea of tradition, the reference to that past as immemorial, and the English tradition of common law often conflated with natural law constitute is also reminiscent of what Jefferson did in an earlier essay entitled "The Rights of British America" (1775). In the essay Jefferson had used the notion of an Anglo-Saxon past as ground for the American independent spirit and resorted to Anglo tradition of common law to make his case (Ferguson 1984; Pocock 1987).

faulty hypotheses and thus invalidate his entire theory. One of these faulty hypotheses or, Jefferson argues, "some other [hypothesis] equally voluntary and inadmissible to cautious philosophy, must be adopted to support the opinion that these are the bones of the elephant" (Peden 1982, 46). These words challenge Buffon's reliability in the very discipline of which Jefferson had previously recognized Buffon to be master.[25]

In the pages of the query that follow, Jefferson proceeds with his indictment of the French naturalist's method. Such a method, Jefferson suggests, lacks the essential features of the Enlightenment scientific culture that it claims to represent: reliance in reason and empirical evidence. Jefferson concludes, "the opinion of a writer [Buffon], the most learned too in the science of animal history," is simply wrong (Peden 1982, 47). A series of comparative tables follows this claim and, in Jefferson's view, show the superiority of the "new" world over the "old" within a frame that stresses the similarity between the two. Once the comparison is drawn, Jefferson directly addresses Buffon's theory of involution and degeneration:

> As if both sides were not warmed by the same genial sun; as if a soil of the same chemical composition, was less capable of elaboration into animal nutriment; as if the fruits and grains from that soil and sun, yielded a less rich chyle, gave less extension to the solids and fluids of the body, or produced sooner in the cartilages, membranes, and fibres, that rigidity which restrains all further extension, and terminates animal growth. (Peden 1982, 47)

The repetition of the words "as if" at the beginning of the first three sentences of this passage accompanies Jefferson's step-by-step refutation

---

[25] The meaning of the word philosophy at the time was the same that it has today, the "study of things and their causes" (Oxford English Dictionary). Natural philosophy was the branch of philosophy that studied the natural world. Its method of inquiry was experimental analysis, which consisted of first discovering all the external facts of nature and then giving them an order through which the natural law underlying them could be reconstructed. Natural history constituted the more descriptive side of the science and aimed at a more general classification of natural data. With the extended list of faults in Buffon's study, Jefferson both shows how Buffon misapplied the method of study and gives an example of an appropriate philosophical analysis and of the form that its results should take. It was a common assumption of the republic of letters' intellectuals that the talented naturalist was he who, in Oliver Goldsmith's phrasing, could assume the attitude, of "A citizen of the world," and as such be open to inquiry outside of his national boundaries and to an unprejudiced encounter with other cultures (Schlereth 1977, 187).

of Buffon's supporting claims and creates an anaphoric rhythm to the passage itself. The use of the classical rhetorical device of the anaphora introduces readers to the subsequent comparison between different uses of eloquence and science. Jefferson prefaces the discussion with a quote in French from Buffon's *Histoire Naturelle* followed by the English translation: "'La nature vivante est beaucoup moins agissante, beaucoup moins forte:' that nature is less active, less energetic on one side of the globe than she is on the other" (Peden 1982, 47). The pairing of the two languages is reminiscent of the pairing of the different speakers at the beginning of the section, and the rhetorical construction, which anticipates the discussion of the espousal of science and eloquence in Buffon's work, is instrumental to Jefferson's scientific refutation. The anaphora that precedes Jefferson's final comparison between his views and Buffon's is now at the service of scientific inquiry.

Just as Jefferson's structure of the passage places rhetorical constructions at the service of science, Jefferson discusses how Buffon has instead placed science at the service of eloquence. Jefferson, in fact, quickly returns to the original topic of the mammoth and its existence. In this new discussion involving the mammoth, Jefferson brings Native eloquence and science together and pits them against Buffon's ideas:

> It may be asked, why I insert the Mammoth, as if it still existed? I ask in return, why I should omit it, as if it did not exist? Such is the œconomy of nature, that no instance can be produced of her having permitted any one race of her animals to become extinct; of her having formed any link in her great work so weak as to be broken. To add to this, the traditional testimony of the Indians, that this animal still exists in the northern and western parts of America, would be adding the light of a taper to that of the meridian sun. Those parts still remain in their aboriginal state, unexplored and undisturbed by us, or by others for us. He may as well exist there now, as he did formerly where we found his bones. (Peden 1982, 53–54)

The question opening the passage is answered by another question, and both are rhetorical and in the affirmative form as if they were both questions and answers.[26] The "œconomy of nature" and the "traditional

---

[26]The recurrence of rhetorical figures, such as the one found in this passage, is a reminder of Jefferson's investment in the role that rhetoric plays in conveying truthful meaning, which he derived from the contemporary rhetorical theories he had embraced (Fliegelman 1993, 30–35).

testimony of the Indian" are on the same level. The indisputable character of the economy of nature and its laws is a direct reference to the argument in favor of a non-evolutionary model of nature Jefferson invokes to counter Buffon's idea of degeneration and its quasi-evolutionary character. Jefferson appeals to the law of nature and to its resistance to change as a fundamental proof of what is wrong in Buffon's views. The idea of a Native rhetoric and his information about the findings of bones combine in this passage to support a non-evolutionary view of nature for which the universe is held together by infinite links that cannot be disrupted without the structure's collapse into utter chaos. At this point, the solemn testimony of the Native American loses its paramount position. The testimony now is "the light of a taper to that of the meridian sun," and, as such, the man's eloquent oratory becomes a tool in the service of Jefferson's empiricism and the scientific ideology it validates.

In an earlier part of "Query VI" Jefferson had already joined the contemporary debates over the power of nature to perform internal changes and taken an anti-evolutionary position. In this section, he addresses the correlation between natural laws and the task of the natural philosopher and he firmly asserts his belief in a vision of a nature that does not admit change to its forms and structures (Schlereth 1977, 32–35). The general context for the comments is a discussion regarding other prehistoric findings. The remains in question are fossilized seashells found in rocks above the sea level, both in North America and in Europe, which he introduces as follows:

> Near the eastern foot of the North mountain are immense bodies of *Schist*, containing impressions of shells in a variety of forms. I have received petrified shells of very different kinds from the first sources of the Kentucky, which bear no resemblance to any I have ever seen on the tide-waters. It is said that shells are found in the Andes, in South-America, fifteen thousand feet above the level of the ocean. This is considered by many, both of the learned and the unlearned, as a proof of a universal deluge. To the many considerations opposing this opinion, the following may be added. The atmosphere, and all its contents, whether of water, air, or other matters, gravitate to the earth; that is to say, they have weight. Experience tells us, that the weight of all these together never exceeds that of a column of mercury of 31 inches height, which is equal to one of rain water of 35 feet high. (Peden 1982, 32)

The precise information and the reference to the empirical approach Jefferson uses to justify his skepticism about the possibility that a deluge could have been the cause for the presence of the shells in elevated areas is directed to a community that knows the idiom Jefferson uses and that shares the same ideas about natural history. He speaks to an audience, the international scientific community, that knows what he is talking about and has the same interest in this apparently inexplicable phenomenon. In the comments that follow, Jefferson's position is strictly empiricist. He argues that the task of the natural philosopher is to find in experience the elements that constitute natural laws and from these laws to reconstruct the paradigms that attend to the structuring of the world. In addition to a prehistoric inundation, Jefferson reports two other contemporary theories that explain the origins of the shells in a lengthy footnote to the text. The two theories argue that a past cataclysm momentarily elevated the levels of seas and lakes, causing the shells to adhere to the earth's surface before the level went down again; and finally, that nature has the power to transform its elements, so rocks can turn into simulacra of animals and plants (Peden 1982, 270). In his conclusion to this discussion, Jefferson writes that none of the answers are viable and: "The three hypotheses are equally unsatisfactory; and we must be contented to acknowledge, that this great phenomenon is as yet unsolved. Ignorance is preferable to error; and he is less remote from the truth who believes nothing, than he who believes what is wrong" (Peden 1982, 33). Because any answer to the question concerning the origins of the phenomenon can only remain in the domain of hypothetical thinking, and because no scientist has collected enough empirical evidence in support of the three theories, the law of nature that has caused the phenomenon cannot be reconstructed and any explication should thus remain unacceptable.

Interestingly, however, Jefferson's position regarding the last of the three theories described above—nature's ability to simulate life in rocks—which Voltaire had proposed in an essay entitled "Coquilles," in *Questions sur l'Encyclopédie*, had not always been one of total skepticism.[27] In the privately printed edition of *Notes* he published in 1785,

---

[27]Voltaire had developed his theory about the shells from the seventeenth-century Jesuit polymath Athanasius Kircher, who had suggested that mountains were primordial features of the surface of the earth. Keith Thomson has noted that Leonardo da Vinci had already argued that the presence of fossilized shells in mountainous areas was the result of sea water covering the mountains (Thomson 2012, 281–282). Caroline Winterer also discusses eighteenth-century philosophes' interest in theories about the presence of fossil shells in elevated territories and Voltaire's theories about them (Winterer 2016, 64–69).

Jefferson had hinted at the possibility that an internal transformation of rocks into lifelike structures might not be wrong. In that context, Jefferson had asked: "Is it more difficult, for nature to shoot the calcareous juices into the form of a shell, then other juices into the forms of Chrystals, plants, animals, …? Have not naturalists already brought themselves to believe much stranger things?" (Peden 1982, 265–266). This initial intention to embrace the French philosopher's hypothesis indicates a propensity to accept a transformative (albeit far-fetched) view of nature on Jefferson's part. This view, however, was promptly reversed after he began to circulate the book's first printed edition around friends and colleagues and the conservative scientific community turned against him.[28] The decision to erase the comments favoring Voltaire's hypothesis, which seems to be dictated by skepticism and the desire to avoid further criticism, reveals Jefferson's ambivalence about his own position, as well as his tendency to privilege natural permanence over mutation. It also throws light on the decision, in the public printing of the book, to embrace a position that, in addition to enabling him to challenge Buffon's claims, allows Jefferson to propose a view that presents American nature to the European readership he wants to attract in terms they would not criticize (Schlereth 1977, 33–35). As it is the case with the possibility of a natural transformation of rocks into shells, the admission of the mammoth's extinction, after having stated its difference in species from other species that can be found in Europe and its outskirts, would produce a transformative reading of nature, possibly reminiscent of Buffon's degenerative model. The criticism that Jefferson's espousal of Voltaire's idea had caused, and his consequent decision to reject transformation in favor of permanence, illustrate the conflict that existed between the longstanding static paradigm, in which nature's order was immutable, and the transformative paradigm for which such order was part of a progressing chain, which Jefferson ultimately rejects. Jefferson's change reveals the ambivalence he felt about replacing one paradigm

---

[28] Jefferson discusses this issue in various contexts and, during a trip to the south of France while minister in Paris, he visited the spot on which Voltaire had observed the shells. See his letters to Chastellaux on June 7, 1785 (Jefferson 1953, 8: 184–186), to Madison on May 11, 1785 (Jefferson 1953, 8: 147–148), and Madison to Jefferson on November 15, 1785 (Jefferson 1954, 9: 38–38). In a letter to David Rittenhouse written on January 25, 1786 (Jefferson 1954, 9: 215–216) Jefferson reiterated his indecisiveness regarding the process (Martin 1961, 146–167; Schachner 1951, 1: 226; Bedini 1990, 165–167).

with the other and it is also indicative of his sense of *Notes* as a work in progress and part of an open dialogue with the European scientific community. The change that took place between 1785 and 1787 reflects *Notes*' involvement in a changing and unstable scientific discourse.

In place of a gesture toward the acceptance of a transformative view of nature, a sternly conservative and static view concludes Jefferson's comments on the new natural findings in the 1787 edition. Jefferson claims that lack of knowledge determines the three theories' lack of authority following a non-transformative view of nature and introducing skepticism as the determining factor in his evaluating process. Although apparently contradicting his later statement that we should believe in the contemporary existence of the mammoth rather than being skeptical of the lack of evidence confirming its life, Jefferson's statement makes sense when aligned with the "chain of being" theory that underscores both comments (Lovejoy 1936, 242–287; Foucault 1970, 166–302). The existence of the mammoth is based on the idea of an uninterrupted and fixed chain of being constituting all natural life—a natural law attending to the workings of nature in general. This is similar to the idea supporting Jefferson's denial that natural evolution had produced the animal remains found in rocks: "no instance can be produced of [nature] having permitted any one race of her animals to become extinct" (Peden 1982, 54). If something has been created a certain way, it cannot be destroyed. Rocks cannot turn into shells and mammoths cannot die out. The lack of specific evidence to prove a species still exists should not generate doubt, because natural laws cannot be questioned (Miller 1988, 47–53).

The dismissal of evolution is accompanied by a reliance on the eloquence of the Native American speaker as a means to assert the validity of Jefferson's empirical method. In other words, Jefferson places eloquence at the service of his empirical method. In the case of the mammoth, rather than measuring a live animal, the association of the Native American voice with the linguistic forms of the republic of letters and the scientific realm of Linnæus and Buffon produces a similar empirical analysis (Dain 2002, 1–39). To those readers who can understand the universalizing language of his static view of nature, Jefferson asks that they trust the eloquent oratory of the Native American because it depends on natural laws. The logic behind Jefferson's assertion of the existence of the mammoth demonstrates how the inclusive language he uses to introduce the speaker and the rhetorical strategy he employs to introduce his word replace the empirical evidence of a living mammoth. With the exception of the initial sentences of the section entitled "Animals," in which he reports the Native American tradition about the existence of the mammoth, in fact, Jefferson does not indicate he has any evidence the animal still exists. He first talks about the animal's remains and when he discusses the animal's existence, he does so in various present perfect forms: the mammoth "may have existed," "has existed," or it "has been," simply leaving open the possibility of such an existence. This possibility becomes a fact when Jefferson appeals to the unquestionable "œconomy of nature" and when he replaces the possibility of changes in time with a form of spatial synchrony that stresses the possibility of the animal's existence in "those parts [that] still remain in their aboriginal state, unexplored and undisturbed by us, or by others for us"(Peden 1982, 54). Jefferson's initial reliance on the oratorical skills of the Native American functions as an appendix to the deistic vision of a nature that refuses to destroy its species. The bones of the mammoth are not the object of speculation regarding its contemporary existence, but become the material evidence of the animal's presence. The rhetorical structure of the claim brings up the notion that nature does not change to the forefront of Jefferson's discussion. And as a consequence of the lack of a surviving living animal, the testimony of the Native American becomes secondary evidence and thus not necessarily questionable.[29]

---

[29] Mitchell Breitwieser has argued that in *Notes*, Jefferson "does join theory and experience ... in an antithetical unity in which the role of experience is to upset theory, to challenge it by exposing its reductiveness, and to instigate further revision, rather than to advertise theory's adequacy." Breitwieser contends that Jefferson supplies Barbé-Marbois with a series of responses that emphasize the arbitrariness of theory whenever it is placed against the mirror of experience. Although this is the case in Jefferson's general confutation of Buffon's argument, Jefferson reverses this point when he decides to embrace the paucity of evidence to support his hypothesis concerning the mammoth. Breitwieser explains this moment as a moment of indecision between the two epistemological paradigms of the time (static and progressive). I see it as moment in which Jefferson arbitrarily assigns fact status to his hypotheses so that his theoretical stand can be supported. In the case in question, in fact, the mammoth's linguistic existence and its potential survival generate the fact. Both these features are arbitrary. Jefferson's testing of experience uncovers the discursive realm in which he bases his theory, an understanding that he puts into use in constructing his own argument against Buffon whenever evidential material is weak. I do agree with Breitwieser's view, though, when he argues against a traditional critical attitude to equate Jeffersonian pragmatism with wisdom when interpreting his perspective on experience and theory in *Notes*. Breitwieser's correct premise is that the instrumental reason expressed in Jefferson's work does not escape historical determination and as such it does not escape ideological bias. His uses of weak evidence in order to frame his argument in favor of a static view of nature confirms it (Breitwieser 2007, 84–121).

Jefferson developed a common epistemological ground to portray America for the international scientific community using Native American oratory and the language the notion of static nature gives him. A relevant feature of this community is that it imagines itself supranational. International cooperation is a component of Jefferson's search for a common understanding between the American natural philosopher and his European counterparts. This cooperation cannot take place unless his portrayal surpasses national boundaries and the political and cultural limitations that they impose. In his concluding argument against Buffon, Jefferson's portrayal further shows how his America is an entity that escapes any form of nationalistic labeling. American nature stands above partisanships, as well as national or pro-European interests and represents the universal uniformity of nature itself. As an ending to his rebuttal, Jefferson places the discussion within the realm of common-sense philosophy and the cosmopolitan ideology that brought the republic of letters together. The language Jefferson uses challenges Buffon at the scientific as well as at the cultural/ideological level and makes America stand out as a supranational entity by making its man a representative of the enlightened republic of letters and its ideals. Jefferson first quotes a long passage from the *Histoire Naturelle* in which Buffon describes the native of the continent as feeble, with "small organs of generation" (Peden 1982, 58), and doomed to physical and social degeneration. Then he harshly comments:

> An afflicting picture indeed, which, for the honor of human nature, I am glad to believe has no original. Of the Indian of South America I know nothing; for I would not honor with the appellation of knowledge, what I derive from the fables published of them. These I believe to be just as true as the fables of Æsop. This belief is founded on what I have seen of man, white, red, and black, and what has been written of him by authors, enlightened themselves, and writing amidst an enlightened people. The Indian of North America being more within our reach, I can speak of him somewhat from my own knowledge, but more from the information of others better acquainted with him, and on whose truth and judgment I can rely. (Peden 1982, 59)

This passage addresses the charge Buffon had made against America, namely the inferiority of the Native American man and the implication, supported in Cornelius de Pauw's work and a number of his followers, that degeneration awaits those who have decided to live in such an environment (Gerbi 1973, 52–156). The passage also establishes a parallel between the false stories about South American natives, Æsop's fiction, and Buffon's work. Against Buffon's "fables," Jefferson opposes his belief, which, he maintains, "is founded on what I have seen of man, white, red, and black, and what has been written of him by authors, enlightened themselves, and writing amidst an enlightened people" (Peden 1982, 59). This sentence sums up all the principles Jefferson has followed to develop his counter-argument. The empiricist appeal to fact and reason, the staples of common-sense philosophy, the most progressive contemporary science of his time, the indirect parallel between Buffon's ideas and Æsop's fictional narrative, and the appeal to an idea of humankind that goes beyond any form of particularism characterize Jefferson's approach to his subject matter (Wills 1978, 19–48).

Jefferson depicts himself as speaking from the vantage point of the Enlightenment intellectual whose words are supported by his scientific expertise and generated within the progressive community of men of letters. The America he depicts in his work represents such a community. As I mentioned earlier in this chapter, a distinguishing trait of this group is that their elite community could speak in a commonly shared idiom rooted in reason and expressed in a broadly understood form. By giving reason and nature aesthetic forms, the republic of letters can express itself and communicate (Schlereth 1977, 25–27). Both Jefferson's claims about his writing and his charges against Buffon in the passage on page 87 rely on this paradigm. The reference to Æsop and the implicit parallel with Buffon's prose challenge Buffon's generic choice, which has exceeded the aesthetic parameters enlightenment culture has established for natural science. To his own strengths (empirical evidence, enlightenment philosophical principles, and a supra-national perspective) Jefferson opposes Buffon's weakness (his fictionalization of the information and his lack of material foundations). These two categorizations determine the parameters for interpreting Buffon's ideas and for developing the rhetorical defense of the Native American man and his society that unfolds in the following pages.

Jefferson responds to Buffon's accusation and defends Native American masculinity, strength, and honor before concluding the discussion of American animals. Toward the end of his digression, he introduces his second Native American speaker, Logan. The speech of the Native chief, the last surviving member of his family, which had been killed by the colonists, has been one of the most quoted passages from *Notes* since its first publication. Logan's speech and his eloquence represent reason and nature's aesthetic power at its best. Logan's eloquence, which, Jefferson writes, could "challenge the whole orations of Demosthenes and Cicero, and of any more eminent orator, if Europe has furnished more eminent" (Peden 1982, 62), is placed against Buffon's attempt to use eloquence to portray the works of reason and nature. Logan's speech, with its Ossianic echoes and Gospel reminiscences, is now what Jefferson pits against Buffon's malicious accusations that American men and the country they inhabit have no future.[30] I appeal to any white man to say, if ever he entered Logan's cabin hungry, and he gave him not meat; if ever he came hot and naked, and he clothed him not. During the course of the last long and bloody war, Logan remained idle in his cabin, and advocate for peace. Such was my love for the whites, that my countrymen pointed as they passed, and said, 'Logan is the friend of white men.' I had even thought to have lived with you, but for the injuries of one man. Col. Cresap, the last spring, in cold blood, and unprovoked, murdered all the relations of Logan, not sparing even my women and children. There runs not a drop of my blood in the veins of any living creature. This called on me for revenge. I have sought it: I have killed many: I have fully glutted my vengeance. For my country, I rejoice at the beams of peace. But do not harbour a thought that mine is the joy of fear. Logan never felt fear. He will not turn on his heel to save his life. Who is there to mourn for Logan?—Not one. (Peden 1982, 63)

---

[30] Here is the text of the speech:
I appeal to any white man to say, if ever he entered Logan's cabin hungry, and he gave him not meat; if ever he came hot and naked, and he clothed him not. During the course of the last long and bloody war, Logan remained idle in his cabin, and advocate for peace. Such was my love for the whites, that my countrymen pointed as they passed, and said, 'Logan is the friend of white men.' I had even thought to have lived with you, but for the injuries of one man. Col. Cresap, the last spring, in cold blood, and unprovoked, murdered all the relations of Logan, not sparing even my women and children. There runs not a drop of my blood in the veins of any living creature. This called on me for revenge. I have sought it: I have killed many: I have fully glutted my vengeance. For my country, I rejoice at the beams of peace. But do not harbour a thought that mine is the joy of fear. Logan never felt fear. He will not turn on his heel to save his life. Who is there to mourn for Logan? —Not one. (Peden 1982, 63)

That Jefferson is not interested in the content of the speech itself as well as in Logan's own words is made evident by the fact that Logan's story is indeed about the end of his people. No member of his family survived the slaughter, and the American Cicero will produce no future generations of orators. So the speech itself ironically confirms Buffon's implication that the human species of the continent are bound to disappear, albeit by the hand of man rather than that of nature!

That Jefferson is not interested in the content of the speech itself as well as in Logan's own words is made evident by the fact that Logan's story is indeed about the end of his people. No member of his family survived the slaughter, and the American Cicero will produce no future generations of orators. So the speech itself ironically confirms Buffon's implication that the human species of the continent are bound to disappear, albeit by the hand of man rather than that of nature!

Buffon's pseudo-science is not the only thing Jefferson counterattacks in his discussion. As what precedes and follows the speech of Logan shows, the rhetorical form of Buffon's charges constitutes the focus of Jefferson's discussions. The notion of eloquence provides Jefferson with a new position from which he can not only critique Buffon's ideas, but also rearrange the form of the text he is rewriting. The text of the speech, a translation that had been circulating since 1774, constitutes the climax of Jefferson's confutation. Logan's words function like the words of the Indian speaker at the beginning of the section. Logan's fluency and eloquence attest to his superiority and to the ideal he represents—an indigenous natural character. Unlike the first Native American speaker, however, Logan's words legitimize Jefferson's argument about early republican American identity in a different, though interrelated, way. In the first example, the chief speaker's oratory legitimized the content of his speech and made it unnecessary for Jefferson to supply other forms of evidence. Native oratory was Jefferson's evidence, and the cultural role of Native Americans' formal interactions with the colonists supported his argument. The form of Logan's speech and Jefferson's following comments support his claim of American moral superiority and frame it with the standard expressive form of the republic of letters—a refined, belletristic prose (Schlereth 1977, 17–22; Goodman 1994, 90–182).

Logan's eloquence stands for Jefferson's. Jefferson delegates his "native" Demosthenes to speak his word and place it against Buffon's. If the reference to the Native American speaker at the beginning of the section helped Jefferson make himself the national scientist, Logan's speech allows Jefferson to become the national bard—the bard who can respond to the European writer whose scientific tract has also borrowed from the literary arts. The first Native American speaker's eloquence had provided Jefferson with the evidence he needed to support his argument; now Logan provides him with the rhetorical tools he needs to construct his argument, eloquence itself. Jefferson passes his authorial agency on to Logan, to then take it in his hands again as a political instrument and from that standpoint respond to Buffon and his followers.

In his final comments on Buffon's work, Jefferson fully deploys this view. He presents America as a space unaffected by nationalistic and political goals and as the ideal ground for dialogue among scientists. And Buffon's work becomes representative of all that *Notes on Virginia* is not. It has a strictly rhetorical foundation, and is motivated by a nationalistic spirit, which, Jefferson implies, goes against the intrinsic cosmopolitan spirit of the scientific community:

> I do not mean to deny, that there are varieties in the race of man, distinguished by their powers both of body and mind. I believe there are, as I see to be the case in the races of other animals. I only mean to suggest a doubt, whether the bulk and faculties of animals depend on the side of the Atlantic on which their food happens to grow, or which furnishes the elements of which they are compounded? Whether nature has enlisted herself as a Cis or Trans-Atlantic partisan? I am induced to suspect, there has been more eloquence than sound reasoning displayed in support of this theory; that it is one of those cases where the judgment has been seduced by a glowing pen: and whilst I render every tribute of honor and esteem to the celebrated Zoologist, who has added, and is still adding, so many precious things to the treasures of science, I must doubt whether in this instance he has not cherished error also, by lending her for a moment his vivid imagination and bewitching language. (Peden 1982, 63–64)

The comment continues in a footnote, "No writer, equally with M. de Buffon, proves the power of eloquence, and uncertainty of theories. [Buffon] takes any hypothesis whatever, or it's [sic] reverse, and furnishes explanations equally specious and persuasive" (Peden 1982, 275). The skepticism of the earlier section toward a transformative view of nature also reappears in Jefferson's final comments on Buffon's work, which Jefferson describes as both non-scientific and politically motivated.

As Jefferson draws a direct connection between nature's partisanship and Buffon's employment of eloquence, he also portrays Buffon's scientific inquiry as driven by a pro-European bias. The French scientist, then, has not simply lent science his oratorical skills and imaginative power; he has done so to bring politics within that realm (by assigning nature a "cis-Atlantic partisanship," and thus a one-sided and partisan perspective).[31] Jefferson's response has done the opposite and has removed America from the nationalistic limitations that such a representation would have produced. In doing so, however, America and its nature in their lack of representativeness as national symbols, have gained a form of exceptionalism that makes them stand, with their roaming mammoths, within and above the standards of the republic of sciences and letters.[32] And this is where Jefferson's cosmopolitanism is both a way to overcome the limits being in the outskirts of the republic of letters produces and a way in which a new form of imperial imagery begins to take shape.

Logan's speech performs the transition necessary for Jefferson's counter-rhetoric to be effective. The Native American's eloquence is what Jefferson describes as "an apt proof" that Buffon's charges of intellectual inferiority are wrong. The eloquence is the tool that starts Jefferson's

---

[31] In the Appendix that he attached to the text in 1800, Jefferson specifies that the implication of Buffon's theories, as the claim of Buffon's follower Raynal also exemplified, is a physical as well as moral degeneration "not excepting even the man, native or adoptive." Such theory, he continues, "so unfounded and degrading to one third of the globe, was called to the bar of fact and reason. Among other proofs adduced in contradiction to this hypothesis, the speech of Logan, an Indian chief, delivered to Lord Dunmore in 1774, was produced, as a specimen of the talents of the aboriginals of this country, and particularly of their eloquence; and it was believed that Europe had never produced any thing superior to this morsel of eloquence" (230). The implicit equation between eloquence and morality shows Jefferson's concern for the social implication that Buffon's charges had. The idea that the moral character of a people depended on their form of government and social institutions was commonly accepted by the *philosophes* of the republic of letters. In his essay "On National Characters" (published in 1748), for instance, David Hume had defined the moral factors contributing to a nation's character as those "circumstances, which are fitted to work on the mind as motives or reasons, and which render a peculiar set of manners habitual to us. Of this kind are the nature of the government, the revolutions of public affairs, the plenty or penury in which the people live, the situation of the nation with regard to its neighbours, and such like circumstances." (Hume 1985, 198) Jefferson's interest in legitimating a portrait of his country's character as compatible with, if not superior to, that of its European counterparts being his primary objective in writing *Notes* underscores his manipulation of the text's linguistic form and his attempts to make it remain within the frame that, he maintains, Buffon has given the representation of the American character.

[32] Matthew Cordova Frankel has pointed out the fundamental importance that aesthetic pleasure and imagination have in Jefferson's understanding of science and politics while considering the relationship between the idea of the sublime and that of citizenship in *Notes* (Frankel 2001, 695–726).

verbalization of the critique to Buffon's central claim. This verbalization reflects the eloquence he is overtly attacking so that, instead of directing the reader's attention away from the idea of artificiality, Jefferson makes it both subject and matter of his own text. It is Jefferson's "bewitching language," introduced via Logan's speech, but not limited to it, that is competing with Buffon's. Moreover, Logan's eloquence, whose superior excellence was recognized on the basis of the judgment of the international community, extends the context from Jefferson's work to that of the transatlantic republic of letters to which the book is addressed and which is complicit in Buffon's criticism of America.

Significantly, the superiority of the speech's eloquence and its transatlantic fame are the two features Jefferson repeatedly evokes in the Appendix he added to the 1800 edition of *Notes*. In the appended text, Jefferson discusses the genesis of his decision to use Logan's speech and illustrates the logic that sustains it. In defense of his decision to adopt the speech to respond to Buffon's accusations of degeneration, Jefferson writes that the speech is what makes America recognizable in the transatlantic context. The "morsel of eloquence," as he calls Logan's words in three different places in the appendix, had been recognized as such once it had "circulated in the newspapers through all the then colonies, through the magazines of Great-Britain, and periodical publications of Europe" (Peden 1982, 230). As a consequence to this vast popularity, Jefferson recalls, the speech was used "as a school exercise for repetition" (Peden 1982, 227) for small children. The speech's eloquence has determined its immediate success, but the British and European presses, Jefferson implies, have as much responsibility for its endurance and recognition. The internationally recognized value of the speech places the American context that produced it at the center of the international stage. To substantiate this initial inference and in defense against the charge of having invented the speech, Jefferson concludes:

> In 1797 however, for the first time, not only the whole transaction respecting Logan was affirmed in the public papers to be false, but the speech itself suggested to be a forgery, and even a forgery of mine, to aid me in proving that the man of America was equal in body and in mind, to the man of Europe. But wherefore the forgery? Whether Logan's or mine, it would still have been American. I should indeed consult my own fame if the suggestion, that this speech is mine, were suffered to be believed. He would have a just right to be proud who could with truth claim the composition. (Peden 1982, 230)

Speaker and writer's identity have become interchangeable.[33] What matters now is the American context that has produced the speech, which, Jefferson has already remarked, was nationally and internationally recognized as a piece of American excellence prior to its publication in *Notes*. The question "But wherefore the forgery?" begins the argument that gives the speech a transcendent American character. It also gives forgery a quasi-poetic value and reminds readers of the original charges against Buffon regarding his "bewitching language." The (almost) magic powers Jefferson had attributed to the language of his French colleague, and which had innately been part of Logan's articulation, are thus to be transferred to Jefferson's own prose, albeit the one he was accused of having invented or the one which he has indeed created when composing *Notes*. The indirect appropriation of eloquence becomes legitimate because Jefferson has established an unquestionable bond between nature, eloquence, and the republic of letters that includes America, and one that Buffon, in his view, had failed to establish.[34]

Jefferson's representation of an American natural environment that surpasses national boundaries serves him in generating a sense of America that is supranational and therefore not bound by the typical limitations that we associate with the idea of a country with borders determined by socio-political entities. This exceptionalism, however, is

---

[33] Jay Fliegelman has read the interchangeability between Jefferson and Logan as "the silent, but proud suggestion that in writing the Declaration he too assumed the role of national poet by producing a text that realized, animated, and invented his people" (Fliegelman 1993, 98). Given the context in which the statement appears, I only see this connection as an induction made possible by the role of national speaker that the rhetorical construction allows Jefferson to assume within *Notes* itself.

[34] Jefferson often talked about the importance that discursive cohesion had for the cohesion of the republic of letters and drew parallels between the latter and the community of scientific societies. In 1809, he wrote to an English correspondent that these societies constituted a tight community, which, unlike that of their nations, was always in peace, and that "Like the republic of letters, they form a great fraternity spreading over the whole earth" (Jefferson 1984, 1201). And like the cosmopolitan idiom that united the members of the republic of letters, the scientific community shared a set of terms, the classifying idiolect of Linnæan taxonomy and the expressive codes of the republic of letters itself, which Jefferson called the "universal language" of this transnational community. When I refer to Jefferson's efforts to remain within the discursive frame of the intellectual community, I mean both the idiolect that its members used to communicate and the ideology that their ideas reflected (Boorstin 1993).

unique because the America Jefferson's words portray is also part of a community that includes other nations, and they are all under the larger umbrella of eighteenth-century Europe. What is clear in Jefferson's representation of America's animals, human inhabitants, and natural environment is that what makes America stand out in the cultural and scientific community that we know as the republic of letters (but that, in fact, existed in the real world of politics and who had influence and power in that world) are the simultaneous participation and exceptional character its natural resources and creatures show. Jefferson's sense of American identity depends on the notion of cosmopolitanism, not in order to transgress an idea of empire (in this case an empire of culture and letters), but to enforce it, in a way not dissimilar to how Franklin's essay on the increase of mankind had in the 1750s. Jefferson's response to Buffon's threatening theories of degeneration makes it possible for him to shift the scientific center and its most powerful features (an exceptional animal that can be studied and claimed as part of one's natural landscape) from the European centers of knowledge to the American soil. Even though the mammoth's size places it on the opposite side of the scale from Franklin's English weeds, they represent the same process of expansion, homogenization, and hegemony.

REFERENCES

Bedini, Silvio. 1990. *Thomas Jefferson: Statesman of Science*. New York: Macmillan.

Boorstin, Daniel J. 1993. *The Lost World of Thomas Jefferson*. Chicago: Chicago University Press.

Breitwieser, Mitchell. 2007. *National Melancholy: Mourning and Opportunity in Classic American Literature*. Stanford, CA: Stanford University Press.

Chinard, Gilbert. 1947. Eighteenth Century Theories on America as a Human Habitat. *Proceedings of the American Philosophical Society* 91: 27–57.

Dain, Bruce. 2002. *A Hideous Monster of the Mind: American Race Theory in the Early Republic*. Cambridge, MA: Harvard University Press.

David, Hume. 1895. Essays: Moral, Political, and Literary. In *Miller*, ed. F. Eugene. Indianapolis, IN: Liberty Fund Inc.

Echeverria, Duran. 1957. *Mirage in the West: A History of the French Image of American Society to 1815*. Princeton, NJ: Princeton University Press.

Faÿ, Bernard. 1927. *The Revolutionary Spirit in France and America*. New York: Harcourt, Brace and Co.

Ferguson, Robert A. 1980. Mysterious Obligations: Jefferson's Notes on the State of Virginia. *American Literature: A Journal of Literary History, Criticism, and Bibliography* 52 (3): 381–406.

Fliegelman, Jay. 1993. *Declaring Independence: Jefferson, Natural Language, and the Culture of Performance.* Stanford, CA: Stanford University Press.

Foucault, Michel. 1970. *The Order of Things.* New York: Random House.

Frankel, Matthew Cordova. 2001. Nature's Nation Revisited: Citizenship and the Sublime in Thomas Jefferson's Notes on the State of Virginia. *American Literature* 73 (4): 695–726.

Gerbi, Antonello. 1973. *The Dispute over the New World*, trans. Jeremy Moyle. Pittsburgh, PA: University of Pittsburgh Press.

Goodman, Dena. 1994. *The Republic of Letters: A Cultural History of the French Enlightenment.* Ithaca, NY: Cornell University Press.

Goring, Paul. 2005. *The Rhetoric of Sensibility in Eighteenth-Century Culture.* Cambridge: Cambridge University Press.

Gustafson, Sandra M. 2000. *Eloquence is Power: Oratory and Performance in Early America.* Chapel Hill, NC: The University of North Carolina Press.

Guthrie, Warren. 1951. The Development of Rhetorical Theory in Colonial America 1635–1850—V the Elocution Movement—England. *Speech Monographs* 18: 17–30.

Howell, Wilbur S. 1971. *Eighteenth-Century British Logic and Rhetoric.* Princeton, NJ: Princeton University Press.

Jefferson, Thomas. 1950. *The Papers of Thomas Jefferson*, ed. James P. McClure et al. Princeton, NJ: Princeton University Press.

———. 1982. *Notes on the State of Virginia*, ed. William Peden. New York: W.W. Norton.

———. 1984. *Thomas Jefferson: Writings*, ed. Merrill D. Peterson.

Jehlen, Myra. 1989. *American Incarnation: The Individual, the Nation, and the Continent.* Cambridge, MA: Harvard University Press.

Kennedy, Jennifer. 2000. Parricide of Memory: Thomas Jefferson's Memoir and the French Revolution. *American Literature* 72 (3): 553–573.

Levin, David. 1988. Giants in the Earth: Science and the Occult in Cotton Mather's Letters to the Royal Society. *The William and Mary Quarterly: A Magazine of Early American History and Culture* 45 (4): 51–770.

———. 1903. *The Writings of Thomas Jefferson*, ed. Andrew A. Lipscomb, and Albert Ellery Bergh, vols. 20. Washington, DC: Thomas Jefferson Memorial Association.

Looby, Christopher. 1987. The Constitution of Nature: Taxonomy as Politics in Jefferson, Peale, and Bartram. *Early American Literature* 22 (3): 252–273.

———. 1996. *Voicing America: Language, Literary Form, and the Origins of the United States.* Chicago: University of Chicago Press.

Lovejoy, Arthur. 2001. *The Great Chain of Being: A Study of the History of an Idea*. Cambridge, MA: Harvard University Press.

Manning, Susan. 1996. Naming Parts; Or, the Comforts of Classification: Thomas Jefferson's Construction of America as Fact and Myth. *Journal of American Studies* 30 (3): 345–364.

Martin, Edwin. 1961. *Thomas Jefferson: Scientist*. New York: Collier.

Miller, Charles. 1988. *Jefferson and Nature: An Interpretation*. Baltimore, MD: The Johns Hopkins University Press.

Mulford, Carla. 2001. New Science and the Question of Identity in Eighteenth-Century British America. In *Finding Colonial America: Essays in Honor of Leo Lemay*, ed. Carla Mulford and David S. Shields, 88–98. Wilmington, DE: University of Delaware Press.

Onuf, Peter. 2000. *Jefferson's Empire: The Language of American Nationhood*. Charlottesville, VA: University of Virginia Press.

Pearce, Roy Harvey. 1988. *Savagism and Civilization: A Study of the Indian and the American Mind*. Berkeley: University of California Press.

Pocock, J.G.A. 1975. *The Machiavellian Moment*. Princeton, NJ: Princeton University Press.

Pocock, J.G.A. 1987. *The Ancient Constitution*. New York: Cambridge University Press.

Schachner, Nathan. 1951. *Thomas Jefferson: A Biography*, vols. 2. New York: Appleton-Century-Crofts.

Schlereth, Thomas J. 1977. *The Cosmopolitan Ideal in Enlightenment Thought:Its Form and Function in the Ideas of Franklin, Hume, and Voltaire, 1694–1790*. Notre Dame, IN: University of Notre Dame Press.

Spahn, Hannah. 2011. *Thomas Jefferson, Time, and History*. Charlottesville, VA: University of Virginia Press.

Thomson, Keith. 2012. *Jefferson's Shadow: The Story of His Science*. New Haven, CT: Yale University Press.

Warnick, Barbara. 1993. *The sixth Canon: Belletristic Rhetorical Theory and its French Antecedents*. Columbia, NC: University of North Carolina Press.

Wills, Garry. 1978. *Inventing America: Jefferson's Declaration of Independence*. New York: Vintage/Random House.

Winterer, Caroline. 2016. *American Enlightenments: Pursuing Happiness in the Age of Reason*. New Haven, CT: Yale University Press.

CHAPTER 4

# Elizabeth Graeme Fergusson's Cosmopolis of Letters

## 1 Fergusson's World of Letters

In the words of her first critic, her friend, and correspondent Benjamin Rush, Philadelphia poet Elizabeth Graeme Fergusson's literary productions and recognition flourished through the salon life she led from her adolescence throughout the years that immediately preceded the War of Independence and the cultures her social practices fostered (1737–1801). In a commemorative essay in the *Portfolio*, Rush wrote:

> Such was the character of Dr. Graeme's family for hospitality and refinement of manners, that all strangers of note who visited Philadelphia were introduced to it. Saturday evenings were appropriated for many years during Miss Graeme's winter residence in the city, for the entertainment not only of strangers, but of such of her friends of both sexes as were considered the most suitable company for them. These evenings were, properly speaking, of the attic type. The genius of Miss Graeme evolved the heat and light that animated them. One while she instructed by the stores of knowledge contained in the historians, philosophers, and poets of ancient and modern nations, which she called forth at her pleasure; and again she charmed by a profusion of original ideas, collected by her vivid and widely expanded imagination, and combined with exquisite taste and judgment into an endless variety of elegant and delightful forms. Upon these

occasions her body seemed to evanish, and she appeared to be all mind. (Rush 1809, 522–523)[1]

Rush's account attests to the active social and intellectual life Fergusson and her family led. The terms Rush uses in this passage remind readers of the universal power of the man of letters possessed to transcend any locality in order to embrace a space of universal knowledge central to the cosmopolitanism examined in this study. Like such a man, the woman Rush depicts makes letters the center of a cosmopolitan universe. Rush's exaltation of her being "all mind" transforms Fergusson into a disembodied entity. As a genderless being of letters, the Elizabeth Graeme Fergusson of Rush's portrayal can move freely within the space of knowledge.

But even more essential to her cosmopolitan identity than identifying Elizabeth Graeme Fergusson with the world of letters is Rush's insistence on her ability to move freely among different linguistic and imaginative realms. Like the cosmopolitan travelers many eighteenth-century fiction writers represented, the cosmopolitan man of letters crossed over diverse literary cultures and times and embraced them all. Fergusson can quote the classics, modern historians, philosophers, and poets. At the same time, she can charm with "a profusion of original ideas." Such a description closely reflects and is reflected in the type of literary works Fergusson produced throughout her long writing career. A largely self-educated poet and scholar, Fergusson read, wrote, and translated poetry all her life. Like many writers of her time, she did not use the printing press to publish much of what she wrote. Instead, her literary works were collected in handwritten commonplace books—books she compiled, exchanged with friends and family, and which she continued to compose and transform by adding new poetry or comments until she died in 1801.

Elizabeth Graeme began her life at the center of a cosmopolitan environment that many mid-eighteenth-century Philadelphians of her socio-economic status inhabited. Her parents' connections were the origin of

---

[1] The Saturday evening gatherings to which Rush refers were held at Graeme Fergusson's house in Philadelphia and at her country estate in Horsham, PA, nineteen miles west of the city. These gatherings began after she returned from an extended period spent in England during the winter of 1765 and continued until 1775, when she found her property in danger of being confiscated due to the loyalism of her English husband, Henry Hugh Fergusson (Ousterhout 2003; Slotten 1984).

Fergusson's own. Her mother, Ann Diggs Graeme, was the stepdaughter of Pennsylvania Governor William Keith. Her father, Thomas Graeme, was a renowned doctor who was the head physician of Philadelphia's port and of the Pennsylvania Hospital. Thomas Graeme also held a variety of political offices throughout his lifetime including that of Naval Officer of Philadelphia and of Justice of the Supreme Court (Ousterhout 2003, 33–35). In her late teens, Elizabeth met William Franklin and began a five-year engagement that ended abruptly in 1759. The tour of Europe she took to recover her physical and mental strength in the aftermath of her breakup with Franklin was cut short by her mother's sudden death. Graeme returned home and never left Pennsylvania again. In 1771, Elizabeth Graeme married Henry Hugh Fergusson, a Scottish immigrant. Their life together was soon interrupted because of Henry Fergusson's open political loyalism. As he was trying to leave for England in order to escape persecution, Fergusson was caught and detained. During the months preceding his departure, Fergusson had also been accused of having had an illegitimate child with the young maid of one of his wife's closest friends. Although he continued to deny the affair, his wife's letters show Elizabeth was profoundly affected and remained dubious. In the end, Elizabeth did not join him and never saw him again (Ousterhout 2003, 163–213).

Fergusson's social position and personal connections formed the context for developing what can be described as the cosmopolitan social attitudes portrayed in Rush's description. Philadelphia made this social cosmopolitanism possible. The trajectory of Fergusson's life took away the social environment that had fostered her early cosmopolitanism.[2] At his death in 1772, Thomas Graeme had left Elizabeth ownership of Graeme Park, the Horsham family estate. Once married, contemporary covertures laws passed the ownership of her inherited property to her husband. Elizabeth risked losing the property to the American government because of Henry Fergusson's loyalty to the British crown and his refusal to turn himself to the republican authorities after he left Pennsylvania and then attempted to return. Elizabeth Fergusson's troubles increased when she was found to be involved in delivering a letter

---

[2] Because the text of all the poems she composed when still Elizabeth Graeme, in the rest of this chapter, I will identify the poet as Elizabeth Fergusson even when talking about work composed before she married Henry Fergusson in 1772.

from Jacob Duché (a long-time family friend and loyalist) to General George Washington asking him to surrender his army to the British troops.[3] All of this made the process of recovering ownership of her family estate difficult. Despite a final court decision to leave her the property, Fergusson lost the ability to make the farm profitable. By the late 1780s, the house was on the market for sale. Her late niece's husband, William Smith, finally bought it and although Smith offered Fergusson the use of the house, she refused and decided to rent rooms from a neighbor. She moved out permanently at the end of 1793 (Ousterhout 2003, 199–258).

During this troubled period, Fergusson began to copy and rewrite her books and continued to do so until the years that preceded her death in 1801.[4] The earliest of the remaining books, a copybook that appears to have been prepared with the intention of submitting to publishers, has a leather binding that reflects the binding style of the late 1770s.[5] Her social interactions and visits to the city of Philadelphia became less and less frequent, but the same cannot be said about her intellectual interactions. It is at this time, in fact, that Fergusson copied and rewrote poems and other passages in the books and at which cosmopolitanism

---

[3] Fergusson handed Washington Duché's letter on October 13, 1777. Washington sent the letter Fergusson had given him to Congress and wrote about it to John Hancock on October 16. In his letter to Hancock, Washington clearly suggested Fergusson's own possible loyalism, an element that contributed to the difficulties in making a case for gaining her property back when confiscated. Here are Washington's words: "I yesterday, through the hands of Mrs Ferguson, of Graham Park, received a letter, of a very curious and extraordinary nature, from Duché, which I have thought proper to transmit to Congress. To this ridiculous, illiberal performance, I made a short reply, by desiring the bearer of it, if she should hereafter, by any accident, meet Mr. Duché, to tell him I should have returned it unopened, if I had had any idea of the contents; observing, at the same time, that I highly disapproved the intercourse she seemed to have been carrying on and expected it would be discontinued. Notwithstanding the author's assertion; but suspect that the measure did not originate with him, and that he was induced to it by the hope of establishing his interest and peace more effectually with the enemy" (Founders Archive 2002).

[4] The manuscript titled "Poemata Juvenilia" that contains her earlier poetry (1750s–1770s) appears to have been compiled in the early 1790s, and two others dated 1787 and 1789 precede it.

[5] I kindly thank the Library Company's Jim Greene for his help in identifying the possible date of the binding.

re-emerges in Fergusson's work.⁶ The commonplace book is the space where Fergusson revives the world that had slipped away from her because of economic and political realities. With her inner circle of friends composed of both loyalists and patriots disrupted, Fergusson's reproduction of poetry in the books replaces the social and cultural exchanges of the cosmopolitan society life that events have caused to disappear. Because of cosmopolitanism's presence as a cultural element of the past and because it functions as a tool to bring the past back to life, Fergusson's writings present two kinds of cosmopolitanism coexisting right next to each other. Fergusson's cosmopolitanism reflects the social and cultural environment that formed her when she lived in colonial Philadelphia. Her cosmopolitanism is the product of her membership in the British Empire and depends on the connections (within and outside of Pennsylvania) that being a member of this empire makes possible. In its re-emergence as a thematic and structural component of her commonplace books, cosmopolitanism becomes a tool to restore many of the socio-cultural ties severed by the revolution.⁷ It also explains Fergusson's ambivalent position towards the American revolutionary cause. In her books, we see cosmopolitanism as a force that resists nationalism because the latter deprived her of the freedoms colonialism and empire had afforded her. Cosmopolitanism curbs the fear of dislocation (physical as well as cultural) brought about by the nationalistic movement for independence with the loss of her husband and the decline of her estate. The words Elizabeth Fergusson used in a letter to her old friend Ann

---

⁶The books are now preserved at the Library Company of Philadelphia, the Pennsylvania Historical Society, the library of Dickinson College in Carlisle, PA, and her family estate Graeme Park in Horsham, PA, which has now been turned into a museum.

⁷Edward Larkin has recently shown that a similar and more overt attitude can be seen in in Hector St. John de Crèvecoeur's *Letters from an American Farmer*. Following Christopher Iannini's suggestion that Crèvecoeur derived his cosmopolitan tendencies from the French natural historian Abbè de Raynal, Larkin convincingly shows that Crèvecoeur's loyalism is based on an idea of empire as an administrative infrastructure that provides the conditions for the cosmopolitanism he believed into exist. In his analysis, Larkin argues that Crèvecoeur's cosmopolitan loyalism in the Letters can be traced from the beginning of the narrative. The revolution and the consequent establishment of the nation-state structure impacts the most fundamental connection the novel is based on, namely the possibility of the correspondence between farmer James and his English correspondent (Iannini 2004, 201–234; Larkin 2016, 40–68).

Ridgeley in 1797 speak to the transition from the cosmopolitanism of her pre-revolutionary life to that of the commonplace books:

> You are very obliging in pointing out a Method to get the manuscripts, which at least my share of them I fear would not repay you for the pains of developing a bad Hand: But I Will not act the Hypocrite: I declare when by peculiar Circumstances I am as it were a Link Cut off from the Chain of that Society both by Birth and Education which I once was taught to expect, and devote my Hours to Retirement and my Pen, I feel a Latent Wish that those whose tasks are congenial to my own, might with the Eye of not *Candor* But *Partiality* see my turn of thought and mode of Life. But you told that "that your Children are fond of Poetry," of Consequence they have read a great deal and under such a monitress as their mother have read the Best, and as they must be devested of that partiality which perhaps you might have, I fear it will be dull work, But my promise is made, and what is still more cogent my Will is on the side of performing it: Tho It may be a considerable time before I put it in Execution, for among the Portions of time I find most tedious where I live, is the *long long* Winter Evenings Once the Joy of my heart when surrounded by a Groupe of Dear Conextions all gone to the Silent abodes of Death. Those Winter evenings I mean in part to devote to sorting; or Copying out such of my little Things; that I think may have a Chance of meeting your and the young Ladies approbation; Therefore rest assured if I live, have my Eyes, Limbs, and faculties between this and the month of May a volume shall make its appearance. (Gratz 1915, 406)[8]

Fergusson's letter reveals how the "peculiar Circumstances" of her economic and social decline as well as the death of close family members and relations became a door into the possibilities of literary production and distribution. By means of the literary activity that her "Pen" engages with, the world that has been lost is turned back into life during her "Hours of Retirement." This activity produces the space for her cosmopolitanism to be revived and as it comes back to life, it also acquires the power to counteract the circumstances behind Fergusson's forced exile.

Although Fergusson is clearly mourning in the passage above, it is impossible not to notice her eagerness to discuss her own literary abilities and the possibilities a new audience might afford her. Susan Stabile has argued that the commonplace book is an analogue of the salon, and,

---

[8] From a letter to Ann Ridgeley (née Moore), September 14, 1797.

in the case of Elizabeth Fergusson, becomes the receptacle of memory when the material objects that surround her disappear. Thus, Stabile argues, the commonplace books become "a kind of poetic autobiography" (Ousterhout 2003, 23).[9] The five extant commonplace books, the didactic translation of François Fénelon's *The Adventures of Telemachus, Son of Ulysses* (1793–1794), the verse adaptation of the Psalms, as well as the body of the letters she exchanged with a number of correspondents, among whom are Benjamin Rush and Francis Hopkinson, all reveal that indeed through those commonplace writings Fergusson continued to live the life she had led while at the center of Philadelphia's social and literary life. Her commonplace writings help us reconstruct that life. They are, as Stabile correctly points out, her "poetic autobiography." It is within the frame of the work she produced and the peculiar temporal and spatial frames of the composition of the books that Elizabeth Fergusson's cosmopolitanism emerges and shows us its power to reopen the avenues closed by the nationalistic enterprise of the revolution.

Since Fergusson did not travel extensively or live a life immersed in different and multicultural environments, one cannot immediately identify her as a cosmopolitan. If a cosmopolitan is one defined by translating into her work a worldview derived from her own experiences around the world among different cultures, languages, and religions, she is not one. Nonetheless, her writings show us how cosmopolitanism had been promoted and fostered by colonialism for individuals who belonged to the English elites. Cosmopolitanism was part of the environment in which figures like Fergusson were immersed and it offered them a model of life and promoted a way of thinking reliant on open borders and relative diversity. The elements that form her cosmopolitanism originate in the socio-economic environment that formed her as a poet and as an intellectual and they are determined by the presence of the British Empire in the American colonies. The cosmopolitanism that characterized the environment that formed her as a writer becomes the underlying principle of the books she compiles, and it gives shape to the poetry they contain.

---

[9] Susan Stabile has described memory as the synthetic conflation of impression. Because such impressions are conveyed through penmanship, Stabile argues, the commonplace books become the embodiment of memory itself. The handwriting that the author uses allows for the transmission of interiority into the exterior space of the page and therefore the body of the work represents the mental effort of remembering itself (Stabile 2004, 85–86).

The elements that form the Enlightenment notion of the cosmopolitan, such as the belief in a universal communication among individuals, the desire to transcend group interests and differences in order to embrace ideals of sympathy, and correspondence among people emerge in her writings, as well as in the way she collected and circulated the texts. The American Revolution blocked Fergusson's access to all of this and, later in life, the cosmopolitanism of Fergusson's writings functions to regain the world that was gone. In this respect, Fergusson's cosmopolitanism shares fundamental elements with the cultural and political loyalism she was accused of sharing with her husband after he formally swore allegiance to the English monarchy. It can also be called "loyalist" when we look at it as the organizing principle of her books and their circulation among her friends and acquaintances in the latter part of her life. Throughout Fergusson's poetry we find traces of the ideological frame her cultural environment helped develop. Her cosmopolitanism can be thus called "creative," as it is what provides Fergusson with poetic imagery and tropes. In the books, Fergusson's commentaries consisting of references, afterthoughts, and historical clarifications, invite the reader to move in an unbounded space in which past and present are combined. They continually reframe the interpretive possibilities offered to the reader and correspondences can be established and changed, which gives the poet and her readers the power to overcome different types of barriers and to have the conversations a real salon would have made possible.

The commonplace books become the locus of the cosmopolitanism that characterized Fergusson's social and intellectual life. The poems and prose she copies and composes for her readers help her move from the local and the familiar into the boundless and the universal. In the later part of her life, Fergusson's commonplace books re-establish both the dynamics of her literary life as well as the intellectual reach her salon and friendships brought her previously. In the opening passage of the diary Fergusson kept for friends and family when she traveled to England in 1764–1765, she uses the metaphor of a circle which moves toward an infinitely open space to describe her departure from home and the familiar and her entrance into a world of personal and worldly discovery and literary freedom. Fergusson describes the first moments of the passage from Philadelphia to Liverpool that took place in June 1764, and depicts the image of the ship in mid-sea this way:

> I could not help observing, that whatever way the Ship moved she appeared to be in the Centre of a Circle, for the Sea seems to be a perfect

Circle, surrounded by Clouds, that look as if they bent down at the Edges to join it, so that our own Eyes form the Horizon, & like Self-Love, we are always placing ourselves in the Middle, where all things move round us.—I saw the Sun set clear, for the first Time, I was reading Priam's Petition to Achilles, for the Body of Hector, I think my Eyes were engaged in one of the finest Sights of the Universe, & my Passions, interested in one of the most pathetic that History or Poetry can paint.— (Wulf 1997, 200–201)[10]

The words Fergusson uses to portray this moment of departure evoke the sense that separation from a place gives an individual new powers to see clearly inward and outward. The woman Fergusson describes maintains her centrality by the continued movement of the ship crossing the ocean. The same movement also allows her to cross over literary and temporary boundaries and join the characters of the Greek epic, implicitly reminding readers that her travels are as much across literary worlds as they are across space. Travel is essential to the individual of the cosmopolitan ideal because it empowers her to learn more about what and who surrounds her, and then to meditate on what is left behind. The image of cruelty and parental suffering the Homeric reference evokes is juxtaposed to the beauty and vastness of the circling ocean. Travel is what allows for a deeper understanding of the ancient epic she is reading, so that her journey is as much for pleasure as it is for learning.[11] The switch from the personal pronoun "I" to a more general "we" when introducing the image of the circle re-enforces the parallel between the

---

[10] The diary itself has been lost, but a series of excerpts were copied in her commonplace book by Milcah Martha Moore.

[11] In his study of the role of civility and polite letters in the formation of colonial American society, David Shields describes the poetry Fergusson wrote after her trip to Britain as having a "cosmopolitan scope of interest and wit." The scholar maintains that such a cosmopolitan quality derives from Graeme's experience abroad, her return to Pennsylvania, and the exercise of a new freedom that her experience has given her. Shields writes that in the poetry she wrote after her travels:

> The place of wit in Graeme's poetics shifts. No longer was it an expression of unfeeling vanity employed in arenas of polite contest; rather, it had become a vehicle of judgment useful in gaining a perspective on the foibles of the world and deflecting the claims of passion. Assuming wit armed Graeme with a self-assurance in mixed company that allowed the sorts of liberties of conversation that marked the Parisian salons. ... Graeme's education as a woman of letters can be seen as an intellectual journey proceeding from the moral earnestness of English sense to a discovery of the social utility of wit as a means of maintaining liberty.

writer and the text she is reading and it unites Fergusson, her writing, and the community that her writing represents. Elizabeth Fergusson's world exists in letters. It exists in the letters she wrote for the epistolary diary she sent home, and in letters in the generic sense of literary compositions. The metaphor of the moving circular ocean Fergusson chooses to describe her departure when writing to her correspondents at home is, like that of the cosmopolitan traveler, one whose center is in motion. When removed from the active life she had lived while younger, the writing of the commonplace books and their traveling from person to person replicate this movement. Fergusson repositions herself at a center similar to the one that this passage describes and from her home she constructs ever-moving circles.

The social and literary correspondences that constitute the foundation of her earlier poetic career find their new prolific ground in the commonplace books that she composes later in life, as well as in the correspondences both Fergusson and her books establish. The cosmopolitan language of universal correspondence permeates Fergusson's work and is enhanced by her recurrent use of the epistolary form and of the theme of friendship that characterize many of her poetic compositions and the marginalia next to them.[12] These elements stand out as essential to the

---

In Shields' description Graeme's ability to employ wit as a means to become a more powerful individual, an individual who masters both knowledge and language at a nonspecifically national level (her salon is based in Philadelphia, but has French features) constitutes the relationship between Graeme and cosmopolitanism that is reflected in her revised use of wit. Graeme's freedom is warranted by the ability to master a language that escapes specific social, gender, and national identification—an ability that Graeme acquires during the time that she travels throughout England (Shields 1997, 138). Susan Stabile reads this passage in terms of gender empowerment. Stabile also suggests that the implicit parallel between the writer and Odysseus situates the poet at the center of her narrative. Stabile, however, continues her analysis by situating her writings within the context of colonial American polite society and its eighteenth-century developments and sees Graeme Fergusson's poems as constructing an early American epic (Ousterhout 2003, 2–6).

[12] When considering the historical and cultural significance of personal writing, rhetorician Susan Miller has argued that our interest in reading any private form of writing from the past such as commonplace books should not mislead us in believing that we can get a real glimpse of what was going on in a person's mind. Rather, the scholar explains, such writings "reveal the intersections of social vectors, forces that produce discursive actions that have simultaneously material, aesthetic, and ideological consequences" (Miller 1998, 2). The compositions we find in the books and the books themselves are as much personal as they are the products of the cultural environment that surrounded and informed their author.

poetic world that she creates. The epistolary correspondences of many of the poems in the commonplace books, as well as the interjections with which Fergusson framed them, such as her thoughts about the poems, the events that took place before she compiled the book, or after she composed a poem or collected a letter all reflect the principle of correspondence that underlines Enlightenment epistemology. The conversation between past and present, and the recalling of the past by means of an act of rewriting make the correspondence visible for the reader of the manuscript. Fergusson's continued manipulation of the books' structure and content and their circulation among friends bring the cosmopolitan character to life when the cosmopolitanism in Fergusson's life begins to fade.

The earliest of Fergusson's extant commonplace books, probably compiled in the late 1770s and suggestively entitled *Poemata Juvenilia*, contains many poems composed during Fergusson's adolescence and early adulthood.[13] The manuscript book also contains many additions dated between the late 1780s and mid-1790s, and it provides a good example of the writer's interaction with her work. The internal side of the book's cover and the front page are filled with added commentary and poems. These additions create an introduction to the collection and they provide us with an example of the role that compiling books, reflecting on the past, and conversing with an audience had for Fergusson, as well as an insight into the way the cosmopolitan ideal affects her poetic compositions. The text and the poems Fergusson transcribed and retranscribed presents us with what I have described as the poet's adaptation of the ideal of universal correspondence, of crossing over boundaries, and universal friendships in order to reproduce the world that the revolution has deprived her of. It is here that we see the conservative aspect of Fergusson's cosmopolitanism. This strategy generates an exchange similar to an epistolary one that enables communication across a variety of borders: linguistic, temporal, cultural, historical, and political. Fergusson's revisionary strategies and her epistolary poems perform a similar task.

The material inserted in the two opening pages of *Poemata Juvenilia* (see Fig. 4.1) show Fergusson's strategy at work. With her retrospective

---

[13] Although the handwriting Fergusson employs indicates that she probably had prepared this copy for submission to a printer or publisher, there is no mention of it in any of her surviving letters or other writings.

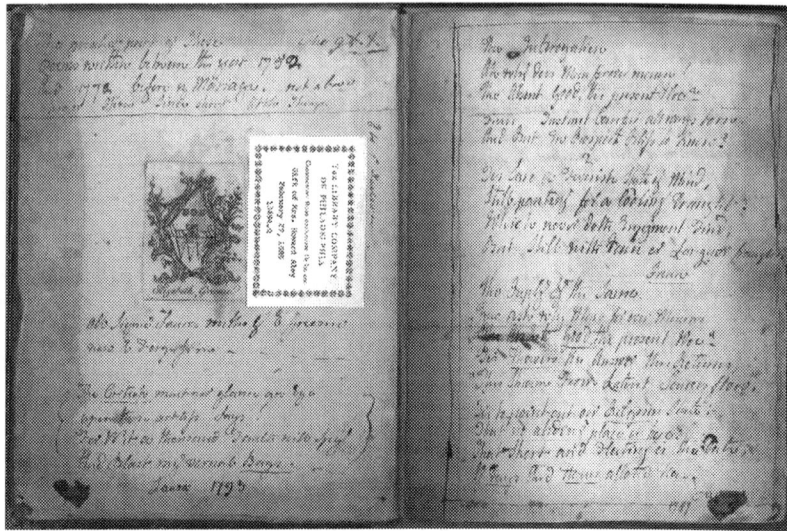

**Fig. 4.1** Inside cover of *Poemata Juvenilia*. The two poems, "The Interrogation" and "An Answer to the Same," are on the right-hand page

additions and comments, the poet generates conversations between texts, between past and present versions of a poem, or between past and present interpretations of the thematic issues that a poem expresses. At the same time, Fergusson positions the poetic voice as an observer who, from a distance, can be an impartial judge of people, places, and time. This voice reflects on the past and is able to provide both commentary and advice. The two poems transcribed on the manuscript's first page are respectively entitled "The Interrogation" and "The Reply to the Same" and they read as follows:

> Oh why does man forever Mourn!
> The absent Good, the present Woe?
> From Instant Comfort always turn:
> And But In Prospect Bliss to know?
> Tis Sure a Feverish State of Mind,
> Still panting for a Cooling Draught?
> Which never doth Enjoyment find,
> But still with Pain or Languor fraught?

"The Reply to the Same" begins with an invocation of those opening lines. It then answers the questions asked in "The Interrogation" and discusses the futility of human worries because of our transient state on earth:

> You ask why Man forever Mourns
> The absent Good, the present Woe?
> Tis *Heaven* the Answer this Returns,
> This Stream from Later Sources flow.
> Tis to point out our *Pilgrim* State:
> That no abiding place is here:
> That Short and Fleeting is the Path,
> Of Days and Hours allottd Here.

The significance of these formulaic poems is not in their poetic form. Their structure is, however, fundamental to understanding how the collected texts they introduce are organized. The two poems stand as a model for most of the works contained in *Poemata Juvenilia*, and, most significantly, they reflect the literary act embodied in writing and collecting her art. The two stanzas of "The Interrogation" are a meditation on man's inability to enjoy life's immediate pleasures and the poem is organized as a series of unanswered questions that begin with the first two lines: "Oh why does Man forever Mourn!/ The absent Good, the present Woe?" The opening invocation in "The Reply" replicates the opening lines "You ask why Man forever Mourns/ The absent Good, the present Woe?" of the previous poem and then performs the task introduced by its title and answers the questions raised in "The Interrogation." The second poem is both a reflection of and a mirroring of the topic of the first poem. The answer discusses the futility of human worries because of our transient state on earth: "our *Pilgrim* State;/That no abiding Place is here:/That short and Fleeting is the Path,/Of Days and Hours allottd here." The poems expect an active reader who will engage in a conversation about the past and the present, compare positions, and evaluate them (Altman 1982). This reader is one who is present in the text, and simultaneously engaged in the outside of it as the potential letter's addressee (MacArthur 1990, 36–116).

Reminiscent of the reflective character of this composition is the reference to the poet's young age at the time of composition implied in the Latin title *Poemata Juvenilia*. The voice of the poet behind the title stands against the voice of the mature poet who writes her poetic responses in the first pages of the book. It also prepares readers to recognize and respond properly to the author's interjections within the text. The reader witnesses and participates in this conversation and is enabled to move from place to place, to overcome cultural and temporal limits in the same way a cosmopolitan traveler moves among different cultures, observes, and understands them. The poems' epistolary/dialogic format is their most notable feature. The voices in the two poems bring past and present together in a conversation. The voice in the second poem is that of a reader who responds to the first writer by reminding her of her question, "You ask." This organization reflects the eighteenth-century practice of reading letters aloud to family members and friends and the function of the book itself, which is written to be circulated and read by those who receive it (Decker 1998; Hewitt 2004; Gaul 2009, 1–14). The collected materials that follow them are meant to be received and responded to, perhaps even rewritten.

Although not letters, the poems I have just cited share many epistolary features. Like letters, they generate a correspondence, they reject finality by asking for a reply and a rewrite (note how the beginning of the second poem repeats the opening lines of the first one), and they ask in fact for the active participation of the reader in the dialogue they establish. Their epistolary/dialogic format is their most notable feature and is immediately visible in the poems that open the collection: two texts in conversation with each other, written in 1752 and in 1789. In these poems change and open-endedness are central thematic and formal features. "A Dream," the first and earliest of the two poems recounts young Elizabeth's entrance in society and her first experience of love. The poem begins with a description of the girl falling asleep and seeing, "a Nymph arise;/Friendship her Name of Social Virtues Queen!" Friendship takes her hand and leads her to a secluded bower in which she introduces the girl to her "favorite Strephon." The nymph tells Strephon Fergusson's name is Truth and leaves her with him without explaining what she should do. Despite her lack of experience and fear of the unknown, the poet tells readers she "found it hard my Strephon to forsake:/I feared some danger if I made delay,/Tho' my Heart Pleaded for a longer Stay." The arrival of the day saves her from making the feared decision and as the "Eastern Light" advances, Strephon leaves her with the shades of the night. In this poem, the fifteen-year-old Elizabeth conflates the discovery of sociability and friendship with her first sentimental involvement. Friendship leads the young girl to the bower and introduces her to love. The features of this process are rewritten when the mature Elizabeth writes a poem in response.

The short poem that immediately follows "A Dream" is written thirty-seven years later and it is its obvious companion. The correlation between the two, as well as the thematic revision that Fergusson made, are evident in the title of the second one, "On the Preference of Friendship to Love":

> Let Girlish Nymphs and Boysh Swains
> Their Amorous Ditties Chant!
> Make vocal Echoing Hills and Plains;
> And Loves frail Passion paint,
> But Friendship's Shady Flame as far;
> Out shines that transient Blaze
> As Midday Sun is a glimmering Star
> Which faintest Beam display.

The response retrieves the three thematic elements of the unit she had established in the earlier poem—friendship, sociability, and love—and reshuffles them in a new picture in which each of them is still present with new connotations. The description of friendship as a "Shady Flame" is ambivalent: the term "shady" could be connected to the colors of an active flame and its reflections, but it appears almost oxymoronic in that the same qualities could be attributed to a sheltering tree and its shadow. At the same time, the power of such flame is like that of a "Midday Sun" that outshines the "transient Blaze of Love." If love and its voices exist within the "Echoing Hills and Plains" and are made larger by refraction, friendship has acquired a new overarching strength as well. Friendship now towers over everything and allows Fergusson to see where each item in the grouping she had done when she was fifteen could be displaced. Now friendship is not imagined as a nymph anymore, in fact, her power and importance are pitted against those of the girlish nymphs who are lost in their "Amorous Ditties" and their chanting. In the second poem, friendship is associated with the poet and is enabled to observe and assess her actions and love's doings.

The peculiar structure of the document that contains the poems enables the poet to become an observer. Scholars have noted the generic hybridity of manuscript commonplace books, such as Fergusson's, and the role hybridity played in defining eighteenth-century social practices.

If, as Stabile argues, Fergusson's commonplace books are a textual analogue of the literary salon, a place in which private and public coexist and embody the mixed social sphere of early America, then the commonplace book is also a site where individuals develop memories to be shared, divided, and continually transformed (Ousterhout 2003, 4–5).[14] Fergusson's interventions like the one above as well as the directives to the reader that indirectly stem from them function in a similar way. They each have the cosmopolitan aim I described earlier. The poetic voice the poem projects onto the first functions as the cosmopolitan observer of texts similar to what I showed happened in Franklin's essays. The poetic self and the space Fergusson inhabits in her manuscripts materialize within the process of production, but the incompleteness of this process makes change and hybridity the product's principal features. All of these are essential components of the Enlightenment cosmopolitan ideal Fergusson has ascribed in her poetics and the hybrid form of her commonplace books. The change and hybridity that these texts engage with and perform link them to the idea of conservative cosmopolitanism that I have described earlier. The possibility of change in social settings and the openness of borders that existed in the past re-emerge as poetic and structural elements of the book that Fergusson composes in later years.

## 2    Past and Present Correspondences

What I have discussed so far shows the dialogic nature of Fergusson's work. This dialogic nature offers the author the possibility to rewrite and transform her work not only by altering its material features. It also gives the reader several interpretive options and possible readings. It frees author and reader from the constraints that a different generic frame would establish. The manuscript nature of the commonplace book facilitates these possibilities and Fergusson's authorial interventions highlight the writer's engagement with the processes of thinking about and responding to texts that is at the foundation of the practice

---

[14] For the early history of commonplace books see Lechner (1974); Crane (1993), 60–63. David Allan's (2010) book contains a particularly useful extended bibliography on the connection between manuscript literature and the history of reading. See also Havens (2001); Justice and Tinker (2002); McKitterick (2005); McGill (2007); Nelson (2007); Hall (2008); Zboray and Saracino Zboray (2009). For Locke see Dacome (2004).

of commonplacing itself.[15] Many of the pages of the books show erasures, additions, rewritings, and other types of commentary. The writer's involvement with the reading and writing processes are central to Fergusson's composition practices. The notion of correspondence is, as I have also noted, reflected in the way in which these processes unfold in the written page and it is visible in the type of authorial interventions she frequently makes. The epistolary form Fergusson often employs for writing her poems is the most visible manifestation of the role correspondence plays in her poetic landscape. These features are obviously a reflection of the socio-cultural practices of the eighteenth-century American elite to which Fergusson belonged (Shields 1997, 11–54). The connection between correspondence and sociability and the value it had for Fergusson is evident in many of her letters. We find an early example in another segment of the diary she sent back home while in England where she writes about her expectations for the future:

> For my Part I think a moderate Fortune, Health, Peace of Mind, & agreable Connections, may be enjoyed in America—there it is I hope to spend my Days—If I have Health, I shall taste those Blessings. ... I know not what my future State of life is to be, but was I to form a Wish it should not be I think Extravagant. I am not particularly attached to any Spot, but while some dear Friends live, I hope it to be in Philad[elphi]a. Health I look on to be the Basis on which we found all Earthly Blessings—a Conscience void of Offence as to gross Crimes (for as to Faults & Foibles, no Life is unsullied with them), A Society of Friends whose Actions are guided by Affection, Chearfulness, Probity & Good-sense—Perhaps if I go any further, you will think me unreasonable in Demands, but this writing diverts me, & I will go. (Wulf 1997, 204, 206)[16]

Fergusson's portrait of what her ideal life should be fits the period's standards of sociability. It highlights the importance that connections to family, friends, and place had for the poet, as well as the inextricability of all of them from each other. The categories of family, friendship, and place are central to the way Fergusson gives meaning to her life, as

---

[15]Book historian Roger Chartier has speculated that the reading practices of seventeenth- and eighteenth-century people might be easily extrapolated from the various forms the commonplace books from these centuries took (Cavallo 2003, 282).

[16]Dated May 31, 1765.

well as to the poetry and prose she wrote, through the themes of family, friendship, and place. Around these themes, Fergusson builds a community both personal and universal. It is in poems centered on personal connections built by family and friendship and on notions of belonging to place that cosmopolitanism emerges as a poetic trope.

In an early example of a poetic epistolary exchange Fergusson represents friendship as the correspondence of feelings. As a central theme to her poem, the particular friendship between the poet and her correspondent is universalized and transplanted from its local manifestation to a series of different and interconnected places. Fergusson wrote this poem to her friend Rebekah Moore in November 1755 and Moore responded with another poem in March 1756.[17] Fergusson later collected the poems in *Poemata Juvenilia*. Although Fergusson's introductory lines describe the poem as "Wrote at the time of the Indian War; Philadelphia Novem '20 1755" and gives the idea that the Indian war is the central theme of the poem, the war is only a pretext to discuss the meaning of friendship and its forms. The opening lines describe the current state of war as a consequence of internal divisions within the colonial world. It is the two correspondents' "wretched" and "unhappy Fate," "To see a bleeding, an expiring State/ Bent with Divisions; and with Civil Broils;/ And Savage Indians glorying in our Spoils." The theme of division and the selfishness from which division derives is already visible in these opening lines. The theme establishes the terms against which Fergusson pits her and Moore's friendship. After praising of Moore's qualities of "Wit, Sense, and good Humor," which friendship's forces bind together, the poem builds the opposition between the true friendship that unites Fergusson and Moore and the empty ones that perform the opposite on the "herds of Mankind:"

---

[17] Moore died during a yellow fever epidemic that killed more than 5000 people in Philadelphia during the summer and early fall of 1793. In a commonplace book that Fergusson composed in the 1790s, the writer commemorated Rebekah Moore Smith's death with a poem followed by a personal note that describes their friendship: "I became acquaintd with her, when I Was 12 and she 14 year old, and each of us till married would have foregone any Scene that the World calls pleasure to have strolld together either at Graeme Park or at Moore = Hall we both had a little Romantic turn as to the Objects of nature we both had a turn for Investigation and dear delightful hour we passd reading. Farwell, farwell Dear Mrs. Smith. Still dearer Becky Moore for they lovd most when R Moore and Betsy Graeme" December 21, 1793.

Long have we known an interchange of Heart,
Felt for each other in the tenderest parts;
Known the Soft Sympathy of Souls refin'd,
The glow delightful of the feeling Mind;
The Social Converse of the ardent Breast
That is by Virtuous tenderness possest.
Friendship's a Theme much spoke of, little known
Love, Innocence with her together flown;
To some lone Hermit Couch and Moss grown Cell
Watching the Midnight Lamps and solemn Bell,
Perhaps beneath some rural Cottage shed;
The best Companions have for refuge fled!
Tired with pursuits; and Sick of Crowds at Court
Where herds of Mankind do with Smiles resort:
At first fair Friendship they did entertain
Till selfish Interest broke the twisted Chain
Interest that Charm which like a Magic Wand
Will every former gentle Tye disband:
My dearest Sylvia from her Laura's side;
To where we go the World may join each name
Nor mention my Miss Moore without her Graeme.

Fergusson associates neoclassical and pastoral images with disinterested friendship and virtuosity. These two elements promote the "Social Converse of the ardent Breast," and make the two young women fitting subjects of eighteenth-century polite society.[18] Using imagery that reminds her readers of Virgil's *Eclogues*, Graeme opposes these defining qualities associated with the rural to the negative ones of urban society, the "Crowds at Court," the "herds of Mankind," as she calls them. Unlike true friends, these individuals interact by using false niceties. The crowds embraced friendship in earnest, but only "till selfish Interest broke the twisted Chain." The contemporary oppositional topos of city versus country is embodied in the corrupted scene of the court and in the pastoral setting of Laura and Sylvia's friendship. The scope of this opposition, however, seems larger than the simple contrast between the

---

[18] Nicole Eustace has recently expanded the connection between politeness and civility to the realm of politics and argued that the eighteenth century was characterized by a similar deep interconnection between politics and sensibility (Eustace 2008, 3–13).

corrupted urban environment and the virtue-inducing countryside. The relationship friendship establishes between the two women restores peace over the political chaos that the opening reference to the colonial conflict had placed to the forefront. But it is ultimately the power of friendship as a universal concept that does not necessarily inhabit the rural space, which is instrumental to achieving the universal peace needed to give friendship's benefits back to the "herds of Mankind." The rural context has served as a refuge for those true friends who would not allow the sickness of the crowds to contaminate them. Laura's observation of Sylvia "thro' fond Friendship's Eyes" detects two distinctive features of the enlightened mind, "wit" and "reason." The sympathetic correspondence friendship establishes possesses a unifying power that could help to bridge the divisions that bend the state during the present conflict. This form of sympathetic correspondence is not made to remain secluded within the rural space that the poem describes as the site of friendship. Such a site, in fact, is called a "refuge" and is connoted as dark and solemn.

A young Fergusson proposes the solution to war and destruction through the opposition of the blinding and anti-cosmopolitan interests. Fergusson's poem exists and is valued as the subject of a sympathetic correspondence between the two friends who perform the exchange. Fergusson's perception of her environment takes place within such a frame, and yet, as the references to the socio-political world of the British Empire show, friendship becomes a universal catalyst. The space the two women inhabit can be displaced anywhere else. Fergusson's poem translates her particular relationship to a realm that crosses the boundaries of the Pennsylvanian countryside, so that the countryside, Philadelphia, colonial America, and the British Empire simultaneously exist as one space.

Place is the other essential thematic category that engages with the cosmopolitan ideal in Fergusson's poetry. One of the poems written after her return from England and the death of her mother and sister represents the poet in the act of writing at Graeme Park, the family estate in Horsham, Pennsylvania. The poem elevates the locality of the country estate and transforms it into a place that is at the same time England and the realm of letters, while remaining rooted in its local natural environment. In her transcriptions, Fergusson introduces the poem as "Some Lines upon my first being at Graeme Park after my return from

England," and titles it "To Memory."[19] The poem begins as a conversation with memory, which is first introduced by a reference to the poet's loss of happiness, and it is followed by a call to memory itself:

> Oh ye white Moments whither are ye flown?
> Hide! Lost forever! Oh forever gone!
> Come <u>Memory</u> come; and with <u>Times</u> Pencils show
> Each former Pleasure; and each poignant Woe:
> Those past Ideas place in strong review,
> When Life was fresh; and all her Senses were new.
> That early dawn; that vernal spring of youth!
> That Snow white Innocence! That artless Truth!
> Pure knowledge opening on the curious Mind
> The Heart all feeling, and the soul all kind!
> Bright <u>Memory</u> range them in my mental Eye
> And Recollection never let them Die.
> The Fairy Landscape let me fend [illegible]
> And try the fleeting flowery Scene to view
> Produce each Page, your simple Book unfold,
> Formd of the Frame of lively Fancys Mold:
> Yet spare the Task or blot out half the Hours;
> Or arm my Heart Ye bright angelic Bowers!

Fergusson invokes a memory of happiness that has been lost in the sorrow her personal loss has caused. The process of remembering the loved ones who have died right before and soon after the writer spent time in England is associated with writing and embodied in the pencil time holds. What Fergusson writes in this exercise of remembering becomes the reality Graeme Park embodies. The poet represents herself as an exile both in America and in England. At the same time, places materialize through the mnemonic act and inscribe this memory in her poetic composition. As the poem continues, memory and letters become one, and memory's power becomes selective and literary. It is not life that it brings back, but its literary representations formed by "the frame of lively Fancys Mold." And it is a literary representation of her experience in England and its materialization within the perimeter of her

---

[19] The poem is collected in *Poemata Juvenilia* and dated August 16, 1766.

Pennsylvania estate that the rest of the poem produces. The remembrance is also a poetic construction in which the poet creates an environment that has no spatial boundaries. The second segment begins with a repudiation of the call to memory that opened the previous one:

> Fly Memory fly! And let Oblivion take!
> With dull Obscurity (her gloomy Mate)
> Your place bright Maid! For but too well I know
> Your presence wakens every former Wo;
> Your Figure Strikes with other Forms so joined
> With kindred Souls to whom my Heart was twined,
> I melt in Sadness lost to every Joy
> Taste every blessing dashd with Griefs Alloy.
> ...
> Ye sweet domestic Joys! Ye spring of Life!
> Exempt from Bustle and from noisy Strife;
> No mean Self Interest ruled; no gloomy Tears;
> No low Suspicion, nor no anxious Cares.
> For Days like these I will call <u>Memory</u> home
> Nor let the Nymph far from my Bosom roam.

Although the poet asks memory to fly away in order to avoid the return of the pain her loss has caused, it is at the end of the same segment of the poem that memory starts to fly back in. This invocation, in fact, marks the beginning of the process of remembrance that starts with the teachings of her deceased mother and the love for her sister. As she mourns both losses, Fergusson develops her self-representation as the poetic analogous of the cosmopolitan traveler. As she observes the familiar scene of Graeme Park she states: "I seem an Exile left, forlorn, alone,/One antient Parent all I claim my own." The image of the exile prepares the ground for the second part of the segment in which she compares her state of mind while she was in England to Ulysses' exile from Ithaca:

> When I the great <u>Atlantic</u> dreary Main;
> Had crossd; the Rosy fingered <u>Health</u> to gain;
> The varging Scene that filld the circling year;
> As pleasing gliding Phantoms did appear;
> All <u>England</u> Joys rushed full upon my View;
> And Pleasure trod in Pleasures ever new.

Yet like <u>Ulysses</u> with his darling spot
The much lov'd Ithaca was ne'er forgot;
My ancient Parents rose before my Sight
And distant lay Contentment; and delight.

The poet's feeling of estrangement is the condition that characterizes both her present and the past that memory brings back. Following this moment Fergusson performs a parallel reading of the British and the American landscapes in an altered form of *translatio studii*.

Prompted by a reference to her maternal family's roots in England, Fergusson describes her literary roots in the poetry of Shakespeare, Milton, and her contemporary Thomson, and then remembers other forms of art, such as the architectural genius of Roman Vitruvius and the pictorial artistry of van Dyck and Rubens. Although recalling memories about the artistic and literary greatness of England causes Fergusson to admit the failure of a *translatio studii* in America, the memory of a memory makes the picture she creates lose clarity as one memory replaces another. Fergusson's remembrance of what she saw in England reminds her of how those very images had made her remember home. Graeme Park, and the memory she has of it, is the place that enables Fergusson to enjoy and understand the importance of artistic production:

When in the Solemn <u>Abbys</u> gloom I walkd
With <u>Shakespeare, Milton,</u> or with <u>Thomson's</u> talkd
Some favorite Passage of their Work occurd;
Some striking Sentence or expressive Word.
Where glowing Genius and warm Fancy fird,
The panting Ardor of a Bard inspird;
The blaze <u>Poetic</u> Shone without Controul
And All <u>Apollo</u> rushd upon the Soul:
All that remaind was polishd Marble-Bust
Or decent Urn to guard the mouldering Dust;
But sure that Heav'nly Spark of Fire divine
Which <u>Poesy</u> terms the raptures of the <u>Nine</u>
Expands and Opens in the Realms above
In Admiration of Scholar's Love!
...
Yet all these Treasures freely I resign
For the dear Circle which I boast are mine.
To the wise World my hasty Course I bear

> When simple Nature claims the largest Share
> And imitative Arts display no standards there.
> When Stow's vast Gardens poured their Sweets around
> When in those walks my wandring Steps I found
> Lost in a wilderness of Bliss I strayd
> And Sunk beneath the lovely rural Shade!
> Another Eden rose before my Eyes,
> And struck each Moment with a fresh Surprise,
> Where Taste, Art, Fortune, and the calmer Hours,
> Pland the retreats of Temples fragrant Bowers.
> Here long Canals in mimick Rivers glide;
> And vernal Beautys paint their mossy Side;
> Where solems Forests, shed a deep brown Shade
> And Phylosophick Melancholy aid.

Fergusson performs another rhetorical translation and describes the mnemonic act as a memory when she tells readers how the secluded bowers of Stowe Gardens are reminiscent of Graeme Park, although admits that arts have failed to be translated in America. The two memories reflect each other so that the physical distance between them is temporarily overcome. The place from which the poem is written and about which it writes are reflected into each other. This poem about memory, in which memory is also remembered, shows how writing produces a form of circularity that allows for space, time, and literary production to be unbounded.

Such ambivalence is sustained by the initial invocation of forgetting in the line "Fly Memory fly" that introduces the long passage dedicated to the remembrance of her English stay. The poem performs a displacement of the act of remembering and of the place where it happens. Fergusson binds Graeme Park, England, and European traditions together. The literary power of memory has generated the necessary correspondences that allow for Fergusson to create a poetic voice that rises above the literary boundaries she claims America has had no power to overcome. By introducing the act of remembering with an invocation to memory to fly away, and by dislocating the spatial referent, Fergusson performs the *translatio studii* she had denied existed in America. *Translatio studii*'s companion, *translatio imperii* seems to be at work here as well, but in an interesting way as, by decentering the place of origin of the literary productions that Fergusson remembers and produces at the same time, she also paradoxically de-centers the place of origin of the artistic and literary productions she refers to in the poem.

The cosmopolitan we find in Fergusson's work is rooted in the place that produced it. The writer sees Graeme Park as a microcosm of the world, and in so doing Fergusson assigns herself as the poet who remembers the type of world citizenship the cosmopolitan subject aspires to.[20] As the poem about memory shows, the boundary between present and past, between one poetic act and the other, are made invisible on the page and they can be overcome. Fergusson's revisions of her poems, which remain on the page together as the ones I have analyzed earlier in this chapter, have a similar function. The editors of William Byrd's commonplace books have talked of them as belonging to a "borderline genre—a genre that existed between the private and the public and in the gray area triangulated by print, writing, and oral performance" (Berland 2001, 79). This borderline status in between categories places Fergusson's poetry and her books in a dialectical relationship with the roles they played in the eighteenth-century culture in which they were published.

In "To Memory," Fergusson engages in a form of translation that is cultural, temporal, and spatial at the same time. Memory and its workings allow the poet to not only move back and forth in time, but also to pull down walls that would otherwise obstruct her access to knowledge and poetic creativity. This process then translates into recovering and reshaping poems and other writings in her commonplace books and it becomes the tool that allows for the cosmopolitanism she integrated in her poetic and social life during the colonial period to be revived after the American Revolution and her social and intellectual exile. The imperial thematic that David Shields has identified as central to so much of the late colonial American poetry, for example, the promise of wealth and cultural refinement extended by the imperial contract, the disputes about metropolitan prerogatives and provincial laws and liberties, as well as the fear of attacks from England's historic enemies, Spain, France, and the latter's provincial allies, the Indians, may have remained marginal or absent from Fergusson's writings, however, those elements are what gives the language of cosmopolitanism its cultural significance (Shields

---

[20] In this respect, the cosmopolitanism that emerges in Elizabeth Fergusson's poetry is the kind that scholars have described as "rooted" in the particularity of human life and in the traditional notion of cosmopolitan that has its origins in the Stoic tradition and imagines its subjects as members of supranational brotherhoods of sorts. See Chap. 1 for a lengthy discussion of these particular aspects of cosmopolitanism.

1990, 1–5). Fergusson's work shows us an essential aspect of the link between cosmopolitanism and the social and cultural infrastructure it had established in early America. Fergusson's cosmopolitanism and especially the form it takes when she compiles and circulates her commonplace books becomes a form of mourning and longing for imperial structures as a warranty of cultural and intellectual freedoms. Fergusson translates cosmopolitanism into her writings as a poetic trope and a lens to examine her more contained world and make it transnational again.

In a letter to her friend Annis Boudinot Stockton, Fergusson reveals how her practice of writing and copying her poetry is an embodiment of the past, an enactment of memory, and a strategy to evoke memory. Her words portray the poetic strategies her poems reveal:[21]

> Remember my dear Friend, that you often ask'd me for my little pieces; And I Have comply'd with your Request. It is time you Said, that if I Surviv'd you you wishd to have them. But I know that you have a Sensibility of Friendship which would make you Sigh at Reading them when this writer of them was no More, But alas when I copy them I find it makes past Ideas very feverishly in my mind: And do what I will the Sigh and the tear obtrudes its Self But I show Patience more than my Genius in these Works of your Obligd Friend, Laura.[22]

As Fergusson says in her address to Stockton, what she reads as she copies the poems in the book "makes past Ideas very feverishly in [her] mind." The poet transcribes her work and maintains the memory alive and, at the same time, the rewriting of the poems triggers the work of memory and brings the past forward into the present.[23] The act of writing about memory in her poem on the same topic re-enacted this process. The process of remembering, of bringing the past back into the

---

[21] Of this dual function of the commonplace book, David Shields has said that it "had a dual function: on one hand it stood as a substitute library, epitomizing literature into its pithiest sentences all conveniently arranged by topic, on the other hand the act of writing sententiae helped fix them in memory" (Shields 1993, 409).

[22] The note opens the manuscript copy of the book at Dickinson College, which was compiled for Annis Stockton in 1789.

[23] Susan Stabile describes memory as the synthetic conflation of impression. Because such impressions are conveyed through penmanship, Stabile argues, the commonplace books become the embodiment of memory itself. The handwriting that the author uses allows for the transmission of interiority into the exterior space of the page and therefore the body of

present in the books, is reflected in the alterations, the commentaries, the notes and footnotes Fergusson adds from version to version of the texts. They are the features that dislocate the work Fergusson produced from its rootedness in the cosmopolitan world of colonial Philadelphia and her family home in Horsham to the contained and constraining world in which the Revolution pushed her. The circle that Fergusson had painted as widening at the beginning of her writing career has become "so narrow that … the next narrower must be that House which no man breaks the Commandment for in Coveting of his neighbor," Fergusson wrote to Annis Stockton in 1794.[24] The world that existed in the past and the spatial freedom it provided can be revived in her rewriting of those moments. The work and its author are citizens of the world again—a world made of letters and that can survive even when the space around it disappears.

With Fergusson's example, we have an insight into the way cosmopolitanism resisted nationalism in one of the latter's pre-nineteenth-century manifestations. Cosmopolitanism functions as a conservative force with which to mourn and reimagine a lost imperial world. The form of resistance against nationalistic impulses in Fergusson's work fits the patterns of how cosmopolitanism manifests itself in eighteenth-century colonial culture. This relationship between colonial cosmopolitanism and nationalism helps us better understand and clarify the difficulty Franklin's memoir presented when attempting to reconcile the cosmopolitanism of his earlier years with the nationalistic message the later parts of the text conveyed. The texts I have examined in Chaps. 2, 3, and herein Chap. 4 show the different ways in which nationalism, empire, and cosmopolitanism are linked in this period. Today, we see nationalism driving imperial projects or as the result of the dismantling of an imperial structure. Undoubtedly these elements are interconnected, but the examples shown so far highlight how the dynamics during this period were different from the dynamics emerging in the following decades when,

---

the work represents the mental effort of remembering itself (Stabile 2004, 86–88). While I find Stabile point useful to understand the role that memory plays in the construction of the poetic apparatus that takes form in Fergusson's books, I am interested in exploring the ways in which the form of the text that contains the poetic object, the material object itself, reproduces the ideas that form the notion of Enlightenment cosmopolitanism.

[24] Letter to Annis Boudinot Stockton, January 16, 1794. Benjamin Rush Papers, Historical Society of Pennsylvania.

for example, the ex-colonies became a nation state. For an eighteenth-century colonial American like Fergusson, the advent of the nationalistic ideology of the revolution destabilizes the freedom, diversity of ideas, and access to international contact that living in imperial America had provided. Franklin could not reconcile the cosmopolitanism of his early years with the nationalistic model of the figure he portrayed in the memoirs, and by the end of the autobiography his past position is inapplicable to the present and can only be presented as a thing of the past. Jefferson's employment of the cosmopolitan ideal in his address to the scientific community in *Notes on Virginia*, although composed after formal statehood had been ratified, did not present this conflict because it addressed an audience whose primary aim was not nation-building per se. The republic of letters' environment could remain cosmopolitan while Jefferson was asserting American uniqueness within its boundaries. With Elizabeth Graeme Fergusson, the conservative side of eighteenth-century colonial cosmopolitanism emerges, and although her position is not dissimilar to that of Kant during the same period and both present cosmopolitanism as the force that can counterbalance nationalism's divisive and discriminatory power, they do so with a different perspective about empire.[25]

REFERENCES

Allan, David. 2010. *Commonplace Books and Reading in Georgian England*. Cambridge: Cambridge University Press.
Anderson, Benedict. 1983. *Imagined Communities*. New York: Verso.
Altman, Gurkin. 1982. *Epistolarity: Approaches to a Form*. Columbus, OH: Ohio State University Press.

---

[25] Studies of nationalism, its forms and its emergence, have been produced in parallel with those of cosmopolitanism, as a consequence of these two phenomena's connections. What I have described here as Fergusson's fear of the rise of nationalism and, more visibly, the subsequent rise of exclusionary cultural and political norms differs, however, from what scholars have identified as the most common reasons for opposing nationalism. The rise of nationalism and nationalistic tendencies are presented as, in large part, the offspring of imperialistic policies throughout the history of the western world and imperial powers are those that are connoted in negative terms (Anderson 1983; Gellner 1983; Hobsbawm 1992; Balibar 1991; Smith 2010; Ignatieff 1995; Balibar 2015). For Fergusson the opposite is the case: Fergusson sees the imperial structure that the national one is replacing in positive terms, as it is what established the cosmopolitan harmony she had experienced when younger.

Balibar, Etienne. 2015. *Citizenship*. Cambridge: Polity Press.
Balibar, Etienne, and Immanuel Wallerstein. 1991. *Race, Nation, and Class Ambiguous Identities*. London: Verso.
Bannet, Eve Tavor. 2006. *Empire of Letters, Letter Manuals and Transatlantic Correspondence, 1688–1820*. Cambridge: Cambridge University Press.
Berland, Kevin, Jan Kirsten Gilliam, and Kenneth A. Lockridge. 2001. *The Commonplace Book of William Byrd II of Westover*. Chapel Hil, NC: University of North Carolina Press.
Cavallo, Guglielmo, and Roger Chartier. 2003. *A History of Reading in the West*, trans. Lydia G. Cochrane. Amherst, MA: University of Massachusetts Press.
Crane, Mary Thomas. 1993. *Framing Authority: Sayings, Self, and Society in Sixteenth-Century England*. Princeton, NJ: Princeton University Press.
Dacome, Lucia. 2004. Noting the Mind: Commonplace Books and the Pursuit of the Self in Eighteen-Century Britain. *Journal of the History of Ideas* 65 (4): 603–625.
Decker, William Merrill. 1998. *Epistolary Practices: Letter Writing in America Before Telecommunications*. Chapel Hill, NC: The University of North Carolina Press.
Eustace, Nicole. 2008. *Passion is the Gale: Emotion, Power, and the Coming of the American Revolution*. Chapel Hill, NC: University of North Carolina Press.
Gaul, Theresa Strouth, and Sharon Harris. 2009. *Letters and Cultural Transformations in the United States, 1760–1860*. Burlington, VT: Ashgate Press.
Gellner, Ernest. 1983. *Nations and Nationalism*. Ithaca, NY: Cornell University Press.
Goldberg, Jonathan. 1990. *Writing Matter: From the Hands of the English Renaissance*. Stanford, CA: Stanford University Press.
Gratz, Simon. 1915. Some Materials for a Biography of Mrs. Elizabeth Fergusson, neé Graeme. *Pennsylvania Magazine of History and Biography* 39: 257–409.
Hall, David D. 2008. *Ways of Writing: The Practice and Politics of Text-Making in Seventeenth-Century New England*. Philadelphia, PA: University of Pennsylvania Press.
Havens, Earle. 2001. *Commonplace Books: A History of Manuscripts and Printed Books from Antiquity to the Twentieth Century*. New Haven, CT: University Press of New England.
Hewitt, Elizabeth. 2004. *Correspondence and American Literature, 1770–1865*. Cambridge: Cambridge University Press.
Hobsbawm, Eric. 1992. *Nations and Nationalism Since 1780: Programme, Myth, Reality*. Cambridge: Cambridge University Press.
Iannini, Christopher. 2004. 'The Itinerant Man': Crevecoeur's Caribbean, Raynal's Revolution, and the Fate of Atlantic Cosmopolitanism. *William and Mary Quarterly* 61 (2): 201–234.
Ignatieff, Michael. 1995. *Blood and Belonging: Journeys into the New Nationalism*. New York: Farrar, Straus & Giroux.

Justice, George L., and Nathan Tinker. 2002. *Women's Writing and the Circulation of Ideas: Manuscript Publication in England, 1550–1800*. Cambridge: Cambridge University Press.
Larkin, Edward. 2016. *The American School of Empire*. New York: Cambridge University Press.
Lechner, Joan Marie. 1974. *Renaissance Concepts of the Commonplaces*. Westport, CT: Greenwood Press. Second edition.
MacArthur, Elisabeth J. 1990. *Extravagant Narratives: Closure and Dynamics in the Epistolary Form*. Princeton, NJ: Princeton University Press.
McGill, Meredith L. 2007. Common Places: Poetry, Illocality, and Temporal Dislocation in Thoreau's. *A Week on the Concord and Merrimack Rivers. American Literary History* 19 (2): 357–374.
McKitterick, David. 2005. *Print, Manuscript and the Search for Order, 1450–1830*. Cambridge: Cambridge University Press.
Miller, Susan. 1998. *Assuming the Position: Cultural Pedagogy and the Politics of Commonplace Writing*. Pittsburgh, PA: University of Pittsburgh Press.
Nelson, Cary. 2007. The Temporality of Commonplaces: A Response to Meredith McGill. *American Literary History* 19 (2): 375–380.
Ousterhout, Anne M. 2003. *The Most Learned Woman in America: A Life of Elizabeth Graeme Fergusson*. University Park, PA: The Pennsylvania State University Press.
Rush, Benjamin. 1809. An Account of the Life and Character of Mrs. Elizabeth Ferguson. *Portfolio* 1: 520–527.
Shields, David S. 1990. *Oracles of Empire: Poetry, Politics, and Commerce in British America*. Chicago: University of Chicago Press.
Shields, David S. 1993. The Manuscript in the World of Print. *Proceedings of the American Antiquarian Society* 102: 403–416.
Shields, David S. 1997. *Civil Tongues and Polite Letters in British America*. Chapel Hill, NC: North Carolina University Press.
Slotten, Martha C. 1984. Elizabeth Graeme Ferguson A Poet in 'The Athens of North America'. *The Pennsylvania Magazine of History* 108: 259–286.
Smith, Anthony D. 2010. *Nationalism, Theory, Ideology, History*, 2nd ed. London: Polity.
Stabile, Susan M. 2004. *Memory Daughters: The Material Culture of Remembrance in Eighteenth-Century America*. Ithaca, NY: Cornell University Press.
Washington, George. 2002. https://founders.archives.gov/documents/Washington/03-11-02-0537.
Wulf, Karin A., and Catherine La Courreye Blecki. 1997. *Milcah Martha Moore's Book*. University Park, PA: The Pennsylvania State University Press.
Zboray, Ronald J., and Mary Saracino Zboray. 2009. Is It a Diary, Commonplace Book, Scrapbook, or Whatchamacallit? Six Years of Exploration in New England's Manuscript Archives. *Libraries & the Cultural Record* 44 (1): 101–123.

CHAPTER 5

# 'A Continual and Almost Exclusive Correspondence': Philip Mazzei's Cosmopolitan Citizenship

My analysis of the writings of Franklin, Jefferson, and Fergusson focused on how cosmopolitanism connected the discourse of empire to the discourse of nation-building when the latter replaced the former during and after the American Revolution. In this chapter and the next, I analyze another way in which eighteenth-century cosmopolitanism connects to the same environment and how two writers who inhabit the margins of the British Empire, for quite different reasons from those of the three previous writers, use the language of the cosmopolitan ideal to identify themselves. The Italian émigré Philip Mazzei and the ex-slave, sailor, and abolitionist Olaudah Equiano do not have much in common except for living on the margins of the culture they are immersed in as expatriates. Yet, cosmopolitanism works similarly in the works of these two writers, namely as a tool that allows them to define an identity that they would be otherwise denied. The marginalization they experience in the colonial culture is different. Mazzei's limitations and marginal position are determined, as I will show, by his linguistic and cultural differences. Equiano's marginality is dependent on his status as a former slave and as an African. Both writers use a cosmopolitan attitude to develop a critical response to the environment surrounding them. What I want us to observe about cosmopolitanism by looking at these writers is twofold: first, imperial culture can at once be exclusive and generate diversity; second, cosmopolitanism can work as a disruptive and critical force that works against that exclusivity. Both Mazzei and Equiano find the language in cosmopolitanism to assert an identity that, by means of its being supranational, resists and dismisses the obstacles they find.

© The Author(s) 2017
C. Cillerai, *Voices of Cosmopolitanism in Early American Writing and Culture*, The New Urban Atlantic, DOI 10.1007/978-3-319-62298-9_5

In many ways, the Italian expatriate Philip Mazzei fits the model of the man Franklin portrayed in the 1720s and 1730s. Mazzei's life trajectory reflects that which the figures like Franklin said were going to bring Pennsylvania civility, politeness, and wealth because of their supranational loyalties and their international experiences. And like that of the figures in Franklin's writings, Mazzei's American cosmopolitan identity was sustainable only in writings representing it. Mazzei's cosmopolitanism was a by-product of the economies and of the social connections that the empire established. By the end of the American Revolution, Mazzei's representation of an American identity based on the cosmopolitan ideal proved ineffective to make him successful economically, politically, and socially within the frame of the newly established republic. The establishment of a state apparatus that developed legislation made it impossible for Mazzei to become the diplomat he had aspired to be, and his cosmopolitan attitude was, in fact, what made the decision to leave the only option for him (Mazzei 1983, 1: 171–172). Right after making the decision to not return to the United States, Mazzei wrote to John Adams words that reveal the conflict between his cosmopolitan attitude and the new national reality:

> I do not conceive that the bad effects of the existing imperfections in our Govt. will affect me; I am old & have no children; but the honest part of the inhabitants of this Globe are my brethren, Posterity my children; & was I to go & spend the remainder of my days in China I would with pleasure, and in compliance with what I think my duty, contribute all my exertions to the forming of an asylum for Mankind from oppression. (Mazzei 1983, 1: 494)[1]

The cosmopolitan ideal in Mazzei's writings—like the cosmopolitan life he led—were the product of the colonial world, just as it was the case for the young men Benjamin Franklin presented as prospective young leaders in the essay on history I examined in Chap. 2. Once the American republic was established, Franklin's ideal national identity became practicable only as a part of the narrative we now call the American dream.

Educated as a medical doctor, Philip Mazzei immigrated to colonial Virginia with the skills his school education gave him and those

---

[1] Paris, September 27, 1785.

developed during more than two decades spent importing "exotic" goods to London from all over Europe and its outskirts. Mazzei is best known because of his friendship with Thomas Jefferson, who was his neighbor in Virginia between 1773 and 1785 and his correspondent throughout his life.[2] Mazzei's life and the writings that recount it have been described as either examples of early Italian immigration and of its origins in the revolutionary period or as stories about the European cosmopolitan man of letters who traveled and corresponded with his international colleagues, and finally wrote about his worldly experiences.[3] Mazzei was both. He rooted his American identity in the Enlightenment cosmopolitan ideal of universal citizenship and correspondence. For Mazzei, being an American, being an Italian expatriate, and being a cosmopolitan were not contradictory possibilities. When Mazzei arrived in Virginia in 1773 he had already crafted his cosmopolitan identity while living in London where he had settled in 1756. His cosmopolitanism is what helped him reshape his image into that of an ideal American. Cosmopolitanism's roots in the colonial ideology that formed him as an intellectual show us the power that cosmopolitanism had to help individuals in the world Mazzei inhabited navigate it and find ways to identify themselves.

---

[2] The Tuscany native left Virginia and followed Jefferson to Paris at the beginning of 1785, when the latter was the minister plenipotentiary in Paris. Unlike Jefferson, however, he did not come back to the United States. His letters and other writings remained forgotten until the bicentennial celebration of the republic, when his autobiography, the microfilm edition of his collected papers, and his only published book were translated into English.

[3] Howard Marraro was the first American scholar who promoted the publication of Mazzei's work. He published selections from Mazzei's correspondence with the Grand Duke of Tuscany, Thomas Jefferson, John Adams, and the King of Poland. Marraro also translated Mazzei's autobiography (Marraro 1942). It was, however, with the celebration of the 200th anniversary of the republic in the late 1970s that the rest of Mazzei's work began to be collected and published. Margherita Marchione translated the first book of Mazzei's *Recherches historiques et politiques sur les États-Unis* which Mazzei had published in France in 1788 (Marchione 1975). The entire text of Mazzei's work on the United States was published as *Researches on the United States* a year later (Sherman 1976). Marchione also collected Mazzei's papers in microfilm (Marchione 1982) and edited a new translation of Mazzei's autobiography entitled *Philip Mazzei: My Life and Wanderings* (Mazzei 1980). A printed edition of his papers was published in three volumes (Mazzei 1983).

Cosmopolitanism in Mazzei's writings is similar to, and different from, that employed by Thomas Jefferson and Benjamin Franklin. Like the other two writers, Mazzei was a member of the European intellectual elite, possessed an extensive knowledge of European culture, mores, and people, and was at ease speaking the idiom of the republic of letters. Unlike Franklin, whose cosmopolitan subjectivity lost its centrality when he inscribed it into his memoirs, Mazzei developed a model of an American national identity during the revolutionary years that was cosmopolitan in nature and purpose. His life experience, however, showed that this form of American identity could only exist within the realm of his writings. His cosmopolitanism, his non-American birth, and his writings were ultimately the reasons why he left his adopted country to never return. The cosmopolitan representation of an American served the purpose of carving out a space for Mazzei within a social and cultural texture that would have otherwise marked him (and in the end did) as an outsider and not allowed for him to imagine American nationhood as inclusive and open to change. The American identity based on cosmopolitan principles that Mazzei represents throughout his writings can exist only when he imagines it in the context of a world whose margins are open and fluid. Philip Mazzei embodies the type of individual represented in Franklin's writing which I analyzed earlier. Similarly to Franklin's virtuous men, Mazzei's identity fails to be manageable when the colonial world turns into a national one. Cosmopolitanism provides figures like Mazzei a frame to define who they are when they are still part of an open-border colonial environment, and produces images of a national self that can exist outside of the political and structural limits of a national state. When those limits are set, cosmopolitanism fails these figures. The supranational stage is key for cosmopolitanism to become a viable feature of a description of national identity. The cosmopolitan American identity that participating in the revolutionary politics of the 1770s had allowed him to develop, and that helped him navigate many encounters in Europe, failed to help him promote his political and socioeconomic advancement in the United States after the revolution was over. His attempts at being assigned a diplomatic post in Europe and at playing a political role within the United States' government failed. In the end, the only cosmopolitan American that Mazzei could be was the one in the memoirs of his time in America that he wrote at the end of his life.

## 1 LETTERS

Cosmopolitanism gave Mazzei the vocabulary to describe what America and Americans are. Mazzei represents a standard American self with imagery connected to the notion of correspondence, one of the features of cosmopolitanism that makes universal understanding and communication possible. Correspondence as a means of exchange and of understanding oneself in comparison to others is integral to the cosmopolitan American self that emerges from Mazzei's work. Letters embody Mazzei's sense of being a part of such a world. Mazzei's letters from and about America employ cosmopolitan and patriotic language and parallel the representation of a sense of identity informed by a colonial and international environment. After Mazzei left London and settled in Virginia in 1773, ideas he had developed in his earlier years as an expatriate provided him with the groundwork for acting and writing in support of the revolutionary project. In the writings Mazzei composed during the revolutionary period, in fact, the epistolary form is not only the chosen genre for most of his writings, but also what he presents to his audience as a model for creating an independent sense of American identity. In Mazzei's American writings, separating from the colonial past and creating a new identity means creating the new subjects of a correspondence.

Before emigrating to the British North American colonies, Mazzei spent sixteen years in London (1756–1772), where he ran an import/export business. Although trained as a medical doctor and having practiced in Smyrna, Turkey, for five years, Mazzei chose the more lucrative career of international commerce when he left the Turkish city. He became part of the circle of colonial businessmen and intellectuals living in London that included Benjamin Franklin (Mazzei 1980, 110–117). The correspondences Mazzei established between the domain of commerce, the republic of letters, and the imperial environment within which he lived and operated, provided a model then applied to the context of revolutionary America. Mazzei established the relationship among these entities as a correspondence, which existed within and as an epistolary medium. The correspondences, which established his status of cosmopolitan intellectual and man of business, intersected and became the basis of Mazzei's representation of his sense of identity.

The notion of correspondence in all its multiplicity of meanings was essential for the Enlightenment intellectual. The use of the idea of correspondence to talk about oneself, one's career, and the relationships between the various aspects of one's life was a peculiar feature of the eighteenth-century realm of letters.[4] The philosophical concept of analogy between impressions and mental ideas under empiricism, for example, was intended as correspondence, and it also shaped the way in which the man of letters perceived himself in his environment. Correspondence between parts defined the way natural philosophy represented the world's organization. The concept of sympathy rested on the idea that people were connecting with one another, and as a consequence, the idea of correspondence defined social interactions. In addition, epistolary exchanges joined people and minds and produced social relations. Contemporary economic theory was based on the notion of exchange of goods and information (Christensen 1987, 11–12). Ultimately, these correspondences helped individuals like Mazzei, who lived in the extended world of the colonial empire, develop a sense of identity that depended on ties and allegiances defined by mobile mediums of exchange, rather than fixed notions of geographical belonging. The eighteenth-century definition of the cosmopolitan as a state of mind allowed individuals to become members of a community that went beyond national borders national loyalties, and their limitations naturally intertwined with various models of correspondence. Epistolary correspondences and the epistolary genre were the main means of communication and expression for eighteenth-century expatriates and colonials like Mazzei. Embodied in the letter and in the ideas of which it is the carrier is Mazzei's representation of his world and of the individuals who inhabit it.

Mazzei's writings consist of personal letters, newspaper articles written in the epistolary form, and, as was the case with Benjamin Franklin, an autobiography written as a personal letter, which he addressed to an Italian friend. One distinctive epistolary feature is the progressive character of text and content.[5] Mikhail Bakhtin's definition of letters as always

---

[4] In the *Preliminary Discourse to the Encyclopedia of Diderot*, for example, Jean Le Rond D'Alembert introduces the work he did with Diderot not as the task of two individuals, but as the product "of a society of men of letters" whose knowledge is distributed from one to the other. A large part of the *Discourse* itself is dedicated to the discussion of the ideology that kept the republic of letters together and what the concept meant for his contemporaries (D'Alembert 1963, 3).

[5] I have provided bibliographical reference on epistolarity in Chap. 4.

"half someone else's" concisely describes how the notion of epistolary correspondence stands on the ideas of incompleteness and lack of closure and depends on the presence of two entities, writer and addressee/receiver, for its existence (Bakhtin 1990, 293). Mazzei's epistolary subjectivity defined itself in correspondence with other selves and in dialogic relationship with his interlocutors. The ideas that a letter conveys are usually ones in progress, part of a written discussion, or possibly subjected to a revision by the response that the letter-writer expects from the correspondent. Mazzei's construction of identity (his own and that of the group to which he belongs) takes place within and re-enacts the spatial and temporary movement of the correspondence that embodies it. Correspondence in the colonial period had important sociological as well as literary roles in the formation of a sense of identity for various groups.[6] Mazzei's work shows how an identity of the early American community founded on the language of correspondence and epistolary dialogue lacks the exclusive features usually associated with the idea of a national community. Exclusion thus emerges as a primary category in the defining terms of national identity after American colonial identity becomes that of the United States of America.

## 2  LETTERS OF EXCHANGE: HOW TO BECOME AN AMERICAN

Mazzei was born in 1730 in Poggio a Caiano, a small village north of Florence, and he died in Pisa in 1816. In the memoir he drafted in 1811, Mazzei explains how his stay in Turkey in the early 1750s introduced him to "consuls and merchants of all European nations" and describes this cosmopolitan community as thriving with life and intellectual excitement (Mazzei 1980, 96). During the sixteen years he spent in London (1756–1772), Mazzei became one of those cosmopolitan intellectuals he had met in Turkey. His career was long and varied. Contemporary to his introduction to the world of international commerce, he became a tradesman himself and a teacher of Italian. He also began to write. After

---

[6] Focusing on the role that letter manuals' generic representativeness, Eve Tavor Bannet, for example, claims that epistolary writings "contributed to forging the nation and the first British Empire as much as improved roads and transportation, the institution of the post office and of regular shipping routes, the periodical press, and national days of celebration and commemoration" (Bannet X).

he relocated to Virginia, he became a farmer, but he was also a journalist, an agent in search of financial support for the revolutionary cause, and eventually an envoy to the last king of Poland, Stanislaus II. During his retirement years in Pisa, he resumed the two activities he had enjoyed in Virginia: writing and gardening.[7]

As I have suggested earlier, the various roles Mazzei assumed during his life evolved along a series of correspondences articulated in the epistolary exchanges that constituted his writings and were finally summarized in the letter he wrote in 1811 to his friend, the lawyer Giovanni Carmignani. Later in the century, the letter was published as his autobiography. In the dedication that opens this work, Mazzei talks about the significance of letter writing in his career. Letters constitute "the story of my life," he begins. As he later mourns the loss of some of those letters during his many travels, he tells his friend that the letters he wrote and received during his lifetime could explain his life because "they would apprise [Carmignani] of my conduct, first in the State of Virginia as a good citizen of my adoptive country, then as its agent in Europe, then as agent of King Stanislaus of Poland, and later as *chargé d'affaires* of the King and Republic of Poland at the French Court" (Mazzei 1980, 25). The subjectivity this letter presents defines Mazzei as a cosmopolitan intellectual. Mazzei uses this same model to represent his autobiographical self.

Mazzei began to publish what he was writing in the years that preceded his emigration to Virginia. The structure of a brief text printed anonymously in London in 1768 shows the extent to which the dynamics of the epistolary form and its cosmopolitanism affected Mazzei's vision of subjectivity and group identity. The rhetorical and formal strategies Mazzei used for the early pamphlet return as a model for the discussion of American national identity in his writings during the revolutionary period. Mazzei portrays the correspondence between an Italian and a British subject in the 1760s. Their commerce of letters ensures the viability of the cultural and legal systems in both England

---

[7]Thomas Schlereth describes this type of eclectic career as the typical one of the eighteenth-century cosmopolite. At times, Schlereth argues, "this did lead to superficial dilettantism and some over generalized (even sloppy) scholarship. Yet, Franklin's international reputation rested, not unjustly, on his varied intellectual activities as scientist, diplomat, journalist, statesman, artisan, economist, man of letters, and philosopher" (Schlereth 1977, 10). And so was Mazzei's life characterized by different intellectual enterprises that went from founding an agricultural society with Jefferson, writing a natural history of the United States, and producing essays on the rights of man.

and Italy. Ultimately letter exchange guarantees the possibility of change and improvement for both sides. The pamphlet is written in English with an Italian translation in the opposite page. The text of *A Letter on the Behavior of the Populace on a Late Occasion, in the Procedure against a Noble Lord from a Gentleman to his Countryman abroad*, despite its wordy title, is brief and consists of an exercise in applying Cesare Beccaria's theories of just punishment and the rightfulness of national laws that protect it.[8] As the title suggests, Mazzei wrote the pamphlet in the epistolary form and imagined it addressed to an Italian correspondent. The narrative strategy he uses to deploy his argument consists of creating a set of three different personas: the original letter writer (who Mazzei does not name, but, who could likely be him because he is imagined as an expatriate living in England), the Italian correspondent, and the English editor in charge of the publication. The subject of the letter emerging from this text is characterized by an ability to translate and reshape its features as they are engaged in the epistolary exchange. The narrative voice takes shape as the letter unfolds and imagines the

[8] In *On Crimes and Punishments* (1963), the Italian jurist Cesare Beccaria developed a theory for transforming the penal system in Europe that was based on a mathematical system. Beccaria's theory proposed to measure all human reactions in terms of pleasure and pain. In Beccaria's view, men have a natural tendency to "abandon the most important regulations" either to the care of common sense or in the hands of "persons who have an interest in opposing the wisest laws." Therefore he argued that:

> It is … only after they have passed through a thousand errors in matters most essential to life and liberty, after they have arrived at the limits of endurance exhausted by the wrongs they have suffered, that men are induced to remedy the disorders that oppress them and to acknowledge the most palpable truths, which, precisely because of their simplicity, escape the attention of vulgar minds accustomed not to analyze things, but to receiving general impressions all of a piece, rather from tradition than through study.

> The process men need to go through in order to understand "the most palpable truths" closely resembles scientific inquiry. Like science, in fact, it requires individuals to organize, analyze, and study the elements that compose the truths and then classify them. Reorganizing old and creating new laws could solve the problems that the general human attitude to generalize engenders. The contemporary forms of punishment adopted in the majority of European countries, Beccaria claimed, reflected the attitude men have of "receiving general impressions" as if they were unquestionable truths, whereas they should have been "analyzed with the geometric precision which the mist of sophisms, seductive eloquence, and timorous doubts cannot withstand" (Beccaria 1963, 10).

responses of its reader. The identity of this subjectivity comprises various aspects of the notion of correspondence. It is an epistolary correspondence and an intellectual exchange. It is also a linguistic correspondence, which Mazzei defines as linguistic and cultural translation and is reflected in the pamphlet's bilingual format.

The 1768 letter is introduced by an editorial note in which the English-speaking editor explains the reasons for publishing such a correspondence and summarizes the terms of the dispute the pamphlet discusses.[9] In this context, the formal relevance of the notion of correspondence is introduced through a reference to linguistic translation:

> As there can hardly be a matter of greater utility to the public of any nation, than its comparing with its own the opinion of other countries, especially on any points relative to its internal administration of justice; the following letter, on a topic, which has taken up so much of the public attention, from a very ingenious gentleman, to a countryman of his, appeared to me so well meant, so dispassionate, so full of candor, and just reasonings, that I imagined the publication of it could not but meet with a favourable reception. (Mazzei 1983, 1: 24)

The passage shows the function of the pamphlet is to establish a correspondence of ideas on a topic that affects writer, editor, and reader. Translation at the linguistic level and at the cultural level is necessary for parties involved to understand each other. The epistolary terms that inform the exchange between writer and correspondent become a metaphor for the pamphlet's subject: a country's internal structure can be transformed only by "comparing with its own the opinion of other countries." The author addresses the Italian correspondent, who embodies

---

[9] It is impossible to know if Mazzei or the publisher wrote the introduction. In the copy of the pamphlet held at the Library of Congress among Jefferson's papers, the introduction is the only part of the text that is only in English, which may be taken as a sign of a different authorship from that of the text and its translation. The title as well as the body of the text are both in English and Italian, with the English translation facing the Italian on the opposite page. Writing pamphlets in epistolary form and publishing them with a note that explained the editorial choice and the history behind the text were common practices of the time. What is most interesting in the use of such a convention in this pamphlet is the conflation it makes between the notions of translation and epistolary correspondence, which Mazzei then places at the basis of his argument about identity formation in the letter that follows.

the original audience of the letter, while the editor in charge of the English translation addresses the extra-textual audience in England. The published work, in its bilingual and epistolary form, is imagined as bringing the two parties together in a conversation that contributes to the enlightenment of both. Mazzei begins to establish cosmopolitanism as the foundational principle through this discursive strategy based on correspondence.

Mazzei begins his letter as if part of an ongoing conversation. He does not provide his audience with any specifics about background he refers to.[10] The letter's addressee, an Italian friend, is reprimanded for a presumed, prior, negative comment about the British system of laws. Mazzei's reprimand begins with a series of references to his own impartial and cosmopolitan perspective:

> What I confess hurts me, is, to find that one of your sense should let himself be carried away with the general error of blaming those laws: I pity

---

[10] Mazzei's pamphlet is part of a series of texts occasioned by a cause célèbre from the previous decade, the kidnapping of a woman named Elizabeth Canning in 1753. After disappearing for over a month, the maid Elizabeth Canning had returned home and accused a gypsy woman and other accomplices of having kidnapped her and forced her into prostitution. Despite the flimsiness of the evidence, the judge in charge of the trial, Henry Fielding, the novelist, had accepted Canning's version of the story and convicted the accused gypsy. The Mayor of London, Sir Crisp Gascoyne, questioned Fielding's decision and reopened the case. The second trial ended with the acquittal of the gypsy woman and Canning's conviction as perjurer. Canning was sentenced to deportation to the British colonies, where she lived in Connecticut until her death in 1773. Public opinion was largely split during the trials and during the months that followed, and both Fielding and Gascoyne wrote their versions of the story. Fielding himself wrote *A Clear Statement of the Case of Elizabeth Canning* to explain his side of the story and two more essays were published that adopted his perspective. Sir Gascoyne, after his acquittal of the presumed kidnappers, was physically assaulted and received death threats. In 1762 Voltaire published *Histoire d'Elisabeth Canning, et de Jean Calas*, which he based on one of the essays written from Fielding's side of the controversy over the verdict (Treherne 1989; Moore 1994). In his pamphlet, Mazzei takes the side of the lord mayor of London (he calls Gascoyne Lord B.) and refers to the attacks against him. Mazzei justifies his ruling against the woman, and explains the reasons for the English public's misunderstanding of his action. It is clear from the beginning, however, that the story (which took place almost fifteen years before the pamphlet was written) is only the occasion for Mazzei's digression on Beccaria's ideas. Mazzei agrees with his correspondent regarding the need to support the woman's conviction, he also believes that Canning was guilty of perjury, but he admonishes his friend for his attack on the English and their laws.

the multitude, but I cannot excuse you. I have traveled much, I have seen many nations, and have observed that everywhere the generality of mankind are too rash in their decisions: Where some great inconvenience has happened to rise from the laws of a country, those laws are immediately condemned, the multitude never standing to consider, that very often that inconvenience could not have been avoided without opening the door to inconveniences still greater in number and quality. (Mazzei 1983, 1: 26)

By placing the fault in the laws, Mazzei argues, his friend places himself on the same ground as the multitudes who accused the judge. Both his friend and the multitudes have shown lack of judgment and of consideration. Here Mazzei draws a line separating himself from the rest of his audience, British and Italian. Mazzei has now placed his perspective against that of the "generality of mankind," of which his friend is now part too. Mazzei has also distinguished his point of view from his friend's and labeled it authoritative and impartial—two characteristics his cosmopolitan experience has given him. Like the editor, who had placed the authority on himself by rhetorically blocking critical responses away from his opinionated statement in the introduction, Mazzei has now reversed his friend's position and excluded him from the one he had theoretically occupied in the past. The only voice of authority both audiences are now to hear is Mazzei's, the citizen of the world who has "traveled much" and "seen many nations." Mazzei becomes the figure of authority, and this authority lies in his ability to exercise an act of cultural and linguistic translation.

The body of the letter develops through a series of comparisons that project various images against each other. As I said above, the letter begins with a reference to the correspondent's criticism of British law protecting the masses at the disadvantage of people of noble heritage, the "nobility" as he calls them. Mazzei rebukes his Italian friend for taking this position. He writes that English laws protect everybody and entitle everybody to express their judgment, and, through the exercise of such laws, maintain people's freedom. His friend's attitude toward common people, Mazzei says, is mistaken and reflects an Italian elitism towards justice in general. The British people who demanded the punishment of somebody who belonged to the highest social ranks for a crime he had supposedly committed was a sign that such a people felt protected by and entitled to use the legal system with which their nation supplied them:

Don't you think that it must be a check to many villains, to be sure that at the cry of a child [,] persons of all ranks and conditions would fall upon them? Yet [you] cannot deny, that the hope of an escape, or pardon, does encourage crimes. You ought then to applaud, and admire that unprejudiced general spirit of a nation, by which everyone thinks himself obliged to pursue a delinquent, even though he were his friend the minute before he committed the crime. Better turn your reproaches against that maxim, which, in our earliest years, we imbibe in our own country, that it is a shame, and an infamy, to assist the officers of justice, and to do their office in putting an offender into the hands of the law. (Mazzei 1983, 1: 26)

Mazzei asserts that legal system gives legitimacy to the people's remonstrations. In fact, it is their resort to such a system that makes the British public's attack legitimate. The Italian reader who thinks that the episode signifies a flaw in the British laws is not looking at the laws from the right cultural standpoint, but he reproduces a pattern that characterizes attitudes of his own country towards the law. The change of first person pronoun from "I" to "we" in the last sentence of the passage is worth noting. It illustrates a peculiar identity Mazzei attributes to himself as letter writer and to the subject of the epistle here. This identity is fluid and can be adapted to varying rhetorical circumstances. The subject of the letter acquires the features of the cosmopolitan man of letters whose position enables him to communicate both inter- and intra-culturally. In order to understand what happened and to provide his friend with the tools for reading and interpreting a different cultural act, Mazzei changes the position of the narrative voice. He now includes himself among those Italians who had previously misjudged other people's customs by applying the wrong interpretive standards and makes his experience the example to follow. Mazzei was misreading and misinterpreting like other Italians he asserts. Once he was able to understand both and move his terms of comparison from one context to the other, his vision expanded. This new narrative voice possesses a compound identity, an identity created through translation from Italian to English, and from English to Italian again. The act of learning a new language and a new interpretive code produces the change and supplies audiences with the method for a better understanding of their reading. Because it is generated in translation, mobility and interpretive fluidity characterize this subject and they are counterbalanced by the fixity of the language he interprets. The letter-writer becomes the interpreter of the systems of laws he presents. He is both judge and the ones being judged as he assumes the Italian identity by switching pronouns.

By conflating the two roles of judge and judged, Mazzei places the narrative subject inside and outside both positions.[11] The duality of such an identity and his ability to adopt either one make Mazzei the ideal translator of the terms employed in the discussion. Textual interpretation and the ability to do it correctly are essential to the functioning of a legal system; and the subjectivity Mazzei has begun to portray is the most apt to cover such a role. Its fluid identity, its ability to shift from one rhetorical paradigm to another, enable it to generate the model interpreter Mazzei is and wants his reader to become. One's interpretive skills are essential to the functioning of a legal system:

> If it was left to the discretion of a justice not to receive the accusation, where it might appear to him evidently calumnious, this might pave the way for corruption; and you cannot deny that the inconveniences which may arise from the severity of the laws, or from some defects in them, are much less evil than those which would arise from the mistakes, or iniquity of such interpreters of them as should be at liberty to depart from their literal sense. I go even further. Were the inconveniences proceeding directly from the letter of the laws ten times greater, than from an arbitrary interpretation of them, I would, nevertheless, chuse [sic] a subjection to the first; because, since things [laws] are nothing in themselves, but as they afflict or rejoice, a small damage caused to us by the iniquity of a judge, would, and ought to grieve us more than a greater one occasioned to us by the severity or the defect of laws equal to all. (Mazzei 1983, 1: 27–28)

The existence of the legal system depends on the concept of interpretation. Laws are "nothing in themselves," Mazzei claims. The notion of arbitrariness inhabits the law, because it cannot exist outside the realm of human understanding and interpretation. In the end, the law exists only in its applications. Its textual character gives the law the status of inanimate object. The law itself, being an object, cannot be damaging unless an agent is manipulating it.

---

[11] The shift is reminiscent of the one I noticed in Franklin's choice to make himself the secretary of the American Philosophical Society in the broadside he wrote in 1743, which similarly allowed him to be simultaneously an insider and outsider to the society and thus be both its member and its judge see Chap. 2.

The syntax of this passage reflects this particular nature of laws and the essential role interpretive acts play in their existence. The expression "laws equal to all" does not appear until the end of the long period that contains it, and it is preceded by a series of coordinated sentences that begin with "because, since things are nothing in themselves." The grammatical elements that precede the expression create a series of syntactical obstacles, which make the appearance of the expression "laws equal to all" dependent on their reading. The equality of the law is intrinsic to the law as inanimate object, as well as to its verbal execution. "It would carry me too far, were I to say all that could be said in praise of the execution of the criminal laws in this country [England]; I say of the execution, because the laws would be good every where, if the executive power was not misruled," Mazzei adds (Mazzei 1983, 1: 28). Unless qualified interpreters perform their task correctly, the objective equality of the law remains only a potential. And the ability to be a good judge depends on reading and understanding the text of the law. Mazzei brings together the notion of the letter of the law and the notions of reading and interpreting, which he uses to reconnect to his initial claim that his reader should know how to use translation and cultural correspondences correctly. The focus Mazzei places on the agent in this passage takes readers back to his representation of the narrative voice in the pamphlet and his ability to see across cultures and thus understand a culture and its features. Mazzei's transnational subject exists because it is the subject of the letter and because the letter allows for the shifts necessary to maintain an open dialogue.

### 3 Transatlantic Correspondences: The American Experience

The early text that I have analyzed in the previous section of this chapter shows that for Mazzei mobility was essential to the making of the proper citizen of the world and this argument reappears in what he wrote after moving to colonial Virginia in 1773. In the writings of this later period, the imagery of mobility, dialogue, and exchange frames the identity an American citizen should adopt when the prospect of separation from England materializes. Mazzei represents himself as an American as the result of identity rooted in exchange and dialogue, and then he eventually transfers this representation onto the image of American society writ large when he becomes involved in the revolutionary project. According to the terms he has set up in "A Letter to the Populace", Mazzei conceives of identity formation as a process that can happen anywhere. Indeed, he produces an American identity before he physically moves to Virginia. While traveling between England and Italy to buy some of the products he wants to sell to support his new American venture, Mazzei projects an already-shaped American identity in the letter he writes to his agent in Virginia:

> After Mr. Griffin's departure there has not been any ship for the American Continent; otherwise I would have lost no time in going to you, as you prudently advise me to do. I have been all this while in expectation of an agreement with Capt. Watts to carry us to Virginia, and to send him back here with a cargo of wheat. This having failed I am upon an uncertainty as to the time of my getting off. We expect every minute Capt. Frederickson from Tunis with a good American built ship; he is my friend and directed to a merchant who is my friend likewise: I hope either with him, or somebody else to sail in about a month, but if all misfortunes should pursue me and prevent me coming to our blessed Land as soon as I desire, I will take the opportunity of the first fishship, which will be about the latter end of October, and in the meantime bear with patience this exile from my dear Country, mine by choise [*sic*], not by chance. (Mazzei 1983, 1: 73)

In this passage, the process of becoming a "national" is conceived as a transnational phenomenon that takes place away from the geographical limits of a country. In fact, not only does Mazzei employ Lockean terminology to invalidate the contemporary assumption that national character is predetermined, but also claims the power of decision as the fundamental feature of his own identity. Identity is chosen and not just given by the chance of birthplace (Gerbi 1973, 268–275). Travel and geographical mobility are necessary conditions to the formation of identity. The sale of the wheat, however, is the other essential factor involved in the process. Mazzei will cover his expenses from the profit of the sale. Mazzei exhorts his correspondent to "engage all your best friends in buying all the wheat you can, and let it be heavy and clean at least as the Philadelphia is" (Mazzei 1983, 46). For Mazzei, identity transformation is equally dependent on the commercial exchange to exercise free choice. The figure of the cosmopolitan subject who can be a citizen of each and every country he establishes himself in and, at the same time, be a citizen of the whole world, is, as was the case with the representation Franklin had produced, equally dependent on intellectual exchange as it is on commercial ones.[12] However, while in Franklin's writing a prospective American subjectivity built on the terms of the cosmopolitan ideal fails to materialize, for Philip Mazzei the War of Independence provides the ideological context for developing a cosmopolitan American identity. When a resident of Virginia, Mazzei retrieves the terms he had used in the 1760s to represent his new identity as a revolutionary American. Beginning with the propagandistic works he composed and published at the onset of the war, Mazzei suggests that by adopting a cosmopolitan subjectivity similar to that of the author of the pamphlet he had written while in London, his fellow Americans and himself will be able to abandon their colonial identity and become representatives of a new independent national character.[13]

As I suggested at the beginning on this chapter, Mazzei's position within the transatlantic intellectual elite and then in the American environment he joined in the mid-1770s was one of both centrality and marginality. His cosmopolitan self-representation of an American identity and being a citizen of the world is affected by this dual positioning. I highlighted the reference to becoming an American by personal choice in the letter quoted above because it is evidence of another important element that affects eighteenth-century cosmopolitanism. Mazzei's words about a chosen connection to a country as opposed to a birth-given one remind his readers of a common concern among eighteenth-century intellectuals related to current climatological theories about the formation of national character. These theories originated in the writings of thinkers such as the Marquis de Montesquieu and claimed national character was determined by climate and that the geographical location of one's birthplace affected the type of individual one would become.

The specific argument which Mazzei questions is that one's natural surroundings determined one's national character. This idea had been

---

[12] Here Mazzei's sense of a subjectivity formed by combining intellectual and commercial exchanges is similar to the one that Franklin had represented for the members of Junto club see Chap. 1.

[13] Philipp Ziesche has analyzed the crisis of cosmopolitanism at the end of the eighteenth-century. Ziesche sees it as a consequence of a stronger nationalistic attitude that countries like France and the United States developed in order to respond to the universal principles to which many of the revolutionary leaders adhered. Mazzei's representation defies this logic and, at the same time, the unfolding of his life does reflect the narrative that Ziesche retraces in his study (Ziesche 2010, 1–3).

made popular by the political arguments of Montesquieu in *The Spirit of the Laws* as well as by the scientific ones made by Buffon in his *Histoire Naturelle*.[14] Writers argued that living in a particular climate affected the way a people developed certain common cultural and sociological traits. Their ideas had then been applied and elaborated by many European writers and popularized through other literary forms that included pamphlets and newspaper articles. Montesquieu, for example, had argued that human laws were not derived exclusively from a choice that people had made by associating into groups in Locke's model of a common agreement through a social contract. Instead, "a variety of wants in different climates [had] first occasioned a difference in the manner of living, and this gave rise to a variety of laws" (Montesquieu 2002, 229). These laws, though not governed by climate, customs, or circumstances, determined fundamental and unbridgeable differences among groups of people and placed them in a hierarchical order of cultural development and achievements. Ultimately, in Montesquieu's views, no human law or custom could exist outside of the laws of the natural environment, and the ability of a group to develop physically and culturally independently from the environmental conditions that surround it becomes very limited. Similarly, Buffon's assumption that the humidity of North America was the cause of a slow, but inevitable, degeneration of its inhabitants had implied their inability to rise both physically and culturally to the levels of European countries.

Because of the vast popularity of these ideas, late eighteenth-century American and some European writers' words often reveal a concern about the power such theories could have to mold public opinion, to affect representations of America, and, consequently, to determine the outcomes of the war between the colonies and England.[15] This

---

[14] See my discussion of Buffon in Chap. 4.

[15] Antonello Gerbi notes Mazzei's interest in both the political aspect of his argument in favor of the United States and the interest that Mazzei had for the issues of natural history of the American continent and writes: "Mazzei shows himself so averse to any Americanistic fanaticism that his own position becomes correspondingly stronger, both in arguing with the critics of the newborn United States and with those of the physical nature of the American continent" (Gerbi 1973, 273). What Gerbi does not address, however, is the interdependence between these two issues in Mazzei's writings and his perception of scientific theories as part of a political discourse that aims at defining America in opposition to Europe.

issue of climate and national character construction affected Mazzei as a future immigrant and as a southern European while waiting to travel to Virginia, and it reappears a few years after Mazzei settled in Virginia when he writes about the representation of the national character of those inhabiting the North American colonial world. Mazzei writes that these climatological theories had been originally articulated by the "greatest names of the literary world," and then had been vastly adopted by European "gazetteers" to describe the national character of Americans and to discredit them. In his view, the process that these writers were following "reflected" upon a national group a set of pre-constructed images, which deprived its members of the power to create their national identity—a power that was, in his eighteenth-century perspective, their right. The newspaper writer performs a similar task. He mechanically reproduces distorted representations of America and, by extension, its most recent inhabitants, and, by propagating these misrepresentations through the print process, ignores the differences of opinion among Americans. Ultimately, this type of writer, Mazzei suggests, denies Americans their civic freedom to speak for or against different issues which might be crucial to determining the national character of their own country. The task of the American writer will be rewriting the representations European writers and misguided journalists have distorted.

In January 1775, Mazzei began a *Virginia Gazette* article with a reference to and a criticism of the theories that, as he tells his audience, had been produced by French philosophers and natural historians.[16] In the article, Mazzei sets up a rejection of the largely accepted idea of a codependence of national character and climate in favor of an idea of national identity as a cultural and political product. Mazzei's association of cosmopolitanism and national identity becomes apparent. In the opening paragraph of the article, significantly entitled "A Letter from a Citizen of the World," Mazzei states:

> Nothing indicates more strongly an illiberal mode of thinking than a propension to throw reflections on individuals because they happen to have first drawn breath in such and such countries, it being roundly asserted by the dealers out of such stuff that certain bad qualities are annexed to

---

[16] Mazzei's more obvious concerns about these issues emerge in the natural history he wrote in the 1780s while living in Paris.

certain climates, and that every person born under them must necessarily inhale, and be infected with, what it would appear from those characterizers of nations, is incorporated with the very atmosphere. (Mazzei 1983, 1: 72)

Mazzei's impersonal and passive rhetoric reflects the passive state of the subject in the stereotype about national character who should be able to decide what national character to assume for himself. The reflections perform the action and construct what appears to be the fact at the basis of an opinion, thus leaving the subject himself unable to exercise any power of choice. Significantly, the passage continues with a reference to the literary character of these theories' claim of veracity: "though this practice [is] warranted by the example of some writers of reputation," it is nonetheless an "ungenerous and contracted mode of argument" (Mazzei 1983, 1: 72).

As Mazzei's introductory words to his *Virginia Gazette*'s article demonstrate, the notions of correspondence and cultural translation as one of its by-products, rewriting, and re-presentation are fundamental to any attempt at asserting one's national identity. A year after the publication of this articles, these elements re-emerge and become the foundation Mazzei provides of how Americans can claim an original national character. In a letter to John Page written on June 16, 1776, Mazzei requests his friend's help with the translation of some papers he wants to publish, feeling that his written English might not be good enough for the press. Mazzei explains in the letter that Page's translation would improve the original writing so that "Several things, I am confident, will be better out, & several others could be added with great propriety. My composition is [I]talian with [E]nglish words." He writes, "You know that what is elegance in one language is sometimes nonsense in another, &c. &c." (Mazzei 1983, 1: 116). In acknowledging his linguistic limitations and asking for help from a native speaker of the English language, Mazzei also proposes a definition of translation that goes beyond the linguistic level. There is a parallel between the request Mazzei makes to Page and the function he attributed to translation in the epistolary pamphlet analyzed earlier in this chapter.

Mazzei's ideas, his words suggest, will be fully developed after having been processed through the filter of a language different from the one of their original articulation. Ideas will be exchanged during this conversation and the text will undergo a linguistic and a cultural development

(Schlereth 1977, 7–9). In his request for help, Mazzei talks about having a second reader as a needed tool to help him "digest" ideas and to enable him to establish a conversation with other intellectuals: "I would take it as a great favour from you Sir, & from any of the Gentlemen," Mazzei writes, "if I was to see upon the News-Papers, my sentiments, not only put in good [E]nglish, but even corrected and improved" (Mazzei 1983, 1: 116). The notion of translation at work in this passage resembles the epistolary exchange between Mazzei and Page that has made it materially possible: it allows dialogue, develops new ideas, and enriches perspectives. The translator's task is to create a linguistic, cultural, and geographical relationship without breaking down national differences. In fact, the permanence of differences becomes a staple of the idea of translation that emerges from Mazzei's text.[17] Translation does not replace the "Italianness" in Mazzei's composition, it articulates and refines it. Translation then becomes performance of difference rather than its erasure. Mazzei's Italian, or perhaps one should simply say his "other" identity, becomes displaced within a new context and acquires new characteristics. In translation, Mazzei's composition would acquire the propriety and the "elegance" it lacked in its original Italian utterance. Page's translation would perform a revisionary process and provide a discursive as well as a cultural context for Mazzei's ideas to mature in a process that parallels the one in the bilingual letter he wrote thirteen years earlier.

In addition, similarly to what the shift in personal pronouns had done in the pamphlet, Mazzei implies that the translation of his words will also produce a subject in the narrative that can be both within and without the narrative itself. The idea of identity as a performance becomes a central feature of the identity Mazzei will then imagine for Americans. In one of the pieces Mazzei published in English in the *Virginia Gazette* a few months after he wrote this letter to Page, he proposes a way for Americans to assert an identity independent from England, based on this model of performance. Mazzei suggests that his American readers revise the terms with which they identified themselves in relation to England, and proposes a national model for the new American citizen—one whose

---

[17] I use the term translation in a loose sense of transference from one place to another or one context to another. Translation itself initiates a process by which the literal translation of words inserts cultural characteristic and habits into a new realm and allows for exchange and transformation (Steiner 1998; Venuti 2008, 1–24).

roots are not based on climatological or philosophical theories, but on a correspondence of ideas and a universal sense of identity. In the pamphlet he had composed while living in London, Mazzei's representation of translation as an instrument to establish a cultural correspondence between nationals implied the identity given him by his native cultural and linguistic background was twofold. Such identity could be both a frame of reference and a potential constraint. It stopped being a frame of reference and it became a limitation when it was not placed in a dialogue with other forms of identity. Mazzei reproduces this argument in another article written while in Virginia. Mazzei's "Observations of a Citizen of the World in answer to an American," in the issue of the *Virginia Gazette* published on August 24, 1776, exemplifies how the process of national identification derives from the power of national subjects to both identify and separate themselves from what defines the national. The structural similarity with the essay he wrote almost a decade earlier is immediate. The essay, written in a form familiar to Mazzei's contemporaries, consists of a combination of two genres, the newspaper article and the familiar letter (Crane 1950, 1–18; Smiths 1988).

The main characteristic of Mazzei's role of "Citizen of the World," as he identifies himself in the title of the article, unfolds as the letter progresses. A prefatory note opens the article and illustrates how the idea of epistolary correspondence has both a formal and a thematic relevance in the essay. In the note, Mazzei explains that the representation of the American situation outlined in the following article had been originally written for a European audience, but, given that its subject was recognizably a representation of Americans, it needs to be brought back in front of an American audience. Mazzei poses as the editor in the introductory passage, an impartial third party whose view is above partisan conflicts. In this passage, Mazzei outlines a strategy of reflection that becomes the rationale with which he envisions the new American identity the following essay illustrates:

> The following is a copy of a letter sent the other side [*sic*] the Atlantic in January last. Although it appears to contain a number of observations for the use of an [A]merican, we believe it was written with the only intent of giving a true account of the situation of things on this continent, to some people in power, who might be induced to interfere, and form their deliberations accordingly; and we have thought proper to publish it, in order that our customers may have an opportunity to see the sentiments of every

member of the community, not only in respect to the present doings, but even to what may probably be expected. (Mazzei 1983, 2: 120)

In this passage, Mazzei makes clear that by observing themselves reflected in the representation the article gives, Americans are enabled to reflect upon themselves as a nation. This strategy of reflection by which Americans are the spectacle for Europeans points to Mazzei's more comprehensive aim in the essay: a new form of self-representation.

As the writer of the letter, Mazzei functions as the middleman in charge of the most important part of the exchange—namely, the writing, translating, and transmitting of a representation of America for insiders and outsiders as well. The correspondence the article establishes is epistolary because it is written as a personal letter, and it takes shape in an exchange of newspaper articles like this one. Mazzei's address to the American audience functions backward. It gains efficacy by being delivered first to a transatlantic audience and then re-routed to the American context. Indeed, the transatlantic context in which the article is circulated becomes the legitimizing one for the argument Mazzei wants to make. According to Mazzei, both the American community and the community across the Atlantic should see the same picture.[18] The result of this process is the creation of a new version of community that is original in the Enlightenment sense of being the result of an ingenious reproduction (Christensen 1987, 3–20).

---

[18]The American audience that Mazzei describes in the introductory letter to the reader has the same features that William Dowling has attributed to the "epistolary audience" in the context of the eighteenth-century verse epistle. This is an audience, Dowling explains "at one remove ... as overhearing or listening in on the epistolary exchange between letter-writer and addressee" (Dowling 1991, 11–12). This characteristic of the verse epistle, Dowling contends, derives from the genre's participation in contemporary ideological debates. The poem, he explains, is seen as a symbolic act with the potential to intervene in the domain of the real. At the same time, Dowling continues, the position of this audience is profoundly ambivalent. It is caught between the demands of a traditional "organic" society and those of the new money or market society that is gaining more and more ground. It seems to me Dowling's idea could be extended to the larger genre of eighteenth-century epistolarity, in particular to its use in early American newspaper writing as a means of revolutionary propaganda. Mazzei's letter takes the shape of an intervention in the identity crisis that the secession from England has generated, and through it, he attempts to provide his public with an alternative form of self representation.

Mazzei also produces the language that Americans should use to represent themselves in the article. What Mazzei does for his audiences parallels what he had wanted John Page to do a few months earlier. He explains things "not only in respect to the present doings, but even to what may probably be expected" (Mazzei 1983, 2: 119). The language Americans need to master could be defined as a discursive fluency in diplomatic politics.[19] This language would free them from the national constraint that identification with England had created and, at the same time, it would define them as a nation that could speak for itself. The retranslating of the letter into English will provide a democratization of opinion by presenting the audience with "the sentiments of every member of the community"—Mazzei's view of the goal of the revolution itself. Mazzei's opening remarks imply that by embodying the image proposed in the letter, Americans will be able to achieve the goal of representing themselves as a solid and independent national body and hence will legitimize themselves in the eyes of their European observers. The interchange the prefatory note suggests should be the foundation of a dialogue between the European and the American audience is described again within the body of the essay that follows it. Mazzei discusses the form of cultural and epistolary correspondence Americans should develop and with which they should exchange cultural representations with Europe. He develops a vision of American identity established on a process of reflection and revision.

The letter begins with a series of conventional images: Mazzei represents the colonial relationship to England in terms of master/servant, and familial imagery. He uses the imagery of slavery to describe the colonists' state of subjugation, whereas he stresses how the British political deceit has violated the intimate relationship between the two countries with the familial imagery and has led the colonists to rebel. Mazzei argues that France and Spain's non-intervention policy at the beginning of the conflict between England and the North American colonies has

---

[19] At the same time that Mazzei is promoting an egalitarian fluency, the process through which the individual can speak, which he describes in the essay, is one that leaves little freedom of choice and one that is directed and staged by the middleman. This view, however, is not at odds with Mazzei's perception of this figure in cosmopolitan terms. Traditionally, fictional cosmopolitan figures are often placed in a similar superior position, which enables them to obtain an overview and develop a thorough judgment of the cultural situation that they observe.

been a positive action. Contrary to the prevailing view, Mazzei explains these two powers' immediate intervention on the American side would not have helped the colonists' cause. In fact, the British would have immediately realized the danger of such an alliance and would have sought a peaceful reconciliation, which would have had the effect of forestalling the American Revolution:

> If those powers [France and Spain] had made the least movement, the British Ministry, as soon as they had received the second and last petition from the General Congress, would have become advocates for the colonies; they would iimmediately have called the Parliament, would have declared that things had been strangely misrepresented, and badly understood by both parties; and that modest Senate, at the first hint from their Master, and without any further examination, would undoubtedly have declared that this was even the case; terms of reconciliation would have been proposed, and you [Americans] would eagerly have embraced them, because the wounds were not as yet so deep as to have eradicated from your hearts that sympathetic affection which arose from a blind veneration for the land that gave birth to your ancestors, and was nourished by the similarity of customs, language, and religion, and by a continual and almost exclusive correspondence. (Mazzei 1983, 2: 120)

With his discussion of reconciliation, Mazzei introduces the images of misreading and misinterpreting that lay at the basis of his project for constructing a new identity for Americans. Once again, the process of interpretation becomes fundamental to the development of identity. The politics of deceptive reconciliation, to which Mazzei refers here, are not exactly political, they are rather rhetorical. In this scenario, the dishonest act with which the British would induce the colonists to trust them— interestingly represented as "exclusive" and therefore negative form of correspondence—would consist of a misrepresentation of the image Americans have of themselves and their relationship to England. As a result of this strategy, the British would have been able to reinstate their power and the colonists would have lost their chance to become an independent nation.

The reference to the ideas of representation and understanding as the tools with which England exercises its power over the colonies, and the implication that England itself has manufactured a representation of America, allows Mazzei to explain that the deceptive reconciliation would take place at the rhetorical level.[20] The English would willingly manipulate the American colonists by appealing to an idea of American identity that they have constructed in language. When Mazzei states "terms of reconciliation would have been proposed, and you [Americans] would eagerly have embraced them," his focus shifts from governmental politics to the politics of interpretation. Within this context, political acts depend on interpretive acts. When Mazzei argues that, besides the ties of blood and ancestry, the colonists have remained attached to England because of an intense and exclusive correspondence, he implies that national identification has two components: Americans have identified with England because of their descent; and England, corresponding with them, has established the cultural and political tie that allowed the colonial system to exist. Mazzei's next step is to produce a new cosmopolitan correspondence, which provides Americans with new terms of identification.

Both Mazzei's recourse to the metaphor of correspondence to describe the identification of the American colonists with England, and his recourse to the epistolary form to write his article reveal how he manipulates this expressive form to draw a new national model. The conceptual conjunction between the notion of literary correspondence and that of national identity is made formally possible by the genre Mazzei adopts to express it, which is itself based upon the combination of two separate categories. When used outside the private realm of personal correspondence, epistolarity conflates the private and the public (MacArthur 1990, 36–116). Mazzei resorts to the features of intimacy associated with the private letter to establish an emphatic correspondence with his reading public. His essay exploits the genre's features to create a literary document with which his audience can establish an intimate connection—indeed a connection of the same type England had nourished during colonial times. A document in the form of a letter creates an intimacy between its writer and reader that encourages the transmission of information to take place in a manner similar to the one produced by the use of the verb "nourished."

---

[20] Leonard Tennenhouse has provided one of the most thorough analyses of the discursive representations of the relationship between America and England. Tennenhouse sees the revolution and the birth of an independent identity as a mainly discursive process that had its roots in the century preceding the War of Independence (Tennenhouse 2007).

Mazzei's decision to write the article as a personal letter shows how he assumes, as writer and translator, a similarly nourishing role. In addition, he complicates and adds authority to this role by adding the cosmopolitan epithet of "Citizen of the World" and by pointing to the political identity Americans would acquire once separated from England. This type of self-representation makes of the cosmopolitan author a controlling and rational figure as well, who has the knowledge necessary to establish a correspondence between different texts and, at the same time, to generate new ones. Mazzei deployed this letter five years after its publication in an effort to convince the French foreign minister the Comte de Vergennes to promote financial support for impoverished Virginia. In the letter he wrote to Vergennes, Mazzei describes the history of the essay and illustrates the peculiar role he had assigned to himself:

> In the paper in question, I pretended I was answering an American and gave an idea of the state of affairs in America then, and of what I thought the House of Bourbon ought to do.
>
> When my friends learned that the first copy had fallen into enemy hands, they thought it advisable to have a translation published in the gazette, for they were convinced it would make a favorable impression on the people at a time when the opposition tried as hard as it could to fill them with prejudices.
>
> What I can assure Your Excellency is that I have very much at heart the honor and prosperity of France and America both by inclination and sense of duty; that I speak as I think; and that in matters concerning America and the character of Americans I feel better qualified to judge than the Americans themselves, for I see without spectacles and weigh on the scale of comparison, which is not likely to be the case, from what I have been able to observe, with someone who was born and lived almost all his life in America. (Mazzei 1983, 1: 290–291)

These extracts illustrate how Mazzei's sense of identity is determined by the textual space that contains it. What he describes as a posture for the article, however, is also the type of identity he assumes in this letter. In Fact, the "I" who addresses Americans and suggests that they take off their spectacles and look at what England has done to them from a different point of view makes of deception—manifested in his exploitation of the fictive role of "Citizen of the World"—the means by which

Americans can find themselves. With this new representation, Americans too will be able to see themselves "without spectacles" and weigh "their position on the scale of comparison" (Mazzei 1983, 1: 119). Like Mazzei, his readers will have assumed a cosmopolitan viewpoint and assumed the identity that best fits the context. Instead of arguing for a separation of the political and the personal realms that the British have merged with their "almost exclusive correspondence," Mazzei actually reproduced this exclusive correspondence in his essay. His use of the epistolary form and his establishment of a transatlantic context as the background for it perform the same function that the British use of sympathetic affection and correspondence had had in the past. The citizen of the world has become the prototypical American.

## 4  Postscriptum

When Mazzei returned to Virginia in 1784, after having attempted and failed to raise money from a number of supporters of the revolutionary cause in Tuscany, France, and the Low countries, he found himself in dire economic straits. Mazzei requested to be assigned a diplomatic position in Europe in hopes to mend his financial problems, but he faced an unforeseen obstacle. Congress, with the support of is closest political ally, Thomas Jefferson, was developing legislation that nullified the very foundation of Mazzei's Americanness: only natives of the North American territories could hold diplomatic positions. The country that was his by choice could not, in the end, be his country in the terms he had defined it. In October 1785, Mazzei candidly wrote to Jefferson: "After my return to Virginia, I realized better than I had ever done before that to be foreign-born and not wealthy tend to exclude one from offices reputed to be honorable and in which one as a zealous and active citizen can be useful to the country even if one is of modest ability" (Mazzei 1983, 1: 499). In Mazzei's words one recognizes the beginning of the exclusivist policies that characterized the establishment of nation-states' geopolitical borders. We also recognize the conflict that imagining national identity in terms of non-belonging and of the universalist ideal of cosmopolitanism generates (Smith 1996, 1–12). Mazzei's ability to construct his identity by performing it as an act of translation originated in his existence within and his understanding of the terms that the imperial culture that informed his views provided.

This very act of imagining an American subjectivity as originating in translation, however, is exactly what cannot be sustained in the America Mazzei himself helped found. As Mazzei wrote in a letter to John Adams dated September 27, 1785, he ultimately felt that "the bad effects of the imperfections existing in our Govt." would not affect him directly. His old age and the lack of any children made it possible for him not to worry about it, at least not enough to do anything other than voice his disappointment with some of his closest friends and correspondents. What worries Mazzei in 1785 is how such a policy dispossesses an American citizen of its most important character, its exemplarity for mankind. So Mazzei continues:

> but the honest part of the inhabitants of this Globe are my brethren, Posterity my children; & was I to go & spend the remainder of my days in China I would with pleasure, and in compliance with what I think my duty, contribute all my exertions to the forming of an asylum for Mankind from oppression (Mazzei 1983, 1: 44). The socio-political realities of the new American republic make it impossible for the type of citizen Mazzei describes in this passage to be an active civic participant and work from within the new national system in order to not only improve the one system but also to use it for the benefit of humankind. His cosmopolitan view of citizenship has failed to find an application and his representation of American citizenship in cosmopolitan terms can only remain a critical form of ideal.

REFERENCES

Bakhtin, M.M. 1990. *The Dialogic Imagination*, ed. Michael Holquist and trans. Caryl Emerson and Michael Holquist. Austin, TX: University of Texas Press.

Beccaria, Cesare. 1963. *On Crimes and Punishments*, trans. Henry Paolucci. New York: The Bobbs-Merrill Company.

Christensen, Jerome. 1987. *Practicing Enlightenment: Hume and the Formation of a Literary Career*. Madison, WI: The University of Wisconsin Press.

Crane, Verner W. 1950. *Benjamin Franklin's Letters to the Press, 1758–1775*. Chapel Hill, NC: The University of North Carolina Press.

D'Alembert, Jean Le Rond. 1963. *Preliminary Discourse to the Encyclopedia of Diderot*, trans. Richard N. Schwabs. New York: Bobbs-Merrill.

Dowling, William C. 1991. *The Epistolary Moment: the Poetics of the Eighteenth-Century Verse Epistle*. Princeton, NJ: Princeton University Press.

Gerbi, Antonello. 1973. *The Dispute over the New World*, trans. Jeremy Moyle. Pittsburgh, PA: University of Pittsburgh Press.
MacArthur, Elisabeth J. 1990. *Extravagant Narratives: Closure and Dynamics in the Epistolary Form*. Princeton, NJ: Princeton University Press.
Marchione, Marcherita. 1975. *Philip Mazzei: Jefferson's "Zealous Whig"*. Morristown, NJ: The American Institute of Italian Studies.
Marraro, Howard. 1942. *Memoirs of the Life and Peregrinations of the Florentine Philip Mazzei, 1730–1816*. New York: Columbia University Press.
Mazzei, Philip. 1976. *Researches on the United States*, trans. Constance D.Sherman. Charlottesville, VA: University of Virginia Press.
———. 1980. *Philip Mazzei: My Life and Wanderings*, ed. Margherita Marchione and trans. S. Eugene Scalia. Morristown, NJ: American Institute of Italian Studies.
———. 1983. *Philip Mazzei: Selected Writings and Correspondence*, vol. 3. Prato: Cassa di Risparmi e Depositi di Prato.
———. 2002. *The Spirit of the Laws*. New York: Prometheus Books.
Moore, Judith. 1994. *The Appearance of Truth: The Story of Elizabeth Canning and Eighteenth-Century Narrative*. Wilmington, DE: University of Delaware Press.
Schlereth, Thomas J. 1977. *The Cosmopolitan Ideal in Enlightenment Thought: Its Form and Function in the Ideas of Franklin, Hume, and Voltaire, 1694–1790*. Notre Dame, IN: University of Notre Dame Press.
Smith, Rogers M. 1996. *Civic Ideals: Conflicting Visions of Citizenship in U.S. History*. New Haven, CT: Yale University Press.
Smiths, Jeffery. 1988. *Printers and Press Freedom: The Ideology of Early American Journalism*. New York: Oxford University Press.
Steiner, George. 1998. *After Babel: Aspects of Language and Translation*, 3rd ed. New York: Oxford University Press.
Tennenhouse, Leonard. 2007. *The Importance of Feeling English: American Literature and the British Diaspora, 1750–1850*. Princeton, NJ: Princeton University Press.
Treherne, John. 1989. *The Canning Enigma*. London: Jonathan Cape Ltd.
Venuti, Lawrence. 2008. *The Translator Invisibility: A History of Translation*, 2nd ed. New York: Routledge.
Ziesche, Philipp. 2010. *Cosmopolitan Patriots: Americans in Paris in the Age of Revolution*. Charlottesville, VA: University of Virginia Press.

CHAPTER 6

# The Cosmopolitan Frame of Olaudah Equiano's *Interesting Narrative*

In the preceding chapters, I have shown how the relevance of the discourse of cosmopolitanism for North American authors depended on the socio-cultural conditions that the imperial structure established. The geographical removal of the colonial territories determined the marginality of the writers I have considered so far. Their socio-economic status, however, gave them a central place among the elites of the time. As an African and a slave, Olaudah Equiano's place in the imperial structure is marginal at both the social and the cultural level. As it was the case for the previous authors, the emergence of cosmopolitanism in his writings shows how it can be a tool of empowerment and a tool to counteract the same forces that allow for its existence. Olaudah Equiano's 1789 self-published book entitled *The Interesting Narrative of the Life of Olaudah Equiano, or Gustavus Vassa, the African, Written by Himself* identifies itself in autobiographical terms. The author—known as Gustavus Vassa while a slave and an ex-slave—adopts his (or the) native Igbo name, Olaudah, to tell the story of his abduction in Africa, his life as a seafaring slave, his manumission, his conversion to Methodism, and other adventures he experienced.[1] Throughout the narrative, the

---

[1] With the use of both the definitive article and the personal pronoun to refer to the Igbo name, I refer here to the recent debates over the veracity of Equiano's claim about his African birth. Question about Equiano's identity and about the reliability of his story have been raised since the publication of the book. If initially Equiano's writing as an exslave and a speaker for the abolitionist movement were behind the questions, in recent

first-person narrator follows the various stages of Equiano's life as it unfolds through the book. Literary critic Cathy Davidson has called the text both autobiographical and novelistic in nature.[2] According to

---

years, questions about identity and veracity were raised by Vincent Carretta's discovery of Equiano's baptismal certificate which claimed he was born in South Carolina (Carretta 2003). Given the loud debates that have taken place during the past few years regarding the authenticity of Equiano's account of the middle passage after Carretta's finding, I would like to say here that I take the same position that Cathy Davidson and Hazel Carby have recently taken (Burnard 2006; Carretta 2007a, b; Lovejoy 2006, 2007; Sensbach 2006; Bugg 2007; Ugwuanyi 2009). According to both scholars, the authenticity of that story is only relatively important (Davidson 2006, 8–51). Carby provides a useful frame for understanding the possibility that Equiano was indeed a native of South Carolina rather than a native African and for the need to understand what the purpose of an autobiographical narrative had for an individual who had been stripped of a legitimate way to claim self-ownership:

> Perhaps we will never know, for sure, on which side of the Atlantic Equiano was born but would the information definitively determine how the narrative is to be read? Even if he was born on the African continent is not Equiano still turning to "invention" to create an African identity? And, if he was born in the New World, cannot we also argue that Equiano is "reclaiming" an African identity? Should not our interpretation of the first chapters of *The Interesting Narrative* be asking what meaning is produced in these processes of invention *and* reclamation? ... I will argue that Equiano's 'detour through the past' enables him to produce himself anew, as a new kind of subject. (Carby 2009, 630)

Carby's argument reminds us of important factors that need to be considered in order to analyze autobiographical narratives in general and this one in particular. Where does the narrative subject of an autobiography coincide with that of its author? Davidson's reading is also along these lines. The scholar reminds us of the eighteenth-century literary convention of founding narratives in truth as a way to explain how the use of artifices is indeed the means writers used in order to provide readers with a truthful rendition of their personal stories. Davidson compares Equiano to contemporaries such as Swift and Rousseau and reminding us that the latter's use of artificiality was at a much higher level than we will ever find in *The Interesting Narrative*. To the comments of these two scholars, I would like to add that I am here considering the literary aspects of this text and I am only relatively interested in discussing the veracity of the facts Equiano refers to as I am to his ability to rhetorically manipulate the linguistic means he uses. And in this respect, I am therefore more interested in the way the rhetorical value of the expressions such as "founded on truth" had than in their factual veracity.

[2] Davidson describes the narrative's generic complexity as combining "(in unequal parts) slave narrative, sea yarn, military adventure, ethnographic reportage, historical fiction, travelogue, picaresque saga, sentimental novel, allegory, tall tale, pastoral origins myth, gothic romance, conversion tale, and abolitionist tract, with different features coming to the fore at different times, and the mood vacillating accordingly" (Davidson 2006, 10).

Davidson, the generic multiplicity and the consequent hybridity of *The Interesting Narrative* reflects Equiano's profound uncertainty about life. The instability manifested at the literary level is not, Davidson argues, the result of literary inability or indecisiveness. It is typical of the two literary genres that frame the narrative, the autobiography and the eighteenth-century novel. The text's literary instability is also the result of the precariousness of the slave's life it recounts. Precariousness maintains its presence even when manumission erases the word slave from the life Equiano lives and from the story he tells. As Davidson correctly points out, slavery's presence is indelibly written in Equiano's complexion and determined by the racist nature of the society in which he lived. Slavery is the central factor in *The Interesting Narrative* and affects all its thematic and rhetorical aspects. The complex interweaving of literary genres and themes central to the story of slavery Equianotells in *The Interesting Narrative* provides evidence for understanding how the narrative shows another aspect of cosmopolitanism in eighteenth-century culture and literature. Equiano's confidence and dexterity with contemporary literary genres and themes reflect an identity rooted in the cosmopolitan. Looking at *The Interesting Narrative* from this perspective does not simply reveal Equiano's cosmopolitanism, it reveals a cosmopolitanism in the context of slavery and the colonial world. It reveals the power the language of cosmopolitanism offered figures like Equiano.

Cosmopolitanism allowed Equiano to exceed the social and cultural limitations slavery imposed on him. Like the multiple and undecidable genres that make up the narrative, a text that cannot be rooted in a specific generic frame and yet contains them all, Equiano was a man whose home was the eighteenth-century world of colonial exchanges, of commerce, of intercultural contacts and dialogues. It was not a world he chose, unlike the other cosmopolitan writers considered here, but a home into which he was forced, and a home he made his own through complex processes of acculturation. To talk about Olaudah Equiano/Gustavus Vassa as a cosmopolitan, however, might seem redundant and obvious. His worldliness and nomadic life, his multilingualism and his multicultural education are just some of the features scholars have described as the markers of his cosmopolitan character. In fact, since Paul Gilroy's description of the black Atlantic in the cosmopolitan terms of a "desire to transcend both the structures of the nation state and the constraints of ethnicity and national particularity," most scholarship on Equiano points to these features in *The Interesting Narrative* (Gilroy

1993, 19; Gerzina 2001; Davidson 2006; Carby 2009; Lowe 2009). Equiano's cosmopolitanism is usually acknowledged, but the significance of his cosmopolitanism to his text is unstudied.[3]

As I have noted earlier, the generic multiplicity that characterizes the narrative is a formal reflection of Equiano's cosmopolitan resistance to rootedness and boundaries. The cosmopolitan model of subjectivity Equiano develops in the narrative most visibly manifests in the way in which the conventions of the genres he employs are transformed in order to allow the narrative subject to express himself outside the boundaries the audiences he speaks to impose on him (Aravamudan 2001). To understand how this transformation works in a more specific way and to see how Equiano manipulates the conventions of the captivity genre throughout the text it is worth paying attention to the book's first three chapters. As a story about slavery, *The Interesting Narrative* is necessarily a story of captivity; in fact, it is more appropriate to call it a story about captivities, about the captives who experience them, and about the way each of the stories Equiano tells us speak to each other. Equiano deploys the captivity narrative's generic features in a way that allows for many rhetorical and ideological inversions, which, in turn, frame the cosmopolitan representation of cultural formation and acculturation he develops in the text. Equiano experiences captivity at multiple levels and in multiple forms. African slave traders first hold him captive and then transport him from his home village to the coast of West Africa to sell him to European slave traders. Then, because of the sale, the captivity transforms itself into new forms of imprisonment without a definite end. This inscription of captivity stories into one another is aligned with Equiano's creation of a cosmopolitan narrative subject who refuses to maintain a fixed position figuratively and rhetorically, as well as geographically. Equiano rewrites himself according to a

---

[3] In describing Equiano as cosmopolitan I am taking a position that differs from that of post-colonial scholars such as Srivinas Aravamudan. Aravamudan describes figures like Equiano as "tropicopolitans" and opposes them to Enlightenment cosmopolitans because of their geographical position and, especially, because they challenge the privilege of contemporary cosmopolitans (Aravamudan 1999, 233–288). I call Equiano a cosmopolitan because I see his developing narrative identity as being generated using terms that belong to the rhetoric of Enlightenment cosmopolitanism. Rather than seeing the narrative subject as working to debunk the concept, I see the narrative reshape the concept itself within its rhetorical frame.

new set of standards by repositioning the subject and thus generating a rhetorical freedom.

## 1 Rewriting the Frame

The first captivity story *The Interesting Narrative* tells takes place between West Africa, Barbados, and Virginia, three geographical markers of the black Atlantic. This narrative includes abduction, removal, and deliverance, and it shares thematic and rhetorical features with both Anglo-American and Barbary captivity narratives. As Equiano relates this experience, he produces an ethnographic description of the African regions he passes through, mostly based on contemporary anti-slavery texts. Native African slave traders take Equiano captive and transport him to the coast to sell him to European traders. The cargo ship on which the white traders place Equiano takes him to Barbados, from where he is soon shipped to a plantation in Virginia. He does not remain in this first captivity for long as he is soon bought by the English Royal Navy lieutenant, Michael Henry Pascal, who is in the colonies not in his official military position, but as a merchant and trader. Equiano's first stage of slavery ends with a deliverance framed as a Christian redemption in line with the genre's conventions:

> I had been some time in this miserable, forlorn, and dejected state, without having no one to talk to, which made my life a burden when the kind and unknown hand of the Creator (who in very deed leads the blind in a way they know not) now began to appear, to my comfort; for one day the captain of a merchant ship, called the Industrious Bee, came on some business to my master's house. (Equiano 2003, 63)[4]

God's providential intervention into chattel slavery in Virginia or the West Indies—embodied in his owner-to-be—takes the shape of a

---

[4] I have chosen to follow Vincent Carretta's edition of Equiano's personal narrative because it is a reprint of the ninth and last edition published during his lifetime. With the changes and additions that Equiano included throughout the years and which Carretta has admirably noted throughout the text, it reflects the progress that the text followed and the development that certain ideas had for the writer throughout the years. Most importantly, it provides us with the reflection of some of the dialogic interactions Equiano had with his public and, consequently, with a certain amount of information about the history of the book that previous and later editions cannot provide.

relatively easier life of a seafaring slave.[5] What appears like an ending is a new beginning. Pascal, the man who purchases Equiano in Virginia, is presented as Equiano's providential savior, but his role is bound to change. Pascal will soon turn into the next captor when he refuses to accept Equiano's payment for his manumission and instead sells him again.

If Equiano's future is not bound to chattel slavery, the bondage that slavery places on him is impossible to be broken by manumission or escape, and the story of Equiano's captivity continues from stage to stage until he realizes the paradox of the concept of freedom for people of African descent when witnessing and experiencing abuse and discrimination in the West Indies where he travels and works. Then, he writes: "Hitherto I had thought only slavery dreadful; but the state of a free negro appeared to me now equally so at least, and in some respects even worse, for they live in constant alarm for their liberty, which is but nominal, for they are universally insulted and plundered without the possibility of redress" (Equiano 2003, 122). The rhetorical freedom Equiano achieves when he employs the terms of cosmopolitanism and rewrites the story of his life in those terms becomes the only effective means of escape, not only for himself as a black subject of the British Empire, but also for the potential readers who want to join him in the rewriting of a cultural frame.[6] Although separate from the larger captivity that is his life in the Atlantic world as both a slave and a free man, the captivity narratives overlap and merge with each other by means of the very story they are part of, that is, Equiano's *Interesting Narrative*.

Captivity in the story of Equiano's life in Africa, as a seafaring slave and as a free black man, is both physical and ideological and is at the center of the narrative as it is at the core of the literary genre to which

---

[5] Jeffrey Bolster in *Black Jacks* discusses extensively the way in which social hierarchies were working differently in seafaring life and how for black men, both slave and free, it was perhaps the least oppressive environment to be in. If for white sailors life at sea was extremely difficult compared to the opportunities they had working on land, the opposite was the case for black sailors (Bolster 1997, 68–101).

[6] In "An enslaved Enlightenment: rethinking the intellectual history of the French Atlantic," Laurent Dubois proposes that we develop a "more integrated intellectual history of the Enlightenment" that considers writers in positions like Equiano's as enabling conversations and proposing new perspectives from which to consider such a history and its making (Dubois 2006, 1–14).

it belongs. As scholarship on captivity narratives and on slave narratives has shown, the two genres are formally and historically interconnected. The popularity and market viability captivity narratives demonstrated throughout the seventeenth and eighteenth centuries were determining factors for the translation of one genre into the other.[7] The first published slave narrative in the North American colonies written by the slave/sailor Britton Hammond, for example, was published because it contained a captivity narrative and was marketed as such by the Boston publisher who printed it. Beginning in the seventeenth century, a number of factors made captivity narratives a popular genre. They replicated and confirmed early modern Protestant beliefs by showing how, through trial and faith, redemption could take place. They legitimized the representation of other groups as evil and savage, and thus allowed the colonial and British public to feel comfortable with the process of taking over lands inhabited by other peoples. They reinforced the opposition between an "us" that represented the good and positive of the civilized world and a "them" that embodied its opposite—savagery and danger—and, consequently, legitimated the violence that took place in the colonial context. Captivity narratives engaged with, and possibly calmed, fears of cultural and religious corruption. This is a common trait that both Anglo-American and Barbary captivity narratives share. They reinforced the opposition between Christianity and other religions, whether Islam or Native American, and confirmed Christianity's strength, righteousness, and legitimate superiority.

All of these elements filter into the narratives African slaves began to publish during the eighteenth century and into the genre that these texts constituted. Unlike the captivity narratives that British Barbary and Anglo-American captives wrote, formerly enslaved narrators also transformed the way they present the enslaved subject. As scholars have extensively shown, slaves or ex-slaves had to legitimize their authority for an audience that in general did not recognize it. This process, of

---

[7] For this overview of the generic interdependence I rely on John Sekora's essay "Red, White, and Black: Indian Captivities, Colonial Printers, and the Early African American Narrative" (Sekora 1993, 92–104). Although Sekora's essay focuses on early American captivity narrative, the recent work done by other scholars on early modern Barbary captivity narrative has provided similar evidence (Matar 1996, 1999; Burnham 1997; Snader, 2000; Vitkus 2001, 1–52; Baepler 2004, 217–246; Haslam and Wright 2005; Voigt, 2009).

course, was not necessary for those individuals of European descent who were held captives by Barbary Muslims or by Native Americans. William Andrews, among others, has argued that the presence of the white reader who can recognize the veracity of the story that the slave tells and thus legitimize it becomes essential to the existence of the slave narrator in the majority of earlier narratives. And it is often what is not said, the unasked questions, as well as an erasure of ethnic and cultural differences that reveals the culturally manipulated story the writer must tell in order to write and publish the account. The plots that often emerge in slave narratives thus are ones in which slavery itself is the path by which God's presence becomes tangible for the slave and therefore captivity is the needed trial, the *sine qua non* of the enlightenment that the unreligious soul needs (Andrews 1986, 32–33; Patterson 1982).

The intersection of the two genres is central to a text such as *The Interesting Narrative*. Equiano's story is one of conversion. It is a story spoken in a language manufactured by and for the abolitionists who were supporting Equiano ideologically and economically in his anti-slavery efforts at the time of the narrative's composition (Carretta 2005, 270–302). The narrative voice presents itself according to accepted standards from the text's very opening when Equiano introduces the ethnographic description of West African people, their cultures, and their country. The material discussed in the first chapter, which Equiano drew in large part from contemporary anti-slavery activists Anthony Benezet, James Field Stanfields, and other works on Guinea and the coast of Africa, is introduced following a formulaic address to the reader, with references to Equiano's low station, his humble social status, and a final appeal to the cause his story stands for, the damage slavery does to society and the need for its abolition (Boulukos 2007, 241–255). Then he begins the geographical description of Guinea. Equiano's account of his people's culture, traditions, and the region's landscape is built around the idea that Africans are the Biblical descendants of Ham and thereby linked to the Jews. Parallels between the Igbo people and the Jews repeatedly emerge to frame his general discussion of Igbo culture.

Equiano assumes a unique type of narrative position in the midst of the conventional beginning of the description of Essaka, the place to which Equiano refers as his native home country. After the authorial humbling and the expected reminder of the providential role in his experience in slavery, Equiano assumes the position of the cosmopolitan observer who does not tie himself to any place but is at home in every country:

> I was born, in the year 1745, in a charming fruitful vale, named Essaka. The distance of this province from the capital of Benin and the sea coast must be very considerable; for I had never heard of white men or Europeans, nor of the sea; and our subjection to the king of Benin was little more than nominal; for every transaction of the government, as far as my slender observation extended, was conducted by the chiefs or elders of the place. (Equiano 2003, 32)

At the same time Equiano introduces his childhood's perspective, he reveals his knowledge of sophisticated modes of political and social organization familiar to his European audience, thus presenting his retrospective analysis as coming from the perspective of the international and educated traveler. Later, he compares other socio-cultural customs. He describes the "spirit and variety" (Equiano 2003, 34) of the local dances and he footnotes his comment with a reference to the dances of Greek inspiration he has observed in the Turkish city of Smyrna. He draws a comparison between the way the natives wear their clothes and the way the Scottish highlanders wear their tartans. The local tobacco pipes are compared to "those in Turkey" (Equiano 2003, 35). As such an observer, Equiano claims ownership of this native place. At the same time, he also distances himself from it by designing a narrative voice that continually moves from within to without the narrative space. The result of this positioning is an observer who stands outside the narrative with his educated, abolitionist, and English-speaking audience but who is also simultaneously present within the story that he tells. The subject avoids any final positioning within one or the other with this strategy, yet he claims and shows the possibility of membership in both realms.

Equiano also makes sure the reader knows the local cuisine's plainness is of a type a British audience could appreciate: "Our manner of living is entirely plain; for as yet the natives are unacquainted with those refinements in cookery which debauch the taste; bullocks, goats, and poultry supply the greatest part of their food" (Equiano 2003, 35). The plain eating habits and foods of the Africans stands out against the French complex and corrupted ones in a comparison that reminds the reader of the commonly circulating stereotypes about the latter. The sophisticated tastes of the French and (assumed) refined eating habits translate into corrupted morals. This brief passage also shows how the narrative voice is in a continual motion grammatically and physically. The subject who tells the story fluctuates between identifying with one or the other side, observing and telling the story by going back and forth between identification and separation from the Native Africans.[8] The sentence that begins with "our manner of living" presents Equiano as a member of the community whose manners he describes, yet within the same sentence, the natives are also the subjects of observation, as he tells readers that "the natives are unacquainted" with French manners. Equiano leaves the groups intermittently to observe them from the outside, so that by the end of the sentence, food is "their" food rather than "ours." Throughout the descriptions of the African geographical and cultural landscape in the first chapter, the pronoun "us" to whom the voice refers is interchangeably an African community or the English-speaking audience. What might look like disengagement and superiority, however, produces an invitation to not look at white and black or Africa and Europe as opposing each other. Rather, Equiano's rhetorical strategies of movement invite his audience to reshape conflict to dialogue. The rhetorical and grammatical mobility finds a parallel in the spatial organization.

The spatial referents "here" and "there" are never immediately identifiable as Africa and England—or vice versa either. Right after having made himself present in the African cultural landscape he describes saying "we live in a country where nature is prodigal to her favours" (Equiano 2003, 36), Equiano switches position. He begins a sentence saying "I can speak from my own knowledge throughout our vicinity,"

---

[8] Susan M. Marren interprets the fluctuation of the subject in the narrative and its transgression as a sign of Equiano's attempt at liberating it from constraints that others would impose on it. However, Marren also argues, Equiano is ultimately unable, or unwilling, to separate the formation of such an independent self from the demands of the abolitionist cause he was writing for. Because of this inability what Equiano produces in the end is an idealized image of Africa and Africans by which the two are the reflection of what his abolitionist audience wants to see, namely a reflection of themselves rather than independent individuals or groups with a separate identity. My reading contends instead that Equiano invites, through the use of a number of different rhetorical strategies, that difference and its understanding be at the basis of a cultural transformation for his audience (Marren 1993, 94–105).

but he then describes the local practice of marking the passing of the year as follows: "The people at the same time make a great noise with rattles, not unlike the basket rattles used by children here" (Equiano 2003, 41). By the end of the sentence it is evident the voice has relocated itself in another place and "here" is not in the African country he has been describing, but where his contemporary non-African audience sits. Equiano's ability to assume different positions allows him to be both the subject who observes and the subject who is observed, not only when he speaks as the child and the younger man whose story he tells, but also as the narrator. As the narrative proceeds, this strategy, by which the narrating subject can move from place to place and from group identification to group identification, produces a reversal of the rhetorical frame, which defines the concept of subjectivity itself. Scholars have linked this continual repositioning of the narrative voice, as well as the split between the Equiano whose story is narrated and the one who narrates it, to a number of different issues such as Equiano's engagement with questions of identification either as an African or as a Briton, with questions about the ways in which *The Interesting Narrative* engages the dichotomies of black and white, freedom and slavery, etc., and questions about the self in terms of eighteenth-century liberal thought, economic theories, and the language of sentiment.[9]

These reversals compel the reader to loosen their interpretive standards in order to replace them with a more open-minded and universalizing sense of humankind and its nature. In continually displacing the narrative voice, Equiano's roots, rather than in the land he portrays in the first chapter of *The Interesting Narrative*, exist outside and in

---

[9] See, for example, the already quoted reading of the narrative by Susan Marren discussed in note 8. In addition Philip Gould, among others, discusses Equiano's double positioning in the context of an analysis of how early black autobiographies engaged in a literary performance of stories that speak to each other, at times contradictorily. Black writers, who were in most cases writing collaboratively and speaking to multiple audiences simultaneously, were also finding a way to manipulate rhetoric and syntax in order to claim a realm in which they could identify themselves. Gould discusses how Equiano, in speaking to two audiences simultaneously, negotiates between the discourses of commerce and abolitionism, of freedom and slavery, and of agency and subjugation (Gould 2003, 136–137). Vincent Carretta has also highlighted how Equiano constructs his narrative persona in a way that is both identifying with and distancing from the audience. Carretta suggests that Equiano employs more than one identity as a process of reclaiming a social status that slavery had taken away from him (Carretta 2000, 389).

between places, between the Africa he says he comes from, the England where he resides, and the ships where most of the stories he tells take place.[10] In so doing he frees the captive subject from the required generic alignment with one of the two cultures. In presenting himself as such a cosmopolitan individual, he asks his audience to participate with him in the movements the narrative voice performs and, consequently, to see things from multiple perspectives.

## 2  Rewriting Captivity in Cosmopolitan Terms

The narrative strategy Equiano developed in the book's first chapter when introducing the ethnographic description of the Igbo country serves as a frame for understanding the story of Equiano's abduction and first captivity with African kidnappers. Generic features of the captivity narrative take central stage here, as does Equiano's engagement with the terms of cosmopolitanism. The chapter starts with a reflection on the previous one and its significance:

> I hope the reader will not think I have trespassed on his patience in introducing myself to him with some account of the manners and customs of my country. They had been implanted in me with great care, and made an impression on my mind, which time could not erase, and which all the adversity and variety of fortune I have since experienced served only to rivet and record: for, whether the love of one's country be real or imaginary, or a lesson of reason, or an instinct of nature, I still look back with

---

[10]Historian Ira Berlin has named individuals like Equiano "Atlantic creoles." With these terms Berlin designates those people who began their life experience in the "netherworld" between Africa, Europe, and the Americas. These individuals, "by their experiences and sometimes by their persons, had become part of the three worlds that came together along the Atlantic littoral. Familiar with the commerce of the Atlantic, fluent in its new languages, and intimate with its trade and cultures, they were cosmopolitan in the fullest sense." Although Berlin refers to an earlier generation of individuals who traveled around the Atlantic world during the seventeenth century, Equiano's life experience and his socio-cultural position is that of the creole that he has described. Berlin, however, claims that with the eighteenth century and the establishment in the English colonial world of a slave society—that is a society in which slavery shaped every relationship—Atlantic creoles became much less prominent figures in the Atlantic world. He notices, however, that such figures did maintain some presence as "interpreters, sailors and *grumetes* on the very ships that transported them to the New World" (Berlin 1996, 254, 283; Berlin 1998; Bolster 1997, 7–43).

pleasure on the first scenes of my life, though that pleasure has been for the most part mingled with sorrow. (Equiano 2003, 46)

This conventional apology introduces the account of Equiano's abduction, his travels to the African coast, the Atlantic passage and his final arrival in Barbados where he is prepared to be sold as a slave. Equiano's opening words remind the reader that the link to one's native country depends on a learning process that begins early in life. At a young age, an understanding of cultural traits is "implanted" in an individual with "great care," Equiano tells his readers. About the nature of this educational process's outcomes Equiano does not seem to be as sure. As he says in the second part of the passage, the love of one's country can have a number of origins and they can be "real or imaginary, or a lesson of reason, or an instinct of nature" (Equiano 2003, 46). The list suggests such an origin is not the point here. Equiano's patriotism depends on the act of remembering and the pleasure it can produce, not wanting to select any of the other categories as the determinant factor in the production of patriotic feeling. This passage on the role of one's patriotic feeling in the perception of one's cultural and geographical origins introduces the story of the physical captivity the young Equiano experiences before being transported to England. One of the most pressing issues Equiano's comments raise is the possibility of developing or maintaining a tie and a connection to one's native country after a traumatic uprooting like the one he experienced. In order to provide an answer to this question, in the following chapter, Equiano provides a different representation of national identity based on a new set of rhetorical terms.

In this discussion of the feelings for one's place of origin and the authority to speak about them, what strikes the reader is the intent on the part of the "I" who speaks these words to stress the separation between the category of patriotism and that of geographical belonging. The words that begin Equiano's second chapter define geographically (as a native of the African region he has previously described) and socially by claiming his allegiance to the place. Yet, he also dismantles the meaning of patriotism and the loyalties the love for one's country should or could inspire by presenting four different possibilities for its origin and then refusing to link any of them to the geographical roots he claims. Equiano links patriotism and place by an act of reconstruction and the pleasure it procures: "whether the love of one's country be real or imaginary, or a lesson of reason, or an instinct of nature, I still look back with pleasure" to those past events and to the feelings they produced. Equiano invokes pleasure that is both authentic and figurative. In the rhetorical space of *The Interesting Narrative*, loyalty to one's country is defined by the disruption of the roots to which the idea of country attaches itself, which also includes the revision of what home country means to individuals, and its subsequent reconstruction in the space of *The Interesting Narrative*. These opening words about his abduction from his home in Africa provide the reader with a sense of the constructed character of notions of cultural identity and of their instability. What is African, or English, or European, or colonial becomes the product of contingency and is affected by the disruptive power the life of an enslaved colonial subject experiences. As the opening words to a story of captivity, these words are particularly significant.

Scholars of captivity narratives agree that behind the popularity of the genre, which started as early as the late sixteenth century for both Anglo-American and Barbary captivities, was the role they played in solidifying individual, as well as group or national sovereignty. These solidifying notions of early captivity narratives played a role in the way scholarship developed. Scholars tend to consider captivity narratives as part of the discourse of nation formation and consequently, have neglected considering captivity narratives written from a perspective opposite to that of the "usual" captives, namely European men or women. Narratives by Native Americans held captive by European settlers, or those written from the perspective of "renegades" who had started out as European and eventually integrated into the capturing culture have only recently become part of the conversation (Sayre 2010). Recently, scholars have discussed how the field is reshaping its scope by thinking about the place and meaning of such narratives (Sayre 2010). The first three chapters of Equiano's *Interesting Narrative*, for example, were the choice selection in a collection of captivity narratives edited in the early 1990s (Sayre 2000). In the introduction to the extract from Equiano's work, the editor places Equiano's representation of captivity within the traditional frame and considers it a typical Anglo-American captivity even if captive's and captor's positions are inverted: the European slave traders embody the traditional cultural "other" and are the captors while the slave-to-be Equiano is the captive. In the end, the editor argues, *The Interesting Narrative*'s subject fits "the more common type of the transcultured captive, for [Equiano] assimilated the religious and mercantile beliefs of his captors" (Sayre 2000, 201). The comment refers to Equiano's experience as a sailor and his contribution to the slave trade while working on a cargo ship that Equiano recounts later in the book and thus correctly points to an important aspect of *The Interesting Narrative*. Such an argument, however, disregards the role played by inversions such as the one I have noted in the way in which Equiano introduces the story of his captivity at the beginning of the book.

Equiano's manipulation of the narrative subject's position in the opening chapter of his book calls for a different understanding of his experience that includes the indictment of all parties involved: his compatriots who are the original kidnappers, the European traders, his own eventual involvement in the slave trade, and the European public who witness the abuses and remain silent. As the transculturation process takes place, Equiano's identity never becomes completely national or identifiable with one specific group, and *The Interesting Narrative*'s narrator remains fundamentally trans-cultural rather than simply national—a quality that enables him to be powerfully critical. Equiano writes with an accent and his position within the culture never become one of complete assimilation (Giunta 2002, 2).[11] When talking about his own Englishness, Equiano uses the adverb "almost" (Equiano 2003, 77). His membership in the cultural and social world of the British Empire is always going to be marked by marginality. Because of the insecurity any form of identification marked by difference generates, Equiano finds new ways to define identification itself (Edwards 1969, V–LXXII).[12]

The various names and qualifiers listed in the title page—*The Interesting Narrative of the Life of Olaudah Equiano, or Gustavus Vassa, the African, Written by Himself*—mark the multiplicity of identities the

---

[11] I borrow the concept of writing with an accent from Edvige Giunta's work. Giunta has described the concept as follows: "I use the word 'accent' to refer to a series of elements—narrative thematic, linguistic—that, collectively, articulate the experience of living between cultures. Such an experience and the modes of its expression vary according to the chronological proximity of one's generation to the departure from the country of origin, the relationship between one's culture of descent and the culture of ascent … as well as one's sense of allegiance to and/or disconnection from one's ethnic community, and other biographical, geographical, social, and cultural factors."

[12] Paul Edwards has in fact shown the actual visibility of such accent and the difference it brings to the material reality of one's life when he discussed how some of Equiano's misspellings in a number of his manuscript writing are signs of West African English speech and reveal the modifications that happen when a non-native speaker internalizes a foreign language.

writer has chosen or, as it is also the case, that someone else has imposed on him. The name, Gustavus Vassa, is the name by which the Western world has recognized him as a slave, a free man, a sailor, and an abolitionist. It is the result of a choice, but not the choice of the subject of *The Interesting Narrative*. Olaudah Equiano is the name that precedes Vassa spatially on the front page and temporally in the story. It is the name that links the author of the narrative to the origins the first chapter describes (Carretta 2000, 386; Jaros 2013, 1–23).[13] The fluidity among the various names with which Equiano chooses to identify and the fluidity in the definition of patriotism he gives in the passage opening the second chapter represent what I identify as Equiano's contribution to the construction of an eighteenth-century cosmopolitan subjectivity and his rewriting of a captivity narrative in the language of cosmopolitanism.[14] This cosmopolitan subject—a subject who is at home in many places and whose allegiances are relative and contingent—has been violently (either physically or figuratively) uprooted and yet chooses to make the world his own place. To do so, however, Equiano prepares the ground to disrupt the perceived interpretive patterns readers use to understand his story. The subject of this narrative is made homeless by someone else's choice via the brutal act of kidnapping and the similarly brutal acts of stripping him of his name and of the figurative link to the land of his birth. With the story he tells in the first chapters of his book, Equiano reconstructs a memory of a place of which he does now chose to be a part and of which he is also an educated observer. The Equiano who tells this story is the cosmopolitan intellectual whose allegiances are to the world and for whom "the interest of humanity" (Equiano 2003, 32), as he says at the end of *The Interesting Narrative*'s first chapter, is paramount. Yet, the trajectory by which he has arrived at this subject position is different from the trajectories cosmopolitans like Benjamin Franklin

---

[13] Carretta has summarized most of the scholarship over the role of Equiano's binomial identity. Carretta argues that Equiano claims an African identity, which he places over his acquired British one because of the political valence it brought him within the abolitionist movement and the ultimate economic importance it also carried for him. Peter Jaros has recently provided an interesting reading of the rhetorical and historical significance of Equiano's choice to use both his names in the title of this personal narrative.

[14] Critics seem to have unanimously agreed on addressing the author of *The Interesting Narrative* as Olaudah Equiano. I will follow this general trend when I refer to both the author and the narrative voice.

followed.[15] The reference to sorrow at the end of the passage—"I still look back with pleasure on the first scenes of my life, though that pleasure has been for the most part mingled with sorrow"—is a reminder of this fundamental difference and of the rational choice Equiano made to return and re-create a public memory of his life. As it was the case for the educational process that Equiano describes in the second sentence of the passage, when he says his memories "had been implanted in me with great care, and made an impression on my mind, which time could not erase," so the reader of *The Interesting Narrative* will be "implanted" (46) with the knowledge necessary to develop a similar worldview to that of the "citizen of the world" that Equiano portrays in this text as the subject of the captivity narrative it recounts. Equiano asks the reader to interpret his story not as a slave, an abolitionist, or a slave owner, but as a citizen of the world.[16]

### 3 Captivities

As the first chapter ends, at the center of the story is not the culture of the African people Equiano has observed so far, but the abduction of a young Equiano and his subsequent journey into slavery. Equiano

---

[15] As scholarship on Equiano's work has increased in the last decades, its cosmopolitanism has also been noticed. Literary scholar Lisa Lowe has recently described him as "a liberal cosmopolitan subject of globalization, a world citizen more at home at sea than residing in a particular nation" (Lowe 2009, 107). Historian Jeffrey Bolster lists Equiano among those black seafaring autobiographers who "did not root their personal narratives in American or European locales," but rather, as one of those "citizens of the world ... [who] were detached from place in a way that the authors of many later slave narratives were not, and in ways that few whites wished to be" (Bolster 1997, 37). With a reference to Bolster's interpretation of African sailors' attitudes, Gretchen Gerzina talks about Equiano using the same terms (Gerzina 2001, 48). Vincent Carretta observes how assuming one or multiple writing personas allows authors like Equiano and Ignatius Sancho to become "citizens[s] of the world, as it were" (Carretta 1998, 80). It is because of this apparent connection, yet explored only in historiographical analyses that link the life experience to the notion of cosmopolitanism such as Bolster's, between Equiano's text and his career and the discourse of cosmopolitanism and its tropes that I want to pursue the analysis of what it means to call him a cosmopolitan.

[16] In this respect, my reading of Equiano's narrative as a cosmopolitan reversal of the tropes that define patriotism and national identity and which aims at educating the reader about alternative worlds within their world parallels that of Cathy Davidson's who sees the *Narrative* as "a profound novelistic conversion narrative whose main objective is the conversion of the reader, not simply the description of the conversion of the author" (Davidson 2006, 43).

recounts his abduction, travels to the coast, the encounter with the slave ship the middle passage, and, finally, his first experience with the American slave market in the body of the second chapter, which replicates some of the movements of the opening section. In the ethnographic description of the Igbo people that opens the narrative, readers followed a narrator who was simultaneously inside and outside the story and observed from various perspectives. In this second section, Equiano's narrator is, again, in and out of the story he tells. He is the small child who observes unfamiliar things and cultures and he is the adult who interprets what his young self has observed from a cosmopolitan perspective. In the process, Equiano inverts the tropes familiar to his audience and distorts the picture he presents of the Europeans who are about to buy the young Equiano from his African traders and take him to the American colonies. As he describes his physical traveling to the coast, Equiano develops a transgressive narrative structure. The comparisons he draws during the first part of this account show his readers the similarities between his culture of origins and the ones he encounters after he has been kidnapped and taken from place to place while owned by different families. This process happens slowly and even by the time readers observe the inversion, it is obvious that none of the original pictures have remained. It is not only the white/black and African/European dichotomies that we see inverted but also distortions of both in the picture that represents Equiano's entrance into the captivity of slavery. The inability of the various groups to communicate and understand each other is bound to become the central issue at stake in this story of captivity.

As he tells how the African kidnappers took him, the youngest of many sons, and his only sister from their home, transported them and sold them to various African slaveholders, Equiano continues in his role of ethnographer. He describes places and people and reminds the reader of the parallels between African ways of working and living and that of his English-speaking audience. Equiano is still the cultured observer here. From the position he has acquired as citizen of the world, he is able to provide a balanced, yet analytical picture of different cultures in order to give his audience a view of all sides. When he describes the activities at his first owner's business, a blacksmith, he discusses the way the African blacksmith worked by claiming the similarities between his practices and those which are familiar to his audience: "The [stoves] were in some respects not unlike the stoves here in gentlemen's kitchens; and were covered over with leather; and in the middle of the leather a stick was fixed, and a person stood up, and worked it, in the same manner as it is done to pump water out of a cask with a hand-pump" (Equiano 2003, 48). As the narration continues, however, similarities and comparisons are progressively used in a different way.

Rather than being used as a means of comparison that produces familiarity and a positive reflection, European manners progressively become representative of the strange and the unusual. As the child progresses in his travels, he finds himself surrounded by people he recognizes less and less as they acquire more and more European traits. The "manners, customs and language" (Equiano 2003, 53), which had been similar and shareable among people until then, become less recognizable. The referents to the pronouns "we" and "they" become harder to identify and require the reader to search for new grounds of comparison:

> I was very much struck with this difference [in the natives he encounters as he moves toward the coast], especially when I came among a people who did not circumcise, and eat without washing their hands. They cooked also in iron pots, and had European cutlasses and cross bows, which were unknown to us, and fought with their fists among themselves. Their women were not so modest as ours, for they ate, and drank, and slept with their men. But above all I was amazed to see no sacrifices or offerings among them. In some of those places the people ornamented themselves with scars, and likewise filed their teeth very sharp. (Equiano 2003, 53–54)

It is easy to recognize in this passage Equiano's effort to draw a parallel between his African people and the Biblical Jews he continually employs throughout this part of the text. His effort to appeal to the abolitionist audience for which he writes is evident in the suggestion of a possible link between the coastal Africans' moral corruption and their adoption of European customs.[17] I would also like to suggest that the visual blurring of the traits that belong to the two groups in this descriptive passage is a further step in an effort to distort the clarity of the images Equiano describes and to provide a new picture that confuses parallels and

---

[17] Vincent Carretta reminds us in one of his editorial notes to the text of *The Interesting Narrative*'s ninth edition that Equiano's depiction of the coastal African as having been negatively influenced by their contact with the Europeans may be rooted in a common contemporary antislavery movement's claim that the encounter with the Europeans had made native Africans morally corrupted (Equiano 2003, 249).

connections between the cultures of those who Equiano and his audience observe and those observing them.

As Equiano describes this new encounter, in fact, the natives morph into a mixed type, which is Europeanized and given monstrous features—features that suggest a cannibalistic tendency anticipating what Equiano will describe by the end of the chapter as his childhood vision of the European slave traders and their actions on the ship that will take him to colonial America. The European utensils they use and the sharply filed teeth these people show make otherwise faceless and irrelevant figures who appear in the middle of his journey to the coast stand out to the reader and preview what will happen later in the chapter. These monstrous figures are caught in between worlds and in between the tropes Equiano uses to identify those worlds.[18] These figures use European artifacts, speak a language that is marked by difference, live promiscuously, and act aggressively to make others become like them: "They wanted sometimes to ornament me in that manner, but I would not suffer them" (Equiano 2003, 54), Equiano tells his readers. The ambiguity of this moment is reminiscent of a common feature of captivity narratives, especially the Barbary ones, in which the prisoner is either forced or tempted to "turn Turk" and embrace the others' religion.[19] The immediate message his comment sends is of course in dialogue with the Christian conversion narrative the book is telling, but it is also contributing to the ambiguity of positions the entire section produces.

---

[18] The hybridization of the coastal people and the corruption of their group's manners and morals are also reminiscent of the representation that Crèvecoeur's gives of the frontier men in revolutionary North America in *Letters from an American Farmer*. The images here seem to be inverted whereas in Equiano's narrative it is the technologically advanced European materials that are taken as symbols of the moral disarray of the coastal Africans, in Crèvecoeur's text the contact with the savage environment of the frontier is at the root of the cultural and moral chaos that he describes.

[19] Nabil Matar discusses the threat that British captives faced and wrote about when kidnapped by Muslim privateers in North Africa and forced to wear clothes and eat food that was different from what represented their national identity: "Nothing revealed conversion and transculturation more than the change in dress. ... Forced to wear the clothes of the Moors, captives were separated from their national heritage, which in the early modern period was frequently based less on ideals or symbols than on tangible markers" (Matar 2001, 36). Equiano's refusal here shows how he applies the same rules. He is refusing to get marked by the scars that would be showing on his forehead as a sign of his conversion to the customs of the semi-cannibalistic people he met in the middle place.

Equiano describes what could be called an indelible marker of difference an "ornament," and thus difference, fear, the grotesque and the rationally incomprehensible come to the fore in the rest of the chapter when Equiano encounters his "other," the European slave traders.

Equiano's journey changes form here; he now travels "sometimes by land, sometimes by water, through different countries, and various nations, till, at the end of six or seven months after I had been kidnapped, I arrived at the sea coast" (Equiano 2003, 54). As readers are reminded of the captivity state of the subject, their attention is also abruptly taken away from the land and its native inhabitants and the object that will determine the course of Equiano's life, the slave ship takes center stage: "The first object which saluted my eyes, when I arrived on the coast was the sea," he writes, "and a slave-ship, which was then riding at anchor, and waiting for its cargo" (Equiano 2003, 55). The sea and the ship will define the terms of his life. Equiano joins the two worlds of slavery and of seafaring at the same time. Both mark his perception of the world around him and both contribute to the cosmopolitanism he represents and constructs. Being both a cosmopolitan and an ex-slave enables Equiano to perform a criticism of slavery that is much more critical than the ones his abolitionist supporters provided for him.

The section of the second chapter that follows describes the middle passage. It is perhaps the most quoted part of *The Interesting Narrative* and one that portrays the suffering and despair men and women experienced in gruesome detail. The scene that opens this part of the chapter continues the inversion of the dichotomies and oppositions with which Equiano's European readership was familiar and which had begun in the previous pages with the representation of the group of natives whose manners had been affected by the contact with the Europeans:

> When I was carried on board I was immediately handled, and tossed up, to see if I were sound, by some of the crew; and I was now persuaded that I had gotten into a world of bad spirits, and that they were going to kill me. Their complexions too differing so much from ours, their long hair, and the language they spoke, which was very different from any I had ever heard, united to confirm me in this belief. ... When I looked around the ship too, and saw a large furnace of copper boiling, and a multitude of black people of every description chained together, every one of their countenances expressing dejection and sorrow, I no longer doubted of my fate, and, quite overpowered with horror and anguish, I fell motionless on the deck and fainted. (Equiano 2003, 55)

The description of the whiteness, the long hair, and the strange language spoken by the European men who are on and around the slave ship is reminiscent of the men with the sharply filed teeth observed earlier. The horror the boy experiences once he observes the scene around him is highlighted by his inability to understand both the words and the actions of those around him. And the linguistic incomprehension foreshadows the central role linguistic fluency acquires in the following chapters when Equiano describes his acculturation in the English-speaking world of colonial America and England.

When the reader is introduced to the image of the deck, different tropes overlap. The savage and the civilized, the strange and the familiar, the safe and the dangerous slide over one another and reflections turn into distortions. Equiano's description of how his first encounter with the white men makes him faint—a scene that presents the overlapping of the tropes of eighteenth-century sensibility and the natural reaction to a frightening sight—shows how there is no possibility for change. When Equiano wakes up from his fainting spell, the glass of liquor he is offered as a means to calm him down causes him more panic.[20] The "spirituous liquor," in fact, throws Equiano "into the greatest consternation at the strange feeling it produced, having never tasted any such liquor before" (Equiano 2003, 56). And what comes afterwards sounds as if Equiano wanted the rest of the picture to be an alcohol-induced hallucination rather than a reality. In fact, drinking the spirituous liquor seems to produce a heightened picture of another type of spirit, the ghost-like slave traders on the ship, whom the young Equiano thinks are cannibals, and the horrifying job they perform.

The image that follows the drink blends together the surreal and the real. The representation of what happens on board the slave ship is realistic and each of its details, which are made more visible by the enhanced use of verbs of vision such as "to see" and "to watch," directs the reader's attention toward the insanity of what takes place on it. Within a short section, such expressions appear ten times. As Equiano describes what he sees on the deck and in the belly of the ship, what readers are

---

[20] Cathy Davidson considers these scenes as pertaining to a pattern of recurring catastrophes that continually befall Equiano and that ultimately reflect a central trope of "trauma and uncertainty" that characterizes *The Interesting Narrative* and that is linked to its pedagogical purpose to convince his readers of the validity of his argument against slavery (Davidson 2006, 20–22).

shown possesses all the traits of the extraordinary, of a reality that should not be real. The verbs related to vision produce an image as intense as it is horrifying: the description that introduces the reader to the living conditions of the people on the cargo ship when they start the last leg of their journey toward slavery. Although verbs of vision were frequent from the beginning of *The Interesting Narrative* because of the narrative voice's position of observer, Equiano's intensified usage in the section describes the beginning of the transatlantic passage and makes evident the reversal process he has started at the beginning of this section of the book to make the reader more responsive toward what is to come. What the reader sees is not a simple reversal of the opposition between Africans and Europeans, between whites and blacks. Instead, what is observed is a dark and almost comedic (if it was not for the topic it treats) encounter between a group of Europeans stepping on board from another ship anchored nearby and the Africans who are already on board the slave ship—an encounter that does not simply speak of good versus bad, but that speaks of ignorance and incomprehension caused by the inability to understand each other at a linguistic, an ideological, and a human-to-human level. The African captives, who are about to enter the living hell that is the belly of the cargo ship that will take them to the American colonies, face the white men who greet them as follows: "Several of the strangers also shook hands with us black people, and made motions with their hands, signifying, I suppose, we were to go to their country; but we did not understand them" (Equiano 2003, 57–58). Equiano's retrospective assessment of the scene and his almost ironic interpretive comment, "I suppose", bring further confusion, the present questioning of the past does not bring any answer except for reinstating the lack of understanding and the perverse irony of such an act. The narrative voice that emerges does not place itself in any specific here or there, he is not among any of the groups who participate in the scene. Here Equiano does not embody the cosmopolitan observer who is able to provide an exhaustive interpretation because of his supra-partisan status either. Rather, this narrative voice acts as a spectator and the role of interpreter is left to the reader who is now asked to perform this task on his or her own. It is this particular strategy, though, that I would like to suggest as the means by which Equiano deploys a cosmopolitan attitude and creates a unique type of cosmopolitan subjectivity. Equiano can be this particular kind of cosmopolitan, not because he has embraced the role of citizen of the world, but because he has been pushed into the world by his condition. He can be a cosmopolitan subject because he is a slave. His cosmopolitanism is produced by his homelessness and exercised through the social status (or lack of it) that slavery gives him and that allows him to reimagine the notion of inclusiveness. The narrator of *The Interesting Narrative* is asking readers to share and imagine this new notion with him and to use it in order to assess the state of their own culture.

The voice that the "I" brings into the picture is one that comes from the margins. The reader is placed at the geographical margins of the African landscape, at the margins of European transatlantic culture, and the actors in the scene are all marginal as well. The voice who speaks at this moment performs what Walter Mignolo has called "critical cosmopolitanism."[21] This cosmopolitan attitude allows for participation in a conversation that would otherwise exclude Equiano as a subject who can effectively produce actions. The communication takes place by invoking a form of silence that the incomprehension between the parties involved in the exchange has produced, and the silence that the differences in the languages spoken by each group have enhanced. But silence here speaks for Equiano and speaks to the audience whose culture is trying to silence voices like his. The "I" that tells the reader what happened retrospectively resituate the exchange between the newly enslaved Africans and the white men. The reader can then comprehend not only the immediate misunderstanding between Europeans and Africans, but also see the profound indictment of the culture that generates this misunderstanding—a culture that does not live up to the standards it professes.

The voice who speaks through the silence, or the cacophony, and through the foreignness of the handshake, is embodied in the Equiano who comments on the scene four decades later. This voice does not call for an inclusion of the black people on the ship in the culture that the white sailors represent. It is by refusing to provide a definitive reading

---

[21] Mignolo uses the expression in order to describe the way in which excluded voices can bring themselves into a conversation, not because they want to be included in it, but because they want to transform it. Mignolo describes the means by which outsiders like Equiano achieve such a goal as "border thinking," which the scholar defines as a transformative act that allows for participation in a cultural system that would otherwise provide no agency for the speaker. "The alternative to separatism," Mignolo argues, "is border thinking, the recognition and transformation of the hegemonic imaginary from the perspective of people in subaltern positions. Border thinking then becomes a 'tool' of the project of critical cosmopolitanism" (Mignolo 2002, 174).

of the exchange that took place on the deck that the cosmopolitan narrator intervenes and produces a powerful meta-commentary. Equiano refuses to use a voice to direct interpretation here; he insists on remaining semi-silent by limiting his commentary to "I suppose." Thus, he forces the reader to take his place. The judgment this narrator provides comes from what he refuses to explain and in the lesson he nudges the reader to interpret. He directs the reader to understand what is wrong in the exchange that takes place and in the cultural frame that is behind it. The cultural presupposition, implicit in the reason for the traders' words and gestures assumes one group's culture (the Europeans') is superior to another (the Africans') and is what the reader should change. Unlike the spokesperson for the abolitionist movement, the Equiano who speaks at this moment is disengaged from all groups, and his disengagement marks him as a true cosmopolitan. Simultaneously, Equiano guides the reader through the learning process needed to become such an observer. In this moment, the narrative voice's interjection not only reminds the reader of the cruelty represented in the picture, which is the foremost message of *The Interesting Narrative* as a participating party in the abolitionist discourse, but it also provides a meta-commentary on the lack of a rational basis for the enterprise of exercising commerce in human lives and on the contradictory nature of the culture that promotes it. The cosmopolitan observer who speaks as Olaudah Equiano, the well-traveled and well-educated ex-slave, reveals the arrogance in the indifference to the fact that no factual communication takes place not at the time of his kidnapping and not at the time of recounting that moment in the memoir. This is how the narrator points out the true lack of voice of people like himself. The marginalized cosmopolitan becomes articulate by speaking through the narrative cracks.

Along with more verbs related to vision that make the contrasts and contradictions stand out in the scene analyzed earlier, the number of Biblical references also increases. Equiano links his cosmopolitanism to his investment in Christian theology through this second set of references, and he generates another series of contrasts and contradictions. Equiano also invokes Christian symbolism and integrates it into his representation of a mutilated and failed cultural interaction in the exchange between the slaves and their white captors. The white slavers' ignorance of—or, their intentional neglect to consider—the most basic elements of Christianity in both this episode and those that take place on board the cargo ship as it sails toward Barbados are highlighted by the rhetorical irony and the meta-commentary the short remark of the narrative voice produces when Equiano says "I suppose" at the beginning of the section recounting the transatlantic passage. The handshake the whites exchange with the slaves on board the cargo ship reminds readers of another moment of deception, the interaction between Jesus and Judas. The white men's friendly action, like Judas' kissing of Jesus, is a preamble to betrayal. In this case, the betrayal is not only of the individuals whose hands they are shaking as the enslaved black men do not understand the language and the symbols attached to the handshake itself. The handshake reflects the sailors' betrayal of their own cultural and religious foundations and of those held by the audience of *The Interesting Narrative*, thus further stressing the hypocrisy of the act. This citizen of the world—who is Christian, educated, knowledgeable, and devoted to mankind and its welfare—provides the reader with a more complex perspective than the society in which he claims membership enacts (Andrews 1986; Costanzo 1987; Marren 1993; Potkay 1994; Elrod 2001).

The farce of the handshake stands against the utter dehumanization described in the following scene set in the belly of the cargo ship where the slaves are amassed on top of each other and experience the slow death that was the middle passage—a death that Equiano presents as physical, emotional, and, with reference to forgetfulness on the part of Europeans, also cultural. The description of what happens under the deck is not accomplished using the visual strategy Equiano employed for the previous scenes. The reader's experience is now olfactory and quasi-tactile. The physical distress and the abomination of the living conditions of the slaves, the "pestilential" and "insupportable" smells as well as the physical proximity that makes it impossible for a person to turn over, materialize in front of the reader until one is taken out of the place and placed back on the deck where Equiano sets the next segment of his story. Equiano returns to Biblical references with the following description of what takes place on the deck to remind readers of the utter betrayal of all the fundamentals of their professed Christianity:

> One day [the sailors] had taken a number of fishes; and when they had killed and satisfied themselves with as many as they thought fit, to our astonishment who were on the deck, rather than give any of them to us to eat, as we expected, they tossed the remaining fish into the sea again, although we begged and prayed for some as well as we could, but in vain; and some of my countrymen, being pressed by hunger, took an

opportunity, when they thought no one saw them, of trying to get a little privately; but they were discovered and the attempt procured them some very severe floggings. (Equiano 2003, 59)

Not only do the white sailors refuse to share their fish, but they refuse to do so when they have an excess. Equiano inverts Gospel imagery of feeding thousands with just a few fishes.[22] The nominally Christian sailors refuse to share the fish with the starving slaves. The lack of Christian piety is accompanied by the breaking of its fundamental principles. At this place in the narrative, Equiano is both among the slaves who are denied the fish and looking back in retrospect as he had in the previous scenes. The Christian and Biblical references here are ascribing Equiano's anti-slavery narrative within the generic and propagandistic frame which he has established from the opening. There is no reticence or attempt to abstain from judgment while allowing the reader to develop his or her own opinion.

Before the chapter closes with the depiction of the slave sale and the dismembering of all the ties they may still hold, the narrative voice brings readers back to the cannibalistic image introduced at the beginning of the captivity narrative. Equiano describes another moment before the landing begins when a group of merchants visit the ship to examine the newly arrived merchandise:

Many merchants and planters now came on board, though it was in the evening. They put us in separate parcels, and examined us attentively. They also made us jump, and pointed to the land, signifying we were to go there. We thought by this we should be eaten by these ugly men, as they appeared to us; and, when soon after we were all put down under the deck again, there was much dread and trembling among us, and nothing

---

[22] This is one of the many examples of chiastic inversions related to the large set of inversions that Equiano performs from the onset of his narrative. Henry Louis Gates has identified the chiasmus as one of the two rhetorical strategies (the other is the use of two separate voices) that Equiano has introduced in the African-American literary tradition. These strategies, Gates argues, "combine to make Equiano's text a representation of becoming, of a development of a self that not only has a past and a present but which speaks distinct languages as its several stages which culminate in the narrative present" (Gates 1988, 153–154). In the context of my search for the usage that Equiano makes of the language of the cosmopolitan in constructing the narrative and its subject, I am interested in analyzing these inversions and the role they play in reframing a reading of Equiano's life experiences.

but bitter cries to be heard all the night from this bitter apprehensions, insomuch that at last the white people got some old slaves from the land to pacify us. They told us we were not to be eaten, but to work, and were soon to go on land, where we should see many of our country people. This report eased us much; and sure enough, soon after we were landed, there came to us Africans of all languages. (Equiano 2003, 60)

The lack of understanding among the groups and, especially, the lack of any interest in generating it except for calming the cries of the people trapped inside the ship, precedes the first direct reference to the central motif of the rest of the captivity narrative that forms the opening three chapters of *The Interesting Narrative*. The misunderstanding during the first encounter between the Europeans visiting the ship in Africa and the new slaves had brought the notion of miscommunication to center stage, thus helping the reader to see what a fundamental problem it was. Now Equiano retrieves the issue and brings it to the heart of the next chapter in the story of captivity he tells. The following chapter, in fact, is centered on Equiano's attempt to make sense of what he hears and what he sees to begin the process of acculturation he must go through as an uprooted individual. The interpreters in the passage above are finally brought on board the ship are complex figures. Although the compatriots described fail to explain what the word "work" means in the context of slavery, they are the first people who break the long silence of the transatlantic passage: "They told us we were not to be eaten, but to work, and were soon to go on land, where we should see many of our country people. This report eased us much; and sure enough, soon after we were landed, there came to us Africans of all languages" (Equiano 2003, 60). The situation, however, is short lived. The presence of all the languages of Africa that Equiano experiences after landing in North America is immediately replaced by silence imposed by his incomprehension of the English language. This silence becomes the central trope of the chapter that follows in which Equiano describes the ending days of his first captivity—a captivity from which he is, ironically, set free when is sold into slavery again.

## 4 Language Acquisition: Becoming "Almost" English

The scenes that describe the ending moments of Equiano's captivity before he is sold to his new English owner and brought to London are condensed in the first few pages of the third chapter of *The Interesting*

*Narrative*. The end of the captivity is introduced by a series of remarks about Equiano's inability to speak to anybody once he arrives at the Virginia plantation. Equiano also describes his brief time spent working in the master's house and observing the household's human and material features in this section. Equiano laments that all the people from Africa he had previously met and who could understand him have been sent to different plantations, and, because he does not yet speak any English, he is not able to communicate with anybody. It is at the end of this short period characterized by a silence which replicates the silence on the ship that he meets his liberator. Equiano describes this moment as divine intervention and it is a moment that marks an introduction to his linguistic as well as cultural proficiency. Equiano uses imagery typical of the genre to characterize the moment when he is about to end his captivity and enter his second one:

> I had been some time in this miserable, forlorn, and much dejected state, without having anyone to talk to, which made my life a burden, when the kind and unknown hand of the Creator (who in very deed leads the blind in a way they know not) now began to appear, to my comfort; for one day the captain of a merchant ship, called the Industrious Bee, came on some business to my master's house. This gentleman, whose name was Michael Henry Pascal, was a lieutenant in the royal navy, but now commanded this trading ship which was somewhere in the confines of the county many miles off. (Equiano 2003, 63)

The encounter and the apparent rescue mark the progressive ending of the silence and miscommunication that had characterized the previous section, and initiate the process of going home. The irony of this entire process is that home is neither Equiano's natal home nor the home of one's choice, as is the case for the traditional Western cosmopolitan subject. However, in the chapter that describes his liberation from the captivity slavery in Virginia would have brought him into and his passage from the North American colony to London, Equiano represents the going home of the captive at the end of his imprisonment. Equiano's representation of going home gives us the evidence to understand how an individual like Equiano found language in cosmopolitanism to construct an alternative form of identity. It also provides a new definition of the concept of home for displaced individuals like Equiano. This unique identity forms on a ship, a place that is in continual motion, and one imposed on the individual by a series of accidents, abuses, dislocations, linguistic shifts, and transformations. London, the place where the ship the *Industrious Bee* is headed, is only a nominal home for Equiano. His life, as *The Interesting Narrative* shows, takes place on board the various ships he sails on. As readers, Equiano has prepared us to see the incoherence of the process of identity formation in the two chapters that precede this. The chapter that describes his passage from Virginia to London gives us further evidence of what is cosmopolitan in Equiano's identity and the story he tells us. The concept of home is written over in terms that make unstable any description of the concept that is rooted in place, because places are either dangerous or not what they appear to be.

Linguistic acquisition and the acculturation it allows are essential to Equiano's transformation into the man he is when by the end of this three-stage journey he becomes "almost" English and settles in London (Equiano 2003, 77). Yet, it is this incomplete status (signified and caused by his conditions as slave, then ex-slave, African, and non-native speaker of the language) that marks him as both an inferior insider of British colonial culture and as the intellectual cosmopolitan. Ultimately, it is the subject emerging from this experience who becomes able to be a true citizen of the world because of all of it, a man who can be at home wherever home is. This perspective is what enables Equiano to recognize the problematic relationship between the socio-cultural standards he is about to internalize and the reality that surrounds them. In the few pages before the meeting with Pascal and the passage on the *Industrious Bee*, Equiano recounts his experience working in his American master's household and gives readers the first insight in his perception of linguistic and cultural acquisitions. The description of what happens in between the arrival in Virginia and the encounter with Pascal shows readers a fundamental flaw in the way in which his new world thinks of communication itself. From the beginning of the chapter, obstacles to communication, linguistic or manmade, continually present themselves and stunt the boy who tries to speak. As we read through the pages of the chapter, these moments show that the ability to express oneself and linguistic fluency are determined by factors both intellectual and cultural, both natural and manmade. The series of examples that this chapter presents show the limits, and ultimately, the lack of necessity, of complete assimilation to such a culture unless the flaws are eliminated. Equiano's rhetorical strategies, placed against the linear discussion of how he, in fact, became an Englishman. Equiano begins the chapter by telling readers that by the time he is about to leave Barbados he "saw few or none of our native Africans, and not one soul who could talk to me" (Equiano 2003, 62). The same happens when he arrives in Virginia. There is nobody to talk to and his attempts at interpreting the significance of several objects with an obvious cultural meaning is central to the episode inside the plantation house that opens this part of the story. At the plantation, he "thought [himself] worse off than any of the rest of [his] companions; for they could talk to each other, but [he] had no person to speak to that [he] could understand" (Equiano 2003, 62). This scene establishes a striking parallel between Equiano's silence caused by the linguistic barrier and the barriers slavery imposes on individuals. Equiano's first described encounter with another human being details this for the reader when he recounts that one of his first tasks was to fan his ailing, sleeping master. Already scared by the assignment, his shock and fear are farther enhanced by the encounter he has on his way to the master's room:

> While I was in this plantation, the gentleman, to whom I supposed the estate belonged, being unwell, I was one day sent for to his dwelling house to fan him: when I came into the room where he was, I was very much affrighted at some things I saw, the more so as I had seen a black woman slave as I came through the house, who was cooking the dinner, and the poor creature was cruelly loaded with various kinds of iron machines; she had one particularly on her head, which locked her mouth so fast that she could scarcely speak; and could not eat nor drink. I was much astonished and shocked at this contrivance, which I afterwards learned was called the iron muzzle. (Equiano 2003, 62–63)

The "various kinds of iron machines" that trap the woman and render her unable to speak, eat, and drink and, one would assume, unable to move except for performing the chores imposed on her, embody the silencing and paralyzing power of slavery and of his own situation. The young Equiano is not physically strapped into a machine of the kind the woman is forced to wear, but, in addition to his status as slave, his linguistic and cultural incompetence become their figurative equivalent. The power of slavery to silence Equiano becomes reflected in his acknowledgement linguistic and cultural incompetence make him completely powerless (Bugg 2006, 1230–1234).[23] The ability to speak the language acquires an even more central role for the young man who enters this world. The encounter with the muzzled woman is shocking and contributes to Equiano's fears when he arrives at the room.

The absence of voices around Equiano is also significant here. The only other two presences are those of the muzzled woman and their sleeping master. Whoever directed him to his job and gave him the fan remains hidden in the silence that surrounds him. The opposition between the sleep-induced silence of the master and the violently forced one of the woman is highlighted in this comparison and becomes a central element in the story Equiano tells here. The voicelessness of the slaves and the invisibility of those who force it upon them parallel the miscommunication Equiano reports between the slave traders and the newly captured Africans in his previous chapter. Miscommunication will remain central to the story of Equiano's voyage to England. The cosmopolitan that Equiano becomes by retelling his story empowers him with this particular voice. What follows when Equiano describes the time he spent in the bedroom fanning the sleeping man is a series of observations that bring in both the voice of the young observer and the cosmopolitan writer. When Equiano enters the master's room to fan him while he is asleep, the young boy is described as indulging in the observation of the room, which he presents as "very fine and curious."

Although the image of the scared boy remains central, it is important to notice that the objects that capture his attentions are also markers of gentility in the culture to which he is introduced, thus merging the observer's voice with the narrator. At this moment, the voice of the cosmopolitan intellectual begins to insinuate itself in the narrative in a way that is as critical as it was in the previous chapters:

> While he was fast asleep I indulged myself a great deal in looking about the room, which to me appeared very fine and curious. The first object that engaged my attention was a watch which hung from the chimney, and was

---

[23] My reading here is similar to that John Bugg has done when discussing the same passage. Bugg has linked this silencing to Equiano's search for a voice that enables him to first persuade his audience of his credibility before he can enunciate the issues he is interested in promoting. As I have discussed in the previous pages of this chapter, however, I see Equiano's silence also working within the parameters of a narrative strategy that creates blank spaces for readers to fill with their own analysis.

going. I was quite surprised at the noise it made, and I was afraid it might tell the gentleman any thing I might do amiss: and when I immediately after observed a picture hanging in the room, which appeared constantly to look at me, I was still more affrighted, having never seen such things as these before. At one time I thought it was something relative to magic; and not seeing it move, I thought it might be some way the whites had to keep their men when they died, and offer them libation as we used to do our friendly spirits. In this state of anxiety I remained till my master awoke, when I was dismissed out of the room, to my no small satisfaction and relief, for I thought that these people were made of wonders. (Equiano 2003, 63)

In this passage the two objects that catch Equiano's attention produce both aesthetic pleasure and fear. They represent what is fine and curious to the eye of the observer, and yet they symbolize the fear the imposed silence and being a slave generate. The objects mark the place of the family's household in society and the power such a place gives them, which includes controlling other human beings as if they were objects themselves.[24] Yet, at the same time, the readers do not hear any of their voices. They are as silent as the woman working in the kitchen. There is no need for an explanation on the part of the narrative voice. The gentility of the objects Equiano notices is evocative of the gentility the portrait of Equiano on the first page of the book evokes. Equiano is, by the time he writes the story of his life, an established gentleman who can afford to have his own likeness painted. From that position, he can understand both its economic and social values as well as its flaws. And as he tells the story, the flaws fully emerge.

On one level, Equiano presents his young self in all his naïveté and cultural ignorance, and shows his budding sense of good taste according to the standards of his time. On another level, through the parallels his observations generate, he is addressing the paradoxes and contradictions of that culture. The watch hanging from the wall in the room, a symbol of Western culture and of its technological power, is given the controlling power of a plantation supervisor. Equiano imagines the clock

---

[24] In his reading of this passage, Henry Louis Gates describes the clock and the portrait as embodiments of the master's eyes. This gaze, Gates then argues, is reflected and spoken back to when later Equiano invokes the image of the talking book—an image that represents Equiano's ability to read and speak back to the culture that aims at silencing him (Gates 1988, 155–158).

as a speaking object that could tell his owner he has not been performing his assigned task.[25] In addition the clock with its ticking mechanism and its technology reminds readers of another mechanical device, the iron machine on the woman's mouth. Both objects are productions of the same world Equiano is about to join. The machine that marks time and that could be the eye observing the young Equiano while he performs his duty is the parallel of the one that keeps the woman from drinking, eating and, most importantly, from speaking. Both mechanical devices embody the power of the word and the power that those who have it exercise over the slaves. The pairing of these two objects in the short space Equiano dedicates to describing his stay at the Virginian plantation becomes the tool for developing a multifaceted reading experience that points out the intricacies of his culture's texture. All the cultural elements participate in the existence of the world Equiano describes. Gentility speaks to the cruelty behind the muzzling of a human being and vice versa. Significantly, the clock can, in the eyes of the young Equiano, speak, unlike the woman, and therefore it potentially places him in her condition as well. The Equiano who tells the story from his adult perspective has mastered the language and can now provide readers with a view of all the things that compose the world represented in the scene.

Equiano introduces his rescue and passage to his new world of words with the image of cultural silencing the opening scene provides—his passage home. The arrival on the *Industrious Bee* marks the first moment informing readers of the relativity and instability of the idea of identity formation connected to Equiano's becoming English.[26] The second transatlantic passage, which Equiano introduces with the description of his liberation from captivity, begins with the announcement that his silence is broken. There is the first hint at the idea that deception is at the root of what is about to happen to him. The deception is semantic as well as pragmatic:

---

[25] Gates calls it the master's "surrogate overseer" (Gates 1988, 155).

[26] Rather than following the often made assumption that Equiano is either embracing or refusing a British identity or an African identity, I suggest that the narrative voice shows a keen awareness of the relativity of national identity and therefore makes it clear that choice or coercion can be the source of such identity and all of it is always circumstantial and relative. See previous footnotes for criticism that assumes that Equiano is either becoming African or English by the end of the narrative.

A few days after I was on board we sailed for England. I was still at a loss to conjecture my destiny. By this time, however, I could smatter a little imperfect English: and I wanted to know as well as I could where we were going. Some of the people of the ship used to tell me they were going to carry me back to my own country, and this made me very happy. I was quite rejoiced at the idea of going back; and thought if I should get home what wonders I should have to tell. But I was reserved on another fate, and was soon undeceived when we came within sight of the English coast. (Equiano 2003, 64)

This passage is important because it illustrates that his limited knowledge and halted understanding of the English language is good enough to allow Equiano to recognize that the reality that surrounds him is one based on deception. His traveling companions are deceiving and making fun of his credulity, but in retelling the story, the readers are made aware that the individual's gullibility is only partial and temporary. Most importantly, the readers notice the incoherence between the way things are named and what they are. What Equiano's shipmates call home might indeed be their home, but it is not his. In fact, the ship is going to be his home by all effects because of his state as personal property of Michael Henry Pascal. It is soon after this moment that Equiano tells the story of how he acquired his slave name Gustavus Vassa. Equiano's arguing with the master that he wants to be called Jacob, his first assigned slave name, only highlights the incoherence of this naming process. The irony in naming a slave after a Swedish freedom fighter combines with the equally strange decision to not allow Equiano to keep the slave name he had been previously assigned and highlights the arbitrariness of the concept of naming as well as of the identifying process.[27]

As part of this process the definition of home that emerges from the chapters describing Equiano's voyage to England is also reversed. If in fact this is the chapter that tells the story of Equiano's travels home, this is also the chapter that, in addition to the previous ones, continues the process of subverting and questioning the concept of home itself. If England becomes the nominal place where Equiano settles, and Pascal

---

[27] As Vincent Carretta points out in a textual note, the use of ironically inappropriate names for slave was a common practice during the period. Carretta also suggests that Equiano might also be expecting his readers to notice the "parallel between the Swedish freedom fighter and the modern leader of his people's struggle against the slave trade, as well as the irony of his initial resistance to his new name" (Equiano 2003, 253).

and his relatives, the two Guerin sisters, become his putative family, the story the chapter sketches makes the ship and his shipmates the representatives of home. The final destination of the second voyage is England and what Equiano calls home, but by the time Equiano tells his readers "it was now between three and four years since I first came to England," readers also know that he had spent most of this time at sea, and that is what the heart of chapter three is about (Bolster 1997, 7–43). His settlement as an Englishman happens at sea. In addition, the American-born Richard Baker, another shipmate and a figure from the imperial margins, becomes Equiano's instructor and the model he uses to become Anglicized. Richard Baker's main function is that of interpreter and teacher. He helps Equiano communicate. When killer whales start circling around the ship and Equiano is scared, for example, Baker, unlike the rest of the shipmates and the captain, provides him with answers Equiano can, albeit still partially, understand and trust: "I took an opportunity to ask [Baker], as well as I could, what these fish were? Not being able to talk much English, I could but just make him understand my question; and not at all when I asked him if any offerings were to be made to them? However, he told me these fish would swallow anybody; which sufficiently alarmed me" (Equiano 2003, 66). As his interpreter, Dick (as the captain calls Baker), helps Equiano to discern the credible from the incredible and to internalize the linguistic and cultural codes that alienate Equiano at the beginning of the journey. Dick is one of the two figures who in the chapter take part in the often-discussed episode of the talking book. He is the one, with Pascal, who Equiano often observes reading:

> I had often seen my master and Dick employed in reading; and I had a great curiosity to talk to the books, as I thought they did; and so to learn how all things had a beginning: for that purpose I have often taken up a book, and have talked to it, and then put my ear to it, when alone, in hopes it would answer me; and I have been very much concerned when I found it remained silent. (Equiano 2003, 68)

In this scene, Dick does not function as an interpreter. It is "when alone" Equiano puts the book to his ear to see if it can speak. Beginning with Henry Louis Gates, scholars have identified this odd moment as a fundamental feature that marks *The Interesting Narrative* as one of the most important texts of African-American literary tradition. More recently, Equiano's description has been interpreted as a marker of the narrative's postcolonial and transgressive literary character. In the context of my analysis, the absence of the figure Equiano introduces as his interpreter, faithful friend, and agreeable companion a few pages earlier takes us back to the idea of cultural relativity and instability that the chapter represents.[28] Despite his absence, however, Dick's presence as "instructor" is still visible in the passage through the rhetoric and imagery produced for an English-speaking audience. The book in question is most likely a bible in that it is the text that explains "how all things had a beginning." And that beginning is in fact a word. At this point, Equiano is acquiring his own words, and, in the process, understanding the corruption and unreliability of the linguistic system they belong to. In fact, Equiano's manipulation of the tenses once again highlights the incongruities of the reality that surrounds him. Within this context, the inconsistent grammar of the passage reflects the odd relationship between seeing and being of the captivity story Equiano has told so far and it leads us back to what I discussed in the previous pages of this chapter about the connections (or disconnections) between national identity, belonging, and cosmopolitanism.

By the time the reader learns that Equiano has assimilated himself to the culture of his "adoptive" country, the idea of assimilation had been constructed as part of the revision of the terms defining nationhood and cosmopolitan belonging:

> It was now between three and four years since I first came to England, a great part of which I had spent at sea; so that I became inured to that service, and began to consider myself as happily situated… From the various scenes I had beheld on shipboard, I soon grew a stranger to terror of every kind, and was in that respect at least almost an Englishman …

---

[28] Henry Louis Gates's well-known reading of the passage suggests that the shift in tense from the simple past to the past perfect "is Equiano's grammatical analogue of this process of becoming—of becoming a human being who reads differently from the child, of becoming a subject by passing a test (the mastery of writing) that no object can pass, and of becoming an author who represents, under the guise of a series of naïve readings, an object's "true" nature by demonstrating that he can now read these objects in both ways, as he once did in the middle passage but also as he does today" (Gates 1988, 157). Srinivas Aravamudan reads the passage and its imagery using a post-colonial frame and argues that they relate to a representation of the talking book as a combination of fetish and fact, an object that is both real and mystified. Reading is both a miracle and a questioning of such a miracle (Aravamudan 1999, 280–281).

> I could now speak English tolerably well and I perfectly understood everything that was said. I now not only felt myself quite easy with these countrymen, but relished their society and manners. I no longer looked upon them as spirits, but as men superior to us; and therefore I had the stronger desire to resemble them, to imbibe their spirit, and imitate their manners; I therefore embraced every occasion of improvement; and every new thing that I observed I treasured up in my memory. I had long wished to be able to read and write; and for this purpose I took every opportunity to gain instruction … Shortly after my arrival, he [Pascal] sent me to wait upon the Miss Guerins, who treated me with much kindness when I was there before; and they sent me to school. (Equiano 2003, 77–78)

With this eloquent description of his decision to revere and embrace what he describes as the culture of superior men, Equiano also tells the reader how he became almost English. What he has learned by going to school and by impressing on his memory all he has seen has made him almost an Englishman. This process enabled him to write this story and write it in the language and rhetorical form to which he has just introduced his readers. Like the "implanted manners and customs" of his native country, the language and manners of his adoptive one are constructed and can be deconstructed. As it was the case at the beginning of the narrative, location and dislocation take place simultaneously and the language of the cosmopolitan has made all of this possible.

## References

Andrews, William L. 1986. *To Tell a Free Story: The First Century of Afro-American Autobiography, 1769–1865.* Urbana: University of Illinois Press.
Aravamudan, Srinivas. 1999. *Tropicopolitans: Colonialism and Agency, 1688–1804.* Durham, NC: Duke University Press.
———. 2001. Equiano Lite. *Eighteenth-Century Studies* 34: 615–619.
Baepler, Paul. 2004. The Barbary Captivity Narrative in American Culture. *Early American Literature* 39 (2): 217–246.
Berlin, Ira. 1996. From Creole to African: Atlantic Creoles and the Origins of African-American Society in Mainland North America. *The William and Mary Quarterly* 53 (2): 251–288.
———. 1998. *Many Thousand Gone: The First Two Centuries of Slavery in North America.* Cambridge, MA: Harvard University Press.
Bolster, W. Jeffrey. 1997. *Black Jacks: African American Seamen in the Age of Sail.* Harvard, MA: Harvard University Press.

Boulukos, George E. 2007. Olaudah Equiano and the Eighteenth-Century Debate on Africa. *Eighteenth-Century Studies* 40 (2): 241–255.
Bugg, John. 2006. The Other Interesting Narrative: Olaudah Equiano's Public Tour. *PMLA* 121: 1424–1442.
———. 2007 Deciphering the Equiano Archive: Reply to Vincent Carretta. *PMLA* 122: 572–573.
Burnard, Trevor. 2006. Goodbye, Equiano, The African. *Historically Speaking* 7: 10–11.
Burnham, Michelle. 1997. *Captivity and Sentiment: Cultural Exchange in American Literature, 1682–1861*. Hanover, NH: University Press of New England.
Carby, Hazel V. 2009. Becoming Modern Racialized Subjects: Detours through Our Pasts to Produce Ourselves Anew. *Cultural Studies* 1: 624–657.
Carretta, Vincent. 1998. Three West Indian Writers of the 1780s Revisited and Revised. *Research in African Literature* 29 (4): 73–87.
———. 2000. Defining the Gentleman: The Status of Olaudah Equiano or Gustavus Vassa. *Language Sciences* 22: 385–399.
———. 2003. Questioning the Indentity of Olaudah Equino, or Gustavus Vassa, the African. In *The Global Eighteenth Century*, ed. Felicity A. Nussbaum. Baltimore, MD: The Johns Hopkins University Press.
———. 2005. *Equiano, the African: Biography of a Self-Made Man*. Athens: University of Georgia Press.
———. 2007a. Response to Lovejoy, Burnard, and Sensbach. *Historically Speaking* 7 (3): 14–17.
———. 2007b. Does Equiano Still Matter? *PMLA* 122: 571–572.
Costanzo, Angelo. 1987. *Surprising Narrative: Olaudah Equiano and the Beginnings of Black Autobiography*. New York: Greenwood.
Davidson, Cathy. 2006. Olaudah Equiano, Written by Himself. *Novel, A Form on Fiction* 40 (1–2): 18–51.
Dubois, Laurent. 2006. *Social History* 31: 1–14.
Edwards, Paul. 1969. *The Life of Olaudah Equiano, or Gustavus Vassa, the African*. London: Dowson of Pall Mall.
Elrod, Eileen Razzari. 2001. Moses and Egyptian: Religious Authority in Olaudah Equiano's Interesting Narrative. *African American Review* 35: 409–425.
Equiano, Olaudah. 2003. *The Interesting Narrative and Other Writings*, ed. Vincent Carretta. New York: Penguin.
Gates, Henry Louis. 1988. *The Signifying Monkey: A Theory of African-American Literary Criticism*. New York: Oxford University Press.
Gerzina, Gretchen Holbrook. 2001. Mobility in Chains: Freedom of Movement in the Early Black Atlantic. *The South Atlantic Quarterly* 100 (1): 41–59.

Gilroy, Paul. 1993. *The Black Atlantic: Modernity and Double Consciousness*. London: Verso.
Giunta, Edvige. 2002. *Writing with an Accent: Contemporary Italian American Women Authors*. New York: Palgrave Macmillan.
Gould, Philip. 2003. *Barbaric Traffic: Commerce and Antislavery in the Eighteenth-Century Atlantic World*. Cambridge: Harvard University Press.
Haslam, Jason, and Julia M. Wright. 2005. *Captivity Subjects: Writing Confinement, Citizenship, and Nationhood in the Nineteenth Century*. Toronto: University of Toronto Press.
Jaros, Peter. 2013. Good Names: Olaudah Equiano or Gustavus Vassa. *The Eighteenth Century* 54: 1–23.
Lovejoy, Paul E. 2006. Autobiography and Memory: Gustavus Vassa, Alias Olaudah Equiano, the African. *Slavery and Abolition* 27: 317–347.
———. 2007. Issues of Motivation—Vassa/Equiano and Carretta's Critique of the Evidence. *Slavery and Abolition* 28: 121–125.
Lowe, Lisa. 2009. Autobiography Out of Empire. *Small Axe* 28: 98–111.
Marren, Susan. 1993. Between Slavery and Freedom: The Transgressive Self in Olaudah Equiano's Autobiography. *PMLA* 108 (1): 94–105.
Matar, Nabil I. 1996. The Traveler as Captive: Renaissance England and the Allure of Islam. *LIT: Literature, Interpretation, and Theory* 7 (2–3): 187–196.
———. 1999. *Turks, Moors, and Englishmen in the Age of Discovery*. New York: Columbia University Press.
———. 2001. Introduction. *Piracy, Slavery, and Redemption: Barbary Captivity Narratives from Early Modern England*, ed. Daniel J. Vitkus, 1–52. New York: Columbia University Press.
Mignolo, Walter. 2002. The Many Faces of Cosmo-polis: Border Thinking and Critical Cosmopolitanism. In *Cosmopolitanism*, ed. Carol A. Breckenridge, Sheldon Pollock, Homi K. Bhaba, and Dipesh Chakrabarty, 157–188. Durham, NC: Duke University Press.
Patterson, Orlando. 1982. *Slavery and Social Death: A Comparative Study*. Cambridge, MA: Harvard University Press.
Potkay, Adam. 1994. Olaudah Equiano and the Art of Spiritual Autobiography. *Eighteenth-Century Studies* 27: 677–693.
Sayre, Gordon. 2000. *American Captivity Narratives*. New York: Houghton Mifflin Company.
Sayre, Gordon. 2010. Renegades from Barbary: The Transnational Turn in Captivity Studies. *American Literary History* 22 (2): 347–359.
Sekora, John. 1993. Red, White, and Black: Indian Captivities, Colonial Printers, and the Early African American Narrative. In *A Mixed Race: Ethnicity in Early America*, ed. Frank Shuffleton. New York: Oxford University Press.
Sensbach, Jon. 2006. Beyond Equiano. *Historically Speaking* 7: 12–13.

Snader, Joe. 2000. *Caught Between Worlds: British Captivity Narratives in Fact and Fiction*. Lexington: University of Kentucky Press.

Ugwuanyi, Ogbo. 2009. Olaudah Equiano and the Question of African Identity. In *Olaudah Equiano and the Igbo World: History, Society and Atlantic Diaspora Connections*, ed. Chima J. Korieh, 117–140. Trenton, NJ: Africa World.

Vitkus, Daniel. 2001. *Piracy, Slavery, and Redemption: Barbary Captivity Narratives from Early Modern England*. New York: Columbia University Press.

Voigt, Lisa. 2009. *Writing Captivity in the Early Modern Atlantic: Circulations of Knowledge and Authority in the Iberian and English Imperial Worlds*. Chapel Hill: University of North Carolina Press.

# INDEX

**B**
Barbé-Marbois, François, 60n, 62–65, 86
  Questionnaire to governors of newly formed states, 60
  Relationship to *Notes on the State of Virginia*, 65
Beccaria, Cesare, 137
  *On Crimes and Punishments*, 137
British Empire, 4, 6, 7, 18, 23, 28, 48, 70, 103, 105, 118, 129, 135, 164

**C**
Captivity narratives, 163–165, 172, 178
Cosmopolitan
  After American Revolution, 4, 6, 103, 106, 123, 129, 130, 153
  First appearance of word, 2
  In Colonial America, 5, 18
  Intersection of cosmopolitan ideology and colonial expansion, 2
Cosmopolitanism
  And American Revolution, 4, 6, 103, 106, 123, 129, 130, 153

Communal identity, 4, 10
  And nationalism, 4–8, 60, 68, 103, 125, 126
  The republic of letters, 5, 9, 17, 23, 49, 59, 62, 67, 68, 76, 87, 90, 92, 126, 132, 133
  Role in 18th century American writings, 6, 26n, 41, 73, 115, 146
Cresap, Colonel, 66, 89

**D**
De Buffon, George Leclerc, 62n, 65, 67, 69, 70, 72, 75, 91
  *Historie Naturelle*, 69, 81, 87, 146
  Jefferson's response to in *Notes on the State of Virginia*, 60, 64
Dee, John
  *General and Rare Memorials pertayning to the Perfect Arte of Navigation*, 2; First use of term *"cosmopolite"*, 2
Diderot, Denis, 25, 42
  *Encyclopédie*, 32; Definition of cosmopolitanism, 32

# E

Elocutionary Revolution, 77
Enlightenment
  Emergence of cosmopolitanism, 3, 37, 44, 47, 50, 54, 55, 159
  Universal concepts, 3, 6, 73, 87
Equiano, Olaudah (also known as Gustavus Vassa)
  Abolition movement/abolitionists, 7, 14, 129, 167, 174, 175, 177, 179, 183
  "Almost English", 186, 196
  Baker, Richard (Dick), 194
  Black Atlantic, 161, 163
  Captivity, 14, 162–164, 166, 170–173, 176, 179, 185–187
  Captivity narratives, 163, 164, 172
  Christianity in work of, 165, 183
  Controversy over birthplace, 139
  Cosmopolitanism; As a construct of alternative identity, 187; As a product of slavery, 152, 161, 163; As a tool of empowerment, 159
  Interesting Narrative of the Life of Olaudah Equiano; Description of books/reading, 194; Description of early life in Africa, 159, 164, 172, 186; Description of liberation from captivity, 192; Description of Virginia plantation, 187, 192; Description of voyage on slave ship, 176, 179–181
  Pascal, Michael Henry; *Industrious Bee*, 163, 187, 188, 192
  Slavery, 161
  Tropicopolitans, 13n
  Veracity of *Interesting Narrative*, 166

# F

Fergusson, Elizabeth Graeme
  Commonplace books, 5, 11, 44, 100, 103–106, 108, 109, 113, 114, 115n, 116n, 124; And cosmopolitanism, 5, 100; Dialogic nature of, 114; As a "poetic biography", 105
  Cosmopolitanism; In colonial Philadelphia, 99, 100, 103, 118, 125; Cosmopolitanism as link to socio-cultural past, 10, 103, 115, 159, 167, 188; In poetry, 5, 11, 100, 106, 116, 118, 123; In postcolonial American, 12, 13, 195; Theme of friendship, 108, 113, 116; Theme of place, 116
  Creative cosmopolitanism, 11; And imperial society, 103
  Diary, 106, 108, 115; Voyage from Philadelphia to Liverpool, 106
  Duché letter, 102
  Early intellectual life, 100, 106
  Engagement to William Franklin, 101
  Epistolary quality of poetry, 108, 109, 112, 115, 116
  Letter to Ann Ridgely, 103
  Moore, Rebecca, 116
  *Poemata Juvenilia*, 109, 111, 116; "A Dream", 112, 113; "On the Preference of Friendship to Love", 113; "The Interrogation", 110, 111; "The Reply", 111; "To Memory", 119, 122, 123. *See also* Some Lines upon my first being at Graeme Park after my return from England;
  "Wrote at the time of the Indian War", 116

Rush, Benjamin, 99, 100, 105
Salons, 107
Fergusson, Henry Hugh, 101
Affair, 101
Loyalism, 101, 106
Franklin, Benjamin
American Philosophical Society, 20, 22–25, 28, 142; Intellectual independence through economic prosperity, 21; Republic of letters, 5, 12, 17, 20, 23–25, 26n; Secretary of, 26
*The Art of Virtue*, 36, 38, 39, 41; Incorporation into *Autobiography*, 36
Autobiography; Part 1, 34, 35, 37, 44; Part 2, 34–37, 41; Part 3, 37; Part 4, 37; Writing of, 34
Cosmopolitanism; As a concept of ethnic superiority, 8; Inclusiveness and homogeneity, 55, 73; As a model for local community, 28, 46; In nation formation, 51; Relationship to Empire, 6
Franklin, William (son), 34; Addressee of Autobiography, 34; Break with, 101
"Jakes on our Tables", 49
Letter to Lord Kames, 38
"Observations Concerning the Increase of Mankind, Peopling of Countries"; Cosmopolitanism and homogeneity in culture and ethnicity, 49, 50, 55
"Observations on my Reading History in Library", 41, 55
*A Proposal for Promoting Useful Knowledge Among the British Plantations in America*, 20
"Rattlesnakes and Felons", 49

"Standing Queries for the Junto", 28. *See also* Leather Apron Club
Society of the Free and Easy, 42, 44
Transnationality, 18, 33, 44, 49, 94n, 124, 143
Virtue as a practical art, 38n, 41
Franklin, William (son) Royal Governor of New Jersey, 34
*Autobiography dedicated to*, 39
Break with Benjamin Franklin, 101
Engagement to Elizabeth Graeme Fergusson, 101
Franklin, William Temple (grandson), 34

G
Graeme, Thomas (father of Elizabeth Graeme Fergusson), 101

H
Hume, David, 25, 62, 92
"On National Characters", 92

J
James, Abel, 35
Author of letter to Franklin that inspired Part 2 of *Autobiography*, 37
James, Henry, 1
Jefferson, Thomas
American exceptionalism, 10, 72, 92, 94
Cosmopolitanism; And inclusiveness, 55, 73; And Native American oratory, 66n, 69, 72–74, 75, 87; And scientific community, 10, 73, 75, 83, 84, 91, 95;

And supra-nationality, 4, 13, 18, 24, 67, 87, 94, 129
Elocutionary revolution, relation to, 77, 78
Native Americans, 76, 90; Logan narrative and accusations of forgery, 67, 88, 89n, 90–92, 93n; Use of tradition of oratory, 69, 70, 73–76, 82, 85, 90
*Notes on the State of Virginia*, 9, 10, 17, 59, 60; Difficulty with translations, 19; Publication of, 64–66, 68n; "Query VI", 67–69, 74, 82; Response to de Buffon, 62n, 67, 69, 95; Use of Barbé-Marbois's questionnaire as a framework, 60, 62n, 63, 65
Republic of letters, 59, 60, 62n, 67, 68, 75, 76, 85, 87, 88, 90, 92, 93n, 126

**K**
Kant, Immanuel, 2, 7, 8, 11, 54, 126
Proposal of cosmopolitan international law as universal right, 8

**L**
Leather Apron Club, 29n
Logan narrative, 66n, 67, 74, 88, 89, 90n, 91–94

**M**
Martin, Luther, 66n
Mather, Cotton, 70, 71, 79
Mazzei, Philip
Adams, John, 130, 157; Letter of September 27, 1785, 157
American identity, 130–132

Carmignani, Giovanni, 136; Letter published as Mazzei's autobiography, 131; Letter to, 144
Correspondence, 129–131, 143; As a form of cosmopolitanism, 139
Cosmopolitanism; And correspondence, 139; As a model of American national identity, 132; As a supra-national identity, 129, 132
Decision to leave America, 130, 155
Diplomatic aspiration, 132, 156; Exclusion based on foreign birth, 132; Letter to John Adams, 133
Italian nationality, 130, 134
"A Letter from a Citizen of the World", 147–149; de Montesquieu's theories on codependence of climate and national character, 145; National identity as a cultural and political product, 147
*A Letter on the Behavior of the Populace on a Late Occasion, in the Procedure against a Noble Lord from a Gentleman to his Countryman abroad*, 137–142; Epistolary format and cosmopolitanism, 112, 115, 135, 136; Cesare Beccaria and theories of punishment, 137
London, 133; Cosmopolitan circle, 133; Import/Export business, 133
"Observations of a Citizen of the World in answer to an American", 150–154; American self–representation, 145, 151, 155; Use of epistolary style and cosmopolitanism, 108, 136

*Recherches historiques et politiques sur les États-Unis*, 131. See *also* Researches on the United States
Training as medical doctor, 130, 133
Turkey, 133, 135; Introduction to cosmopolitanism, 133; Medical practice, 133
Virginia, 130, 136, 143, 156; Friendship with Thomas Jefferson, 131; Relocation to, 136
Montesquieu, Marquis de, 145
*The Spirit of the Laws*, 146
Morellet, Abbé André, 64

**N**
Native Americans, 66n, 74–76, 78–88
*Notes on the State of Virginia*, 62, 64–68
Oratory as part of emerging American identity, 73, 76n, 90

**P**
Pascal, Michael Henry, 163, 187, 188, 193, 194
*Industrious Bee*, 163, 187, 188
Postcolonial theory and study, 12, 13n
Cosmopolitanism before and after European empires, 12

**R**
Republic of letters, 5, 9, 12, 17, 18, 20, 21, 49, 59, 60, 62–68, 75, 85, 93–95, 126, 132–134
Rush, Benjamin, 99, 105

**S**
Society of the Free and Easy, 42–44
St. John Crèvecoeur, Hector, 61n, 107
Stockton, Annis Boudinot, 124

**T**
Transnationality, 11, 18, 33, 44, 49, 124, 143, 144
Tropicopolitans, 13n

**V**
Vaughan, Benjamin
Part 2 of Franklin's *Autobiography*, 34

Printed in the United States
By Bookmasters